Taste of Home
VEGETARIAN
made easy

TASTE OF HOME BOOKS • RDA ENTHUSIAST BRANDS, LLC • MILWAUKEE, WI

© 2020 RDA Enthusiast Brands, LLC.
1610 N. 2nd St., Suite 102
Milwaukee, WI 53212-3906

Visit us at tasteofhome.com for other
Taste of Home books and products.

International Standard Book Number:
978-1-61765-931-7
Library of Congress Control Number:
2019954151

Executive Editor: Mark Hagen
Senior Art Director: Raeann Thompson
Editor: Christine Rukavena
Designer: Arielle Jardine
Senior Editor, Copy Desk: Dulcie Shoener
Copy Editor: Sara Strauss
Senior Food Editor: Peggy Woodward, RDN

Cover
Photographer: Dan Roberts
Senior Food Stylist: Shannon Norris
Senior Set Stylist: Melissa Franco

Pictured on front cover:
Black Bean & Rice Enchiladas, p. 42
Pictured on spine:
Tasty Lentil Tacos, p. 26
Pictured on back cover:
Favorite Deep-Dish Pizza, p. 58; Market Basket Soup,
p. 157; Slow-Cooked Stuffed Peppers, p. 24; Italian
Cheese Loaf, p. 90; Veggie Bean Burgers, p. 105;
Cheesy Spinach-Stuffed Shells, p. 76
Pictured on flap:
Black Bean & Sweet Potato Rice Bowls, p. 142

Printed in China
3 5 7 9 10 8 6 4

195

282

275

163

CONTENTS

Must-Try Main Dishes 8

Pizza & Pasta Favorites.......................52

Burgers, Sandwiches & Wraps 86

Grain Dishes & Bowls 126

Heartwarming Soups 150

Sides & Salads................................... 182

Brunch Time....................................... 208

Small Bites & Snacks 244

Room for Dessert...............................280

Index... 316

Meat Lover Options 320

AT-A-GLANCE ICONS

Icons throughout the book indicate
freezer-friendly, five-ingredient,
quick-to-fix, slow-cooked, and
pressure-cooker fare.

MORE WAYS TO CONNECT WITH US:

157

WHY GO MEATLESS?

There are many reasons to choose a vegetarian (or sometimes-vegetarian) lifestyle. Here are a few of the more popular intentions.

Health: A plant-based diet is rich in antioxidants, high in fiber and low in cholesterol. Many choose vegetarian food to reduce cholesterol and lower blood pressure; to help prevent many cancers such as colon, breast, stomach, esophageal, lung and prostate; and to help control diabetes.

Weight Loss: With a well-balanced vegetarian diet, weight loss is possible. However, just like any other diet, a vegetarian diet high in calories from nuts, full-fat dairy and junk food may result in weight gain.

Budget: Forgoing meat for more economical staples, such as dried legumes and grains, can lower grocery store bills.

Respect for Life: Many vegans feel that all living beings, including animals, have value. Vegans oppose using animals to serve any human need, whether for food, clothing, household goods or product testing.

Environmental Concerns: Many people refrain from consuming meat to help the environment. These people believe humans should eat grains or crops rather than using farmland to grow a vast quantity of grain or grass to produce a smaller overall volume of animal protein. Animals raised for food use resources and create waste. A vegetarian diet helps reduce a person's carbon footprint.

Religious Beliefs: Dietary guidelines of various religions restrict the consumption of some or all meat.

Types of Vegetarian Diets

While all vegetarians exclude meat, some also eliminate other animal products from their diets. Here are some common guidelines.

Vegetarian
A broad term for a diet that does not include meat or fish; may or may not include other animal products, such as eggs or dairy

Lacto-Ovo Vegetarian
Meatless diet that includes both dairy products and eggs

Vegan
No meat, fish, dairy or eggs; no products made by animals (such as honey)

Pescatarian
May include fish but no other type of meat

Flexitarian
A mostly vegetarian diet that occasionally includes meat or fish, with an emphasis on fresh, nutrient-dense foods

Vegetarian Made Easy is appropriate for many vegetarian lifestyles. While some recipes include dairy products, eggs or honey, many do not. Further, none of the recipes here include gelatin, Worcestershire sauce or other ingredients that are made with meat products.

EASY WAYS TO EAT MEATLESS MORE OFTEN

Changing your diet overnight is an unrealistic goal; however, taking small, positive steps toward a healthier, more balanced diet is quite achievable. If you want to include more plants in your diet, here are some tips:

Swap meat-based protein for plant-based meals like those found in this book. Try going meatless on Monday to start, and work your way from there.

Sneak in more vegetables—shoot for three types of veggies at each meal. Aim to fill at least half of your plate with vegetables.

Try a delicious new plant-based recipe every week. Get the family involved in choosing what to try for dinner success.

Enjoy a veggie-rich breakfast. This could mean greens in your smoothie, a glass of tomato juice with your toast or raiding the produce drawer for your next omelet.

Add a leafy side salad to your meals. Plan for it when grocery shopping.

Remember, it's all about making small, long-term, sustainable changes. That means lifestyle choices you feel good about, so they're easy to live with!

MEAT LOVER OPTION
PAGE 320

For some, it's just not a meal without meat. To help, this icon highlights recipes that are easy (and tasty) to customize by adding a cooked protein such as beef or poultry.

Prep one recipe and satisfy everyone with the Meat Lover Option.
(See chart on p. 320 for dozens of choices.)

93

IMPORTANT NUTRIENTS

Be sure your meatless diet doesn't skimp on these essentials.

Protein is essential for the proper growth and maintenance of body tissue. Eating a variety of foods each day such as whole grains, legumes, soy products, seeds and vegetables will help ensure adequate intake of essential and nonessential amino acids. So long as you eat a variety of foods throughout the day, it is not necessary to eat complementary proteins in the same meal.

Calcium is needed for building strong bones and teeth. If your diet does not include dairy, look to other sources of calcium such as broccoli; dark green leafy vegetables like kale and collard or turnip greens; calcium-fortified soy-based products like tofu, milk and yogurt; and calcium-fortified cereal.

Vitamin D helps absorb calcium. Egg yolks and vitamin D-fortified milk are some of the best sources. If your diet excludes milk, consider vitamin D-fortified soy milk, orange juice or yogurt. If you think you need a supplement, be sure to check with your physician.

Omega-3 Fatty Acids are key to cardiovascular health, brain function and vision. Fish and eggs are good sources. If your diet excludes them, consult your physician about taking a supplement.

Vitamin B-12 is crucial for red blood cells and nerve function. It is found in animal protein. If your diet does not include dairy products or eggs, look for foods fortified with vitamin B-12, such as cereals and soy-based products. Ask your physician about taking a supplement.

Iron helps form hemoglobin, which carries oxygen in the blood. Iron comes from both animal and plant foods, but the iron in plant foods is more difficult for the body to absorb. Vitamin C-rich foods like citrus fruits help with iron absorption and should be combined with iron-rich foods, such as dark green leafy vegetables, blackstrap molasses, prune juice and dried fruits.

Zinc is an essential trace mineral. It has many functions in the body, such as repairing and building immune cells. It helps with digestion, and zinc is used to make insulin to regulate blood sugar. Zinc comes from both animal and plant foods, but it is more difficult for the body to absorb zinc from plants. Like iron, zinc is best absorbed when eaten with vitamin C-rich foods like citrus. Foods that are rich in zinc include soy products, whole grains, legumes and nuts.

Getting Enough Protein on a Vegetarian Diet

A good rule of thumb for calculating your daily protein need is to multiply your body weight in pounds by .4 grams. For example, a 150-pound person needs about 60 grams of protein daily. Here are some popular meatless sources of protein.

PROTEIN SOURCE	GRAMS OF PROTEIN
1 cup cooked black beans	15g
1 cup cooked chickpeas	12g
1 cup cooked lentils	18g
1 cup cooked quinoa	8g
4 oz. tofu	10g
1 large egg	7g
1 cup cottage cheese	24g
1 cup flavored Greek yogurt	18g
1 cup dairy milk	8g
1 cup plain soy milk	7g
1 oz. cheddar cheese	7g
1 oz. almonds	6g
2 Tbsp. peanut butter	7g

FAVORITE WAYS TO CREATE SATISFYING VEGETARIAN DISHES

1 Go Meaty with Mushrooms. With their rich taste and meaty texture, mushrooms make vegetarian meals that are wonderfully satisfying.

PORTOBELLO MELTS, P. 102

Portobello caps make great vegetarian "burgers." The stems are tough and woody, though. Discard them, or use well-rinsed and coarsely chopped stems in homemade vegetable broth.

2 Get to Know Tofu. Also called soybean curd or bean curd, tofu is made from soy milk the same way cheese is made from dairy milk. Soy milk is mixed with calcium or magnesium salt to create curds. The more liquid (whey) is pressed from the curd, the firmer the tofu will be.

ASPARAGUS TOFU STIR-FRY, P. 49

While tofu has a pretty neutral taste, it acts as a blank flavor canvas, absorbing the flavors of surrounding ingredients. It's a natural in veggie-rich stir-fries and soups, as well as a great way to add satisfying protein and fiber to breakfast smoothies.

3 Reach for Lentils & Other Legumes. Billions of people around the world rely on these vegetarian sources of protein in their diets. Lentils and beans are a major food source throughout the Americas, Caribbean, Mediterranean and parts of Asia.

LENTIL LOAF P. 17

Lentils use few resources to grow and, calorie for calorie, produce only 2.5% as much greenhouse gas carbon dioxide as beef and 10% as much carbon dioxide as tofu. That makes lentils one of the greenest crops there is—especially when you factor in their high protein content.

4 Add an Egg. Eggs are a protein powerhouse. If your diet includes eggs, try adding one to breakfast potatoes, ramen soup, pad thai or even a vegetarian burger.

SOUTHWEST HASH WITH ADOBO-LIME CREMA, P. 217

5 Use Smoky Spices. Ground chipotle pepper and smoked paprika add complexity to many dishes. They lend sweetness, heat and smoky notes, letting you enjoy a bacony taste without the unwanted calories, fat or meat.

SPICY LENTIL & CHICKPEA STEW P. 171

Popular Legumes for Meatless Meals

Stock your pantry with these go-to beans and lentils in canned or dried forms. They're affordable, healthy and convenient for making hearty vegetarian dinners.

◄ **BLACK BEANS** Small and black; widely available and a staple in many Latin American dishes

CANNELLINI BEANS ► Large, white Italian kidney beans; used most often in salads and soups

◄ **CHICKPEAS** Also known as garbanzo beans; medium-size, tan and acorn-shaped; featured in Middle Eastern and Mediterranean dishes

GREAT NORTHERN BEANS ► Large, kidney-shaped and mild; best in stews, dips and classic French cassoulets

◄ **KIDNEY BEANS** Large, light or dark pink or red; used most often with rice and in chilis, stews and soups

GREEN OR BROWN LENTILS ► Small and round; does not need soaking. Green lentils taste slightly peppery; use in salads or as a side dish. Brown lentils have an earthy flavor; great in soup

◄ **RED OR YELLOW LENTILS** Small, split legume; no soaking needed; common in Indian, Mediterranean and Middle Eastern cuisines; soft texture; use in soups and stews

MUST-TRY MAIN DISHES

Discover a world of exciting dinners, from Indian curries and Mexican entrees to down-home American casseroles and potpies. Explore a new cuisine tonight, or try a vegetarian take on dishes the family already loves.

EASY CHANA
MASALA, PAGE 40

QUINOA & BLACK BEAN-STUFFED PEPPERS

If you're thinking about a meatless meal, give these no-fuss filled peppers a try. They come together with a just few ingredients and put a tasty spin on a low-fat dinner!
—*Cindy Reams, Philipsburg, PA*

Takes: 30 min. • **Makes:** 4 servings

1½ cups water
1 cup quinoa, rinsed
4 large green peppers
1 jar (16 oz.) chunky salsa, divided
1 can (15 oz.) black beans, rinsed and drained
½ cup reduced-fat ricotta cheese
½ cup shredded Monterey Jack cheese, divided

1. Preheat oven to 400°. In a small saucepan, bring water to a boil. Add quinoa. Reduce the heat; simmer, covered, until all the water is absorbed, 10-12 minutes.

2. Meanwhile, cut and discard tops from peppers; remove seeds. Place in a greased 8-in. square baking dish, cut side down. Microwave peppers, uncovered, on high until crisp-tender, 3-4 minutes. Turn peppers cut side up.

3. Reserve ⅓ cup salsa; add remaining salsa to quinoa. Stir in beans, ricotta cheese and ¼ cup Monterey Jack cheese. Spoon mixture into peppers; sprinkle with remaining cheese. Bake stuffed peppers, uncovered, until filling is heated through, 10-15 minutes. Top with the reserved salsa.

1 stuffed pepper: 393 cal., 8g fat (4g sat. fat), 20mg chol., 774mg sod., 59g carb. (10g sugars, 10g fiber), 18g pro.

SOUTHWEST TORTILLA PIE

I found this entree a while ago but decreased the cheese and increased the herbs originally called for. It's one of my toddler's favorite meals. She always smiles when she sees it on the table ready for her.

—*Wendy Kelly, Petersburg, NY*

Prep: 50 min. • **Bake:** 15 min.
Makes: 6 servings

- 1   Tbsp. olive oil
- 1   medium green pepper, chopped
- 1   medium onion, chopped
- 1   tsp. ground cumin
- ¼   tsp. pepper
- 3   garlic cloves, minced
- 2   cans (15 oz. each) black beans, rinsed and drained
- 1   can (14½ oz.) vegetable broth
- 1   pkg. (10 oz.) frozen corn, thawed
- 4   green onions, sliced
- 4   flour tortillas (8 in.)
- 1   cup shredded reduced-fat cheddar cheese, divided

1. Preheat oven to 400°. In a large skillet, heat oil over medium-high heat. Add green pepper, onion, cumin and pepper; cook and stir until vegetables are tender. Add garlic; cook 1 minute longer.

2. Stir in the beans and broth. Bring to a boil; cook until liquid is reduced to about ⅓ cup, stirring occasionally. Stir in corn and green onions; remove from heat.

3. Place 1 tortilla in a 9-in. springform pan coated with cooking spray. Layer with 1½ cups bean mixture and ¼ cup cheese. Repeat the layers twice. Top with remaining tortilla. Place pan on a baking sheet.

4. Bake, uncovered, until heated through, 15-20 minutes. Sprinkle with the remaining cheese. Loosen sides from pan with a knife; remove rim from pan. Cut into 6 wedges.

1 slice: 353 cal., 9g fat (3g sat. fat), 14mg chol., 842mg sod., 53g carb. (6g sugars, 8g fiber), 17g pro.

CREAMY LENTILS WITH KALE ARTICHOKE SAUTE

I've been trying to eat more meatless meals, so I experimented with this hearty saute and served it over brown rice. It was so good even the non-kale lovers gobbled it up.

—*Teri Lee Rasey, Cadillac, MI*

Takes: 30 min. • **Makes:** 4 servings

- ½   cup dried red lentils, rinsed and sorted
- ¼   tsp. dried oregano
- ⅛   tsp. pepper
- 1¼   cups vegetable broth
- ¼   tsp. sea salt, divided
- 1   Tbsp. olive oil or grapeseed oil
- 16   cups chopped fresh kale (about 12 oz.)
- 1   can (14 oz.) water-packed artichoke hearts, drained and chopped
- 3   garlic cloves, minced
- ½   tsp. Italian seasoning
- 2   Tbsp. grated Romano cheese
- 2   cups hot cooked brown or basmati rice

1. Place first 4 ingredients and ⅛ tsp. salt in a small saucepan; bring to a boil. Reduce heat; simmer, covered, until the lentils are tender and liquid is almost absorbed, 12-15 minutes. Remove from heat.

2. In a 6-qt. stockpot, heat oil over medium heat. Add kale and remaining salt; cook, covered, until kale is wilted, 4-5 minutes, stirring occasionally. Add artichoke hearts, garlic and Italian seasoning; cook and stir 3 minutes. Remove from heat; stir in cheese.

3. Serve lentils and kale mixture over rice.

1 serving: 321 cal., 6g fat (2g sat. fat), 1mg chol., 661mg sod., 53g carb. (1g sugars, 5g fiber), 15g pro.

TEST KITCHEN TIP

Lentils don't require soaking, but they should be rinsed and sifted through to look for stones before cooking them.

SWEET POTATO & MUSHROOM POTPIES

The last time I was in the U.S., I was served an amazing mushroom and beer potpie at a small brewpub. It was so rich and comforting that I tried many versions when I got home, and I think I've come pretty close!

—*Iben Ravn, Copenhagen, Denmark*

- -

Prep: 45 min. • **Bake:** 30 min.
Makes: 8 servings

- ⅓ cup olive oil, divided
- 1 lb. sliced fresh shiitake mushrooms
- 1 lb. sliced baby portobello mushrooms
- 2 large onions, chopped
- 2 garlic cloves, minced
- 1 tsp. minced fresh rosemary, plus more for topping
- 1 bottle (12 oz.) porter or stout beer
- 1½ cups mushroom broth or vegetable broth, divided
- 2 bay leaves
- 1 Tbsp. balsamic vinegar
- 2 Tbsp. reduced-sodium soy sauce
- ¼ cup cornstarch
- 3 to 4 small sweet potatoes, peeled and thinly sliced
- ¾ tsp. coarsely ground pepper
- ½ tsp. salt

1. Preheat oven to 400°. In a Dutch oven, heat 1 Tbsp. oil over medium heat. Add the shiitake mushrooms and cook in batches until dark golden brown, 8-10 minutes; remove with a slotted spoon. Repeat with 1 Tbsp. oil and the portobello mushrooms.

2. In same pan, heat 1 Tbsp. oil over medium heat. Add onions; cook and stir 8-10 minutes or until tender. Add garlic and 1 tsp. minced rosemary; cook 30 seconds longer. Stir in the beer, 1 cup of broth, bay leaves, vinegar, soy sauce and sauteed mushrooms.

3. Bring to a boil. Reduce the heat; simmer, uncovered, 10 minutes. In a small bowl, mix cornstarch and remaining broth until smooth; stir into mushroom mixture. Return to a boil, stirring constantly; cook and stir the mixture until thickened, 1-2 minutes. Discard the bay leaves; transfer the mushroom mixture to 8 greased 8-oz. ramekins. Place on a rimmed baking sheet.

4. Layer sweet potatoes in a circular pattern on top of each ramekin; brush with the remaining oil and sprinkle with pepper, salt and additional rosemary. Bake, covered, until potatoes are tender, 20-25 minutes. Remove cover and bake until the potatoes are lightly browned, 8-10 minutes. Let stand 5 minutes before serving.

1 serving: 211 cal., 10g fat (1g sat. fat), 0 chol., 407mg sod., 26g carb. (10g sugars, 4g fiber), 5g pro.

TEST KITCHEN TIP

An easy way to cover these potpies for the first portion of their baking? Simply invert another rimmed baking sheet over the top. Gently remove it with oven mitts to check whether sweet potatoes are tender.

🕐 GNOCCHI WITH PESTO SAUCE

Perk up your gnocchi and vegetables with a flavorful pesto sauce. If you don't have pine nuts for topping you can use another nut.
—Taste of Home *Test Kitchen*

- -

Takes: 25 min. • **Makes:** 4 servings

1	pkg. (16 oz.) potato gnocchi
2	tsp. olive oil
1	cup diced zucchini
½	cup chopped sweet yellow pepper
¼	cup prepared pesto
1	cup chopped tomatoes
	Toasted pine nuts, optional

1. Cook gnocchi according to the package directions; drain.
2. Meanwhile, in a large skillet, heat oil over medium-high heat; saute zucchini and pepper until zucchini is tender.
3. Add pesto and gnocchi, stirring gently to coat. Stir in tomatoes. If desired, top with toasted pine nuts.
Note: Look for potato gnocchi in the pasta or frozen foods section.
1 cup: 327 cal., 9g fat (2g sat. fat), 8mg chol., 682mg sod., 52g carb. (10g sugars, 4g fiber), 9g pro.

MEAT
LOVER
OPTION
PAGE 320

⏰ EDAMAME & SOBA NOODLE BOWL

Toothsome soba noodles are made from buckwheat flour.

—*Matthew Hass, Ellison Bay, WI*

Takes: 30 min. • **Makes:** 6 servings

- 1 pkg. (12 oz.) uncooked Japanese soba noodles or whole wheat spaghetti
- 2 Tbsp. sesame oil
- 2 cups fresh small broccoli florets
- 1 medium onion, halved and thinly sliced
- 3 cups frozen shelled edamame, thawed
- 2 large carrots, cut into ribbons with a vegetable peeler
- 4 garlic cloves, minced
- 1 cup reduced-fat Asian toasted sesame salad dressing
- ¼ tsp. pepper
  Sesame seeds, toasted, optional

1. In a 6 qt. stockpot, cook noodles according to package directions; drain and return the noodles to pan.

2. Meanwhile, in a large skillet, heat oil over medium heat. Add broccoli and onion; cook and stir until crisp-tender, 4-6 minutes. Add the edamame and carrots; cook and stir until tender, about 6-8 minutes. Add garlic; cook for 1 minute longer. Add vegetable mixture, dressing and pepper to the noodles; toss to combine. Sprinkle with toasted sesame seeds if desired.

1⅓ cups: 414 cal., 12g fat (1g sat. fat), 0 chol., 867mg sod., 64g carb. (12g sugars, 4g fiber), 18g pro.

TEST KITCHEN TIP

Edamame are immature green soybeans. You can purchase them still in pods or already shelled and ready to use in recipes like this.

VEG JAMBALAYA

I first made this dish when I was craving Creole food but didn't have the usual meats that I like to use on hand. Canned beans take their place in this flavorful dinner that's now in my regular rotation.

—*Crystal Jo Bruns, Iliff, CO*

Prep: 10 min. • **Cook:** 30 min.
Makes: 6 servings

- 1 Tbsp. canola oil
- 1 medium green pepper, chopped
- 1 medium onion, chopped
- 1 celery rib, chopped
- 3 garlic cloves, minced
- 2 cups water
- 1 can (14½ oz.) diced tomatoes, undrained
- 1 can (8 oz.) tomato sauce
- ½ tsp. Italian seasoning
- ¼ tsp. salt
- ¼ tsp. crushed red pepper flakes
- ⅛ tsp. fennel seed, crushed
- 1 cup uncooked long grain rice
- 1 can (16 oz.) butter beans, rinsed and drained
- 1 can (16 oz.) red beans, rinsed and drained

1. In a Dutch oven, heat oil over medium-high heat. Add the green pepper, onion and celery; cook and stir until tender. Add garlic; cook 1 minute longer.

2. Add the water, tomatoes, tomato sauce and seasonings. Bring to a boil; stir in rice. Reduce the heat; cover and simmer for 15-18 minutes or until liquid is absorbed and rice is tender. Stir in beans; heat through.

1⅓ cups: 281 cal., 3g fat (0 sat. fat), 0 chol., 796mg sod., 56g carb. (6g sugars, 9g fiber), 11g pro.

FARMERS MARKET ENCHILADAS

These vegetarian enchiladas use a lot of garden favorites in a quick weeknight meal. Feel free to substitute whatever vegetables you have from your garden—yellow summer squash, eggplant and corn all taste great here, too.

—*Elisabeth Larsen, Pleasant Grove, UT*

Prep: 20 min. • **Bake:** 45 min.
Makes: 7 servings

- 3 **medium zucchini, quartered lengthwise and sliced**
- 1 **poblano pepper, seeded and chopped**
- 8 **oz. sliced fresh mushrooms**
- 8 **oz. cherry tomatoes**
- 1 **Tbsp. olive oil**
- 1 **tsp. ground cumin**
- ½ **tsp. salt**
- ¼ **tsp. cayenne pepper**
- 2 **cups shredded Monterey Jack cheese**
- 1 **cup crumbled queso fresco or feta cheese, divided**
- ½ **cup minced fresh cilantro, divided**
- 2 **Tbsp. lime juice**
- 14 **corn tortillas (6 in.), warmed**
- 1 **can (15 oz.) enchilada sauce**

1. Preheat oven to 400°. In a large bowl, combine zucchini, poblano, mushrooms and tomatoes; drizzle with oil and sprinkle with cumin, salt and cayenne. Toss to coat. Divide vegetable mixture between 2 lightly greased 15x10x1-in. baking pans. Roast 15 minutes; rotate the pans top to bottom. Roast an additional 10 minutes or until vegetables are tender. Return to bowl and cool slightly.
2. Stir in Monterey Jack cheese, ½ cup queso fresco, ¼ cup cilantro and lime juice. Place a scant ½ cup vegetable mixture off center on each tortilla. Roll up and place in a greased

13x9-in. baking dish, seam side down. Top with enchilada sauce; sprinkle with remaining queso fresco.
3. Bake, uncovered, until heated through and cheese is melted, about 20 minutes. Top with remaining cilantro.

2 enchiladas: 346 cal., 17g fat (9g sat. fat), 40mg chol., 780mg sod., 33g carb. (5g sugars, 5g fiber), 18g pro.

TEST KITCHEN TIP

Roasting the veggies before making the enchiladas takes extra time, but it adds so much flavor! Don't skip it.

LENTIL LOAF

This lentil loaf is so hearty and flavorful, you might think it contains meat. And it's packed with fiber, protein and nutrients.
—*Tracy Fleming, Phoenix, AZ*

Prep: 35 min. • **Bake:** 45 min. + standing
Makes: 6 servings

- ¾ cup brown lentils, rinsed
- 1 can (14½ oz.) vegetable broth
- 1 Tbsp. olive oil
- 1¾ cups shredded carrots
- 1 cup finely chopped onion
- 1 cup chopped fresh mushrooms
- 2 Tbsp. minced fresh basil or 2 tsp. dried basil
- 1 Tbsp. minced fresh parsley
- 1 cup shredded part-skim mozzarella cheese
- ½ cup cooked brown rice
- 1 large egg
- 1 large egg white
- ½ tsp. salt
- ½ tsp. garlic powder
- ¼ tsp. pepper
- 2 Tbsp. tomato paste
- 2 Tbsp. water

1. Place lentils and broth in a small saucepan; bring to a boil. Reduce heat; simmer, covered, until tender, about 30 minutes.
2. Preheat oven to 350°. Line a 9x5-in. loaf pan with parchment, letting ends extend up sides. Coat paper with cooking spray.
3. In a large skillet, heat oil over medium heat; saute carrots, onion and mushrooms until tender, for about 10 minutes. Stir in herbs. Transfer to a large bowl; cool slightly.
4. Add the mozzarella cheese, rice, egg, egg white, seasonings and lentils to vegetables; mix well. Mix tomato paste and water; spread over loaf.
5. Bake until a thermometer inserted into the center reads 160°, 45-50 minutes. Let stand 10 minutes before slicing.
1 slice: 213 cal., 5g fat (3g sat. fat), 43mg chol., 580mg sod., 29g carb. (5g sugars, 5g fiber), 14g pro. **Diabetic exchanges:** 2 lean meat, 1½ starch, 1 vegetable, ½ fat.

CAULIFLOWER & TOFU CURRY

Cauliflower, chickpeas and tofu are subtle on their own, but put together they make an awesome base for curry. We have this dish weekly because one of us is always craving it.
—*Patrick McGilvray, Cincinnati, OH*

Takes: 30 min. • **Makes:** 6 servings

- 1 Tbsp. olive oil
- 2 medium carrots, sliced
- 1 medium onion, chopped
- 3 tsp. curry powder
- ¼ tsp. salt
- ¼ tsp. pepper
- 1 small head cauliflower, broken into florets (about 3 cups)
- 1 can (14½ oz.) fire-roasted crushed tomatoes
- 1 pkg. (14 oz.) extra-firm tofu, drained and cut into ½-in. cubes
- 1 cup vegetable broth
- 1 can (15 oz.) chickpeas, rinsed and drained
- 1 can (13.66 oz.) coconut milk
- 1 cup frozen peas
  Hot cooked rice
  Chopped fresh cilantro

1. In a 6-qt. stockpot, heat oil over medium-high heat. Add carrots and onion; cook and stir until onion is tender, 4-5 minutes. Stir in the seasonings.
2. Add cauliflower, tomatoes, tofu and broth; bring to a boil. Reduce heat; simmer, covered, 10 minutes. Stir in chickpeas, coconut milk and peas; return to a boil. Reduce the heat to medium; cook, uncovered, stirring the mixture occasionally, until slightly thickened and cauliflower is tender, 5-7 minutes.
3. Serve with rice. Sprinkle with cilantro.
1⅓ cups: 338 cal., 21g fat (13g sat. fat), 0 chol., 528mg sod., 29g carb. (9g sugars, 7g fiber), 13g pro.
Health tip: One-half cup cooked cauliflower provides nearly half the daily value for vitamin C, not to mention many sulfur-containing compounds that may help protect against certain cancers.

CHILI-LIME MUSHROOM TACOS

I used to make this dish with beef, but then substituting portobello mushrooms turned it into my family's vegetarian favorite. It's quick, nutritious, low in fat and tasty.
—*Greg Fontenot, The Woodlands, TX*

Takes: 25 min. • **Makes:** 4 servings

- 4 large portobello mushrooms (about ¾ lb.)
- 1 Tbsp. olive oil
- 1 medium sweet red pepper, cut into strips
- 1 medium onion, halved and thinly sliced
- 2 garlic cloves, minced
- 1½ tsp. chili powder
- ½ tsp. salt
- ½ tsp. ground cumin
- ¼ tsp. crushed red pepper flakes
- 1 tsp. grated lime zest
- 2 Tbsp. lime juice
- 8 corn tortillas (6 in.), warmed
- 1 cup shredded pepper jack cheese

1. Remove stems from the mushrooms; if desired, remove gills using a spoon. Cut the mushrooms into ½-in. slices.
2. In a large skillet, heat oil over medium-high heat; saute mushrooms, pepper and onion until mushrooms are tender, 5-7 minutes. Add garlic, seasonings, lime zest and juice; cook and stir 1 minute. Serve in tortillas; top with shredded cheese.
2 tacos: 300 cal., 14g fat (6g sat. fat), 30mg chol., 524mg sod., 33g carb. (5g sugars, 6g fiber), 13g pro. **Diabetic exchanges:** 2 vegetable, 1½ starch, 1 medium-fat meat, ½ fat.

CHEDDAR BEAN BURRITOS

My family goes meatless several nights a week, and this recipe is one of our favorites. I usually puree a can or two of chipotles in adobo and freeze in ice cube trays so I can use a small amount when I need it.
—*Amy Bravo, Ames, IA*

Takes: 25 min. • **Makes:** 6 servings

- 2 tsp. canola oil
- 1 Tbsp. minced chipotle pepper in adobo sauce
- 2 garlic cloves, minced
- 2 tsp. chili powder
- 1 tsp. ground cumin
- ⅛ tsp. salt
- 2 cans (15 oz. each) black beans, rinsed and drained
- 2 Tbsp. water
- ½ cup pico de gallo
- 6 flour tortillas (8 in.), warmed
- 1 cup shredded cheddar or Monterey Jack cheese
- ½ cup sour cream
  Additional pico de gallo and sour cream, optional

1. In a large skillet, heat oil over medium heat; saute chipotle pepper, garlic and seasonings 2 minutes. Stir in beans and water; bring to a boil. Reduce heat; simmer, uncovered, until the flavors are blended, 5-7 minutes, stirring mixture occasionally.
2. Coarsely mash bean mixture; stir in pico de gallo. Spoon onto tortillas; top with cheese and sour cream. Roll up. If desired, serve with additional pico de gallo and sour cream.
Freeze option: Cool filling before making burritos. Individually wrap burritos in paper towels and foil; freeze in an airtight container. To use, remove foil. Place a paper towel-wrapped burrito on a microwave-safe plate. Microwave individual burrito on high until heated through, 4-6 minutes, turning once. Let stand 2 minutes.
1 burrito: 410 cal., 16g fat (7g sat. fat), 23mg chol., 726mg sod., 50g carb. (2g sugars, 8g fiber), 16g pro.

MEAT
LOVER
OPTION
PAGE 320

CONTEST-WINNING EGGPLANT PARMESAN

Baking the eggplant instead of frying it makes this favorite dish much healthier! Prep time is a little longer than for some recipes, but the classic Italian flavors and rustic elegance are well worth it.
—*Laci Hooten, McKinney, TX*

Prep: 40 min. • **Cook:** 25 min.
Makes: 8 servings

- 3 large eggs, beaten
- 2½ cups panko bread crumbs
- 3 medium eggplants, cut into ¼-in. slices
- 2 jars (4½ oz. each) sliced mushrooms, drained
- ½ tsp dried basil
- ⅛ tsp. dried oregano
- 2 cups shredded part-skim mozzarella cheese
- ½ cup grated Parmesan cheese
- 1 jar (28 oz.) spaghetti sauce

1. Preheat oven to 350°. Place the eggs and bread crumbs in separate shallow bowls. Dip eggplant in eggs, then coat in crumbs. Place slices on baking sheets coated with cooking spray. Bake 15-20 minutes or until tender and golden brown, turning once.
2. In a small bowl, combine mushrooms, basil and oregano. In another small bowl, combine mozzarella and Parmesan cheeses.
3. Spread ½ cup sauce into a 13x9-in. baking dish coated with cooking spray. Layer with a third of the mushroom mixture, a third of the eggplant, ¾ cup sauce and a third of the cheese mixture. Repeat layers twice.
4. Bake eggplant Parmesan, uncovered, at 350° for 25-30 minutes or until heated through and cheese is melted.
1 serving: 305 cal., 12g fat (5g sat. fat), 102mg chol., 912mg sod., 32g carb. (12g sugars, 9g fiber), 18g pro.

VEGGIE POWER CRISPY TACOS

We eat meatless meals a few times a week, so I replaced the beef with nutty brown rice to bulk up these tacos. Sometimes I like to swap in quinoa for the rice.
—*Kristin Rimkus, Snohomish, WA*

Takes: 30 min. • **Makes:** 4 servings

- 1   medium onion, finely chopped
- 1   medium green pepper, finely chopped
- 1   small sweet red pepper, finely chopped
- 1   can (15 oz.) black beans, rinsed and drained
- 2   large tomatoes, seeded and chopped
- 2   cups shredded cabbage
- 1   cup fresh or frozen corn
- 2   Tbsp. reduced-sodium taco seasoning
- 2   Tbsp. lime juice
- 2   garlic cloves, minced
- 1   cup ready-to-serve brown rice
- 8   taco shells, warmed
- ½   cup shredded reduced-fat Mexican cheese blend
- ½   cup reduced-fat sour cream

1. In a lightly oiled large nonstick skillet, saute onion and peppers until crisp-tender. Add the black beans, tomatoes, cabbage, corn, taco seasoning, lime juice and garlic. Cook and stir over medium heat until vegetables are tender, 8-10 minutes. Stir in rice; heat through.
2. Spoon bean mixture into taco shells. Top with cheese and sour cream.
2 tacos: 423 cal., 12g fat (4g sat. fat), 20mg chol., 682mg sod., 64g carb. (12g sugars, 10g fiber), 17g pro.

PRESSURE-COOKER LENTIL STEW

This tasty vegetarian stew lets you take a break from meat. Adding cream at the end gives it a lovely smoother texture.
—*Michelle Collins, Suffolk, VA*

Prep: 45 min. • **Cook:** 15 min. + releasing
Makes: 8 servings (2¾ qt.)

- 2   Tbsp. canola oil
- 2   large onions, thinly sliced, divided
- 8   plum tomatoes, chopped
- 2   Tbsp. minced fresh gingerroot
- 3   garlic cloves, minced
- 2   tsp. ground coriander
- 1½ tsp. ground cumin
- ¼   tsp. cayenne pepper
- 3   cups vegetable broth
- 2   cups dried lentils, rinsed
- 2   cups water
- 1   can (4 oz.) chopped green chiles
- ¾   cup heavy whipping cream
- 2   Tbsp. butter
- 1   tsp. cumin seeds
- 6   cups hot cooked basmati or jasmine rice
      Optional: Sliced green onions or minced fresh cilantro

1. Select the saute setting on a 6-qt. electric pressure cooker. Adjust for medium heat; add oil. When the oil is hot, cook and stir half the onions until crisp-tender, 2-3 minutes. Add tomatoes, ginger and garlic, coriander, cumin and cayenne; cook and stir 1 minute longer. Press cancel. Stir in the broth, lentils, water, green chiles and remaining onion.
2. Lock the lid; close pressure-release valve. Adjust to pressure-cook on high for 15 minutes. Let pressure release naturally. Just before serving, stir in cream. In a small skillet, heat butter over medium heat. Add cumin seeds; cook and stir until seeds are golden brown, 1-2 minutes. Add to lentil mixture.
3. Serve with rice. If desired, sprinkle with green onions or cilantro.
1⅓ cups stew with ¾ cup rice: 497 cal., 16g fat (8g sat. fat), 33mg chol., 345mg sod., 73g carb. (5g sugars, 8g fiber), 17g pro.

QUICK VEGGIE POTPIES

My family loves potpies, and with this recipe, no one even misses the meat. It's that tasty.
—Annette Woofenden, Middleboro, MA

Prep: 15 min. • **Bake:** 25 min.
Makes: 4 servings

- 1 small onion, chopped
- 6 Tbsp. butter
- 2 garlic cloves, minced
- 6 Tbsp. all-purpose flour
- ½ tsp. salt
- ¼ tsp. pepper
- 3 cups vegetable broth
- 2 cups frozen mixed vegetables, thawed
- 1 can (15 oz.) chickpeas, rinsed and drained
- 1¼ cups frozen cubed hash brown potatoes
- ¼ cup heavy whipping cream
- ¾ tsp. Italian seasoning
- 1 sheet refrigerated pie crust

1. Saute onion in butter in a large saucepan until tender. Add garlic; cook 1 minute longer. Stir in the flour, salt and pepper until blended. Gradually add broth; bring to a boil. Cook and stir for 2 minutes or until thickened.

2. Stir in the vegetables, chickpeas, potatoes, cream and Italian seasoning. Divide mixture among 4 ungreased 10-oz. ramekins.

3. Unroll crust; divide into 4 portions. Roll out each portion to fit ramekins; place crust over filling. Trim, seal and flute the edges. Cut slits in crust. Place ramekins on a baking sheet.

4. Bake at 400° for 25-30 minutes or until the crust is golden brown.

1 potpie: 680 cal., 39g fat (20g sat. fat), 76mg chol., 1518mg sod., 72g carb. (10g sugars, 9g fiber), 11g pro.

 GRILLED CAPRESE QUESADILLAS

This is a quick and healthy summer recipe with ingredients right from the backyard garden. Feta or mozzarella cheese can be substituted for the goat cheese. We also enjoy it with grilled chicken.
—Amy Mongiovi, Lititz, PA

MEAT LOVER OPTION PAGE 320

Takes: 20 min. • **Makes:** 2 servings

- 4 whole wheat tortillas (8 in.)
- 6 oz. fresh mozzarella cheese, sliced
- 2 medium tomatoes, sliced and patted dry
- 1 3 cup julienned fresh basil
- ¼ cup pitted Greek olives, chopped
  Freshly ground pepper to taste

1. Layer one half of each tortilla with cheese and tomatoes; sprinkle with basil, olives and pepper to taste. Fold tortillas to close.

2. Grill, covered, over medium-high heat until tortillas are lightly browned and the cheese is melted, 2-3 minutes per side.

1 quesadilla: 535 cal., 25g fat (13g sat. fat), 67mg chol., 665mg sod., 52g carb. (5g sugars, 8g fiber), 25g pro.

⓼ SHEET-PAN CURRY DINNER
When there's not much time to cook, try roasting potatoes and cauliflower with chickpeas for a warm-you-up dinner. Add chicken or tofu to the sheet pan if you like.
—*Pam Correll, Brockport, PA*

Prep: 15 min. • **Bake:** 30 min.
Makes: 4 servings

- 2 lbs. potatoes (about 4 medium), peeled and cut into ½-in. cubes
- 1 small head cauliflower, broken into florets (about 3 cups)
- 1 can (15 oz.) chickpeas or garbanzo beans, rinsed and drained
- 3 Tbsp. olive oil
- 2 tsp. curry powder
- ¾ tsp. salt
- ¼ tsp. pepper
- 3 Tbsp. minced fresh cilantro or parsley

1. Preheat oven to 400°. Place the first 7 ingredients in a large bowl; toss to coat. Transfer to a 15x10x1-in. baking pan coated with cooking spray.
2. Roast until the vegetables are tender, for 30-35 minutes, stirring occasionally. Sprinkle with cilantro or parsley.
1½ cups: 339 cal., 13g fat (2g sat. fat), 0 chol., 605mg sod., 51g carb. (6g sugars, 8g fiber), 8g pro. **Diabetic exchanges:** 3 starch, 2 fat, 1 vegetable, 1 lean meat.

SALSA SPAGHETTI SQUASH

If you want pasta but are avoiding gluten or trying to keep a lid on carbs, spaghetti squash is a flavorful alternative. Subtly sweet, tender and satisfying—and with a southwestern twist—this is one wonderful and surprising "spaghetti" dish.
—*Clara Coulson Minney,*
Washington Court House, OH

Takes: 30 min. • **Makes:** 4 servings

- 1 medium spaghetti squash
- 1 medium onion, chopped
- 2 cups salsa
- 1 can (15 oz.) black beans, rinsed and drained
- 3 Tbsp. minced fresh cilantro
- 1 medium ripe avocado, peeled and cubed

1. Cut the squash lengthwise in half; discard seeds. Place squash on a microwave-safe plate, cut side down. Microwave, uncovered, on high for 15-18 minutes or until tender.
2. Meanwhile, in a lightly oiled nonstick skillet, cook and stir onion over medium heat until tender. Stir in salsa, beans and cilantro; heat through. Gently stir in avocado. When the squash is cool enough to handle, use a fork to separate strands. Top with salsa mixture.
1 cup: 308 cal., 9g fat (2g sat. fat), 0 chol., 822mg sod., 46g carb. (6g sugars, 16g fiber), 8g pro.

SLOW-COOKED STUFFED PEPPERS

My favorite kitchen appliance is the slow cooker, and I use mine more than anyone else I know. Here's a tasty good-for-you dish.
—*Michelle Gurnsey, Lincoln, NE*

Prep: 15 min. • **Cook:** 3 hours
Makes: 4 servings

- 4 medium sweet red peppers
- 1 can (15 oz.) black beans, rinsed and drained
- 1 cup shredded pepper jack cheese
- ¾ cup salsa
- 1 small onion, chopped
- ½ cup frozen corn
- ⅓ cup uncooked converted long grain rice
- 1¼ tsp. chili powder
- ½ tsp. ground cumin
   Reduced-fat sour cream, optional

1. Cut and discard tops from the peppers; remove seeds. In a large bowl, mix beans, cheese, salsa, onion, corn, rice, chili powder and cumin; spoon into peppers. Place in a 5-qt. slow cooker coated with cooking spray.
2. Cook, covered, on low until the peppers are tender and the filling is heated through, 3-4 hours. If desired, serve with sour cream.
1 stuffed pepper: 317 cal., 10g fat (5g sat. fat), 30mg chol., 565mg sod., 43g carb. (6g sugars, 8g fiber), 15g pro. **Diabetic exchanges:** 2 starch, 2 lean meat, 2 vegetable, 1 fat.

READER RAVE

"I first made this at home and loved it. The next time I didn't stuff the peppers, but instead I added two chopped peppers to the bean mixture. My potluck group loved it, vegetarians and meat-eaters alike."
—MOXIEWOMAN, TASTEOFHOME.COM

TASTY LENTIL TACOS

My husband has to watch his cholesterol. Finding dishes that are healthy for him and yummy for our five children is a challenge sometimes, but this fun taco recipe is a huge hit with everyone.

—*Michelle Thomas, Bangor, ME*

Prep: 15 min. • **Cook:** 40 min.
Makes: 6 servings

- 1 tsp. canola oil
- 1 medium onion, finely chopped
- 1 garlic clove, minced
- 1 cup dried lentils, rinsed
- 1 Tbsp. chili powder
- 2 tsp. ground cumin
- 1 tsp. dried oregano
- 2½ cups vegetable or reduced-sodium chicken broth
- 1 cup salsa
- 12 taco shells
- 1½ cups shredded lettuce
- 1 cup chopped fresh tomatoes
- 1½ cups shredded reduced-fat cheddar cheese
- 6 Tbsp. fat-free sour cream

1. In a large nonstick skillet, heat oil over medium heat; saute onion and garlic until tender. Add lentils and seasonings; cook and stir 1 minute. Stir in broth; bring to a boil. Reduce heat; simmer, covered, until lentils are tender, 25-30 minutes.

2. Cook, uncovered, until the mixture is thickened, 6-8 minutes, stirring occasionally. Mash lentils slightly; stir in salsa and heat through. Serve in taco shells. Top with the remaining ingredients.

2 tacos: 365 cal., 12g fat (5g sat. fat), 21mg chol., 777mg sod., 44g carb. (5g sugars, 6g fiber), 19g pro. **Diabetic exchanges:** 2½ starch, 2 lean meat, 1 vegetable, 1 fat.

GNOCCHI WITH WHITE BEANS

Here's one of those no-fuss recipes you can toss together and cook in one skillet. It's ideal for a busy weeknight, and it's also good with crumbled Italian chicken sausage if you want to please meat lovers.

—*Juli Meyers, Hinesville, GA*

Takes: 30 min. • **Makes:** 6 servings

- 1 Tbsp. olive oil
- 1 medium onion, chopped
- 2 garlic cloves, minced
- 1 pkg. (16 oz.) potato gnocchi
- 1 can (15 oz.) cannellini beans, rinsed and drained
- 1 can (14½ oz.) Italian diced tomatoes, undrained
- 1 pkg. (6 oz.) fresh baby spinach
- ¼ tsp. pepper
- ½ cup shredded part-skim mozzarella cheese
- 3 Tbsp. grated Parmesan cheese

1. In a large skillet, heat oil over medium-high heat. Add onion; cook and stir until tender. Add the garlic; cook 1 minute longer. Add gnocchi; cook and stir 5-6 minutes or until golden brown. Stir in the beans, tomatoes, spinach and pepper; heat through.

2. Sprinkle with cheeses; cover and remove from heat. Let stand 3-4 minutes or until the cheese is melted.

Note: Look for potato gnocchi in the pasta or frozen foods section.

1 cup: 307 cal., 6g fat (2g sat. fat), 13mg chol., 789mg sod., 50g carb. (10g sugars, 6g fiber), 13g pro.

MEAT LOVER OPTION PAGE 320

PRESSURE-COOKER CHICKPEA & POTATO CURRY

Here's a classic Indian dish made quick in the pressure cooker. The seasonings are gentle but you can adjust to suit yourself.
—*Anjana Devasahayam, San Antonio, TX*

Prep: 25 min. • **Cook:** 5 min. + releasing
Makes: 6 servings

- 1 Tbsp. canola oil
- 1 medium onion, chopped
- 2 garlic cloves, minced
- 2 tsp. minced fresh gingerroot
- 2 tsp. ground coriander
- 1 tsp. garam masala
- 1 tsp. chili powder
- ½ tsp. salt
- ½ tsp. ground cumin
- ¼ tsp. ground turmeric
- 2½ cups vegetable stock
- 2 cans (15 oz. each) chickpeas or garbanzo beans, rinsed and drained
- 1 can (15 oz.) crushed tomatoes
- 1 large baking potato, peeled and cut into ¾-in. cubes
- 1 Tbsp. lime juice
  Chopped fresh cilantro
  Hot cooked rice
  Optional: Sliced red onion and lime wedges

1. Select the saute setting on a 6-qt. electric pressure cooker. Adjust for medium heat; add oil. When oil is hot, cook and stir onion until crisp-tender, 2-4 minutes. Add garlic, ginger and dry seasonings; cook and stir 1 minute. Add stock. Cook for 30 seconds, stirring to loosen browned bits from pan. Press cancel. Stir in chickpeas, tomatoes and potato.
2. Lock the lid; close pressure-release valve. Adjust to pressure-cook on high 3 minutes. Let pressure release naturally for 10 minutes; quick-release any remaining pressure.
3. Stir in the lime juice; sprinkle with cilantro. Serve with rice and, if desired, red onion and lime wedges.
1¼ cups: 240 cal., 6g fat (0 sat. fat), 0 chol., 767mg sod., 42g carb. (8g sugars, 9g fiber), 8g pro.

CHEESY CHILE CASSEROLE

A short list of ingredients packs full flavor in this easy casserole. Serve it as the star of your next meal.
—*Phyllis Bidwell, Las Vegas, NV*

Prep: 10 min. • **Bake:** 40 min.
Makes: 8 servings

- 2 cups shredded Monterey Jack cheese
- 2 cups shredded cheddar cheese
- 1 can (7 oz.) whole green chiles, rinsed and seeded
- 2 large eggs
- 2 Tbsp. all-purpose flour
- 1 can (12 oz.) evaporated milk
- 1 can (8 oz.) tomato sauce or 1 cup fresh salsa, drained, divided

1. In a large bowl, combine cheeses. In a greased 2-qt. baking dish, layer cheese and chiles. Whisk the eggs, flour and milk; pour over cheese mixture.
2. Bake at 350° for 30 minutes. Top with half of the tomato sauce or salsa; bake 10 minutes longer or until heated through. Let stand for 5 minutes before serving. Serve with the remaining sauce.
1 serving: 304 cal., 21g fat (14g sat. fat), 125mg chol., 538mg sod., 9g carb. (5g sugars, 0 fiber), 18g pro.

DELICATA SQUASH BOATS

My colorful boats with quinoa, chickpeas and pumpkin seeds use delicata squash, a winter squash with edible skin that's cream-colored with green stripes.

—*Lauren Knoelke, Des Moines, IA*

Takes: 30 min. • **Makes:** 8 servings

- 4 delicata squash (about 12 oz. each)
- 3 tsp. olive oil, divided
- ⅛ tsp. pepper
- 1 tsp. salt, divided
- 1½ cups vegetable broth
- 1 cup quinoa, rinsed
- 1 can (15 oz.) chickpeas or garbanzo beans, rinsed and drained
- ¼ cup dried cranberries
- 1 green onion, thinly sliced
- 1 tsp. minced fresh sage
- ½ tsp. grated lemon zest
- 1 tsp. lemon juice
- ½ cup crumbled goat cheese
- ¼ cup salted pumpkin seeds or pepitas, toasted

1. Preheat oven to 450°. Cut each squash lengthwise in half; discard seeds. Lightly brush cut sides with 1 tsp. oil; sprinkle with pepper and ½ tsp. salt. Place on a baking sheet, cut side down. Bake until tender, 15-20 minutes.

2. Meanwhile, in a large saucepan, combine broth and quinoa; bring to a boil. Reduce the heat; simmer, covered, until the liquid is absorbed, 12-15 minutes.

3. Stir in the chickpeas, cranberries, green onion, sage, lemon zest, lemon juice and the remaining oil and salt; spoon into squash. Sprinkle with cheese and pumpkin seeds.

1 stuffed squash half: 275 cal., 8g fat (2g sat. fat), 9mg chol., 591mg sod., 46g carb. (9g sugars, 10g fiber), 9g pro. **Diabetic exchanges:** 3 starch, 1 lean meat, ½ fat.

57 POLENTA CHILI CASSEROLE

We created this delicious vegetarian bean and polenta bake that combines spicy chili, mixed veggies and homemade polenta.
—*Dan Kelmenson, West Bloomfield, MI*

Prep: 20 min. • **Bake:** 35 min. + standing
Makes: 8 servings

- 4 cups water
- ½ tsp. salt
- 1¼ cups yellow cornmeal
- 2 cups shredded cheddar cheese, divided
- 3 cans (15 oz. each) vegetarian chili with beans
- 1 pkg. (16 oz.) frozen mixed vegetables, thawed and well drained

1. Preheat oven to 350°. In a large heavy saucepan, bring water and salt to a boil. Reduce heat to a gentle boil; slowly whisk in cornmeal. Cook and stir with a wooden spoon 15-20 minutes or until polenta is thickened and pulls away cleanly from the sides of the pan.
2. Remove from heat. Stir in ¼ cup cheddar cheese until melted.
3. Spread into a 13x9-in. baking dish coated with cooking spray. Bake, uncovered, for 20 minutes. Meanwhile, heat chili according to package directions.
4. Spread vegetables over polenta; top with chili. Sprinkle with remaining cheese. Bake for 12-15 minutes longer or until the cheese is melted. Let stand 10 minutes before serving.
1 serving: 297 cal., 7g fat (4g sat. fat), 20mg chol., 556mg sod., 43g carb. (7g sugars, 12g fiber), 19g pro.

ASIAN TOFU

This tasty Asian tofu was the first meatless recipe my fiance ever made for me. It's a wonderful light protein and so easy to pair with broiled or grilled veggies such as eggplant, asparagus or even tomatoes.
—*Emily Steers, Los Angeles, CA*

Prep: 10 min. + marinating • **Broil:** 10 min.
Makes: 4 servings

- ¼ **cup olive oil**
- 3 **Tbsp. reduced-sodium soy sauce**
- 2 **green onions, chopped**
- 2 **garlic cloves, minced**
- ¼ **tsp. ground cumin**
- ¼ **tsp. crushed red pepper flakes**
- 1 **pkg. (14 oz.) extra-firm tofu**

1. Whisk together first 6 ingredients. Cut the tofu lengthwise into ⅜-in. thick slices; cut each slice in half diagonally to make triangles. Place tofu and marinade in a large shallow dish; turn to coat. Cover and refrigerate for 3-5 hours, turning occasionally

2. Preheat broiler. Reserving marinade, place tofu in a 15x10x1-in. pan. Drizzle remaining marinade over tops. Broil 5-6 in. from heat until lightly browned and heated through, about 10 minutes.

2 slices: 208 cal., 18g fat (3g sat. fat), 0 chol., 440mg sod., 4g carb. (1g sugars, 1g fiber), 9g pro. **Diabetic exchanges:** 3 fat, 1 lean meat.

TOMATO-GARLIC LENTIL BOWLS

An Ethiopian dish inspired this feel-good dinner that's tangy, creamy and sure to give you comfort.

—Rachael Cushing, Portland, OR

Takes: 30 min. • **Makes:** 6 servings

- 1 Tbsp. olive oil
- 2 medium onions, chopped
- 4 garlic cloves, minced
- 2 cups dried brown lentils, rinsed
- 1 tsp. salt
- ½ tsp. ground ginger
- ½ tsp. paprika
- ¼ tsp. pepper
- 3 cups water
- ¼ cup lemon juice
- 3 Tbsp. tomato paste
- ¾ cup fat-free plain Greek yogurt
  Optional: Chopped tomatoes and minced fresh cilantro

1. In a large saucepan, heat oil over medium-high heat; saute onions 2 minutes. Add garlic; cook 1 minute. Stir in the lentils, seasonings and water; bring to a boil. Reduce the heat; simmer, covered, until the lentils are tender, 25-30 minutes.

2. Stir in lemon juice and tomato paste; heat through. Serve with yogurt and, if desired, tomatoes and cilantro.

¾ cup: 294 cal., 3g fat (0 sat. fat), 0 chol., 419mg sod., 49g carb. (5g sugars, 8g fiber), 21g pro. **Diabetic exchanges:** 3 starch, 2 lean meat, ½ fat.

Health tip: Cup for cup, lentils have twice as much protein and iron as quinoa.

🕐 MEDITERRANEAN CHICKPEAS

Add this to your meatless Monday lineup. It's great with feta cheese on top.
—*Elaine Ober, Brookline, MA*

Takes: 25 min. • **Makes:** 4 servings

1	cup water
¾	cup uncooked whole wheat couscous
1	Tbsp. olive oil
1	medium onion, chopped
2	garlic cloves, minced
1	can (15 oz.) chickpeas or garbanzo beans, rinsed and drained
1	can (14½ oz.) no-salt-added stewed tomatoes, cut up
1	can (14 oz.) water-packed artichoke hearts, rinsed, drained and chopped
½	cup pitted Greek olives, coarsely chopped
1	Tbsp. lemon juice
½	tsp. dried oregano
	Dash pepper
	Dash cayenne pepper

1. In a small saucepan, bring water to a boil. Stir in couscous. Remove from heat; let stand, covered, 5-10 minutes or until water is absorbed. Fluff with a fork.

2. Meanwhile, in a large nonstick skillet, heat oil over medium-high heat. Add the onion; cook and stir until tender. Add garlic; cook 1 minute longer. Add remaining ingredients; heat through, stirring occasionally. Serve with couscous.

1 cup chickpea mixture with ⅔ cup couscous: 340 cal., 10g fat (1g sat. fat), 0 chol., 677mg sod., 51g carb. (9g sugars, 9g fiber), 11g pro.

GRILLED CHEESE & TOMATO SOUP BAKE

This casserole brings together two classic comfort foods: grilled cheese sandwiches and tomato soup. There's no need for hands to get messy dipping into a bowl of hot soup. Best of all, my picky-eater husband devours every bite.

—*Megan Kuns, Perrysburg, OH*

Prep: 25 min. • **Bake:** 25 min. + standing
Makes: 6 servings

3	oz. reduced-fat cream cheese
1½	tsp. dried basil, divided
12	slices Italian, sourdough or rye bread (½ in. thick)
6	slices part-skim mozzarella cheese
6	Tbsp. butter, softened
½	cup tomato paste
1	garlic clove, minced
¼	tsp. salt
¼	tsp. pepper
1¾	cups 2% milk
2	large eggs
1	cup shredded Italian cheese blend or part-skim mozzarella cheese

1. Preheat oven to 350°. In a small bowl, mix cream cheese and 1 tsp. basil until blended; spread onto 6 of the bread slices. Top with mozzarella cheese and remaining bread. Spread outsides of sandwiches with butter. Arrange in a greased 13x9-in. baking dish.

2. In a small saucepan, combine the tomato paste, garlic, salt, pepper and remaining basil; cook and stir over medium heat for 1 minute. Gradually whisk in the milk; bring to a boil. Reduce heat; simmer, uncovered, 4-5 minutes or until thickened, stirring frequently. Remove from heat.

3. Whisk eggs in a large bowl; gradually whisk in a third of the milk mixture. Stir in remaining milk mixture; pour over sandwiches. Sprinkle with Italian cheese blend.

4. Bake, uncovered, 25-30 minutes or until golden brown and cheese is melted. Let stand 10 minutes before serving.

1 serving: 485 cal., 29g fat (17g sat. fat), 137mg chol., 918mg sod., 33g carb. (7g sugars, 2g fiber), 23g pro.

TEST KITCHEN TIP

When this casserole comes out of the oven it's best to let it sit for the full 10 minutes, if not a little longer. You'll end up with a rich, creamy texture similar to a breakfast strata or a savory bread pudding.

EGGPLANT ROLLATINI

These authentic eggplant roll-ups may take some time to prepare, but the end result is restaurant-quality and just right for a special occasion. I think your family will request this dish time and again.

—Nancy Sousley, Lafayette, IN

Prep: 1 hour • **Bake:** 30 min.
Makes: 5 servings

- 1   large eggplant
- 1   Tbsp. salt

SAUCE

- 1   small onion, chopped
- ¼   cup olive oil
- 2   garlic cloves, minced
- 1   can (15 oz.) tomato sauce
- 1   can (14½ oz.) diced tomatoes
- ½   cup chicken broth
- ¼   cup tomato paste
- 2   Tbsp. minced fresh parsley
- 2   tsp. sugar
- ½   tsp. salt
- ½   tsp. dried basil
- ¼   tsp. pepper
- ⅛   tsp. crushed red pepper flakes

FILLING

- 1   carton (15 oz.) ricotta cheese
- 1   cup shredded part-skim mozzarella cheese
- ½   cup grated Parmesan cheese
- ¼   cup minced fresh parsley
- 1   large egg, lightly beaten
- ⅛   tsp. pepper

COATING

- 3   large eggs, lightly beaten
- 1   cup seasoned bread crumbs
- 1   cup grated Parmesan cheese, divided
- 2   garlic cloves, minced
- 2   Tbsp. minced fresh parsley
      Dash each salt and pepper

1. Peel and slice eggplant lengthwise into fifteen ⅛-in.-thick slices. Place in a colander over a plate; sprinkle with salt and toss. Let stand 30 minutes.

2. Meanwhile, for sauce, in a large saucepan, saute onion in oil. Add garlic; cook 1 minute longer. Stir in remaining sauce ingredients. Bring to a boil. Reduce the heat; simmer, uncovered, until flavors are blended, stirring occasionally, 20-25 minutes. Rinse and drain eggplant slices.

3. In a large bowl, combine filling ingredients; set aside.

4. Place eggs in a shallow bowl. In another shallow bowl, combine bread crumbs, ½ cup Parmesan cheese, garlic, parsley, salt and pepper. Dip eggplant in eggs, then in bread crumb mixture.

5. In an electric skillet, heat ½ in. of oil to 375°. Fry eggplant in batches until golden brown, 2-3 minutes on each side. Drain on paper towels.

6. Preheat oven to 375°. Spoon 1 cup of sauce into an ungreased 13x9-in. baking dish. Spread 2 rounded Tbsp. filling over each eggplant slice. Carefully roll up and place seam side down in the baking dish. Spoon the remaining sauce over roll-ups. Sprinkle with the remaining Parmesan cheese. Cover and bake until bubbly, 30-35 minutes.

3 pieces: 726 cal., 48g fat (15g sat. fat), 181mg chol., 3182mg sod., 44g carb. (19g sugars, 7g fiber), 35g pro.

VEGGIE-CASHEW STIR-FRY

Getting my meat-loving husband and two sons, ages 5 and 7, to eat more veggies was always a struggle until I whipped up this stir-fry one night. I was shocked when they cleaned their plates and asked for seconds.

—Abbey Hoffman, Ashland, OH

Prep: 20 min. • **Cook:** 15 min.
Makes: 4 servings

- ¼   cup reduced-sodium soy sauce
- ¼   cup water
- 2   Tbsp. brown sugar
- 2   Tbsp. lemon juice
- 2   Tbsp. olive oil
- 1   garlic clove, minced
- 2   cups sliced fresh mushrooms
- 1   cup coarsely chopped fresh baby carrots
- 1   small zucchini, cut into ¼-in. slices
- 1   small sweet red pepper, coarsely chopped
- 1   small green pepper, coarsely chopped
- 4   green onions, sliced
- 2   cups cooked brown rice
- 1   can (8 oz.) sliced water chestnuts, drained
- ½   cup honey-roasted cashews

1. In a small bowl, mix soy sauce, water, brown sugar and lemon juice until smooth; set aside.

2. In a large skillet, heat oil over medium-high heat. Stir-fry garlic 1 minute. Add vegetables; cook until the vegetables are crisp-tender, for 6-8 minutes.

3. Stir soy sauce mixture and add to pan. Bring to a boil. Add rice and water chestnuts; heat through. Top with cashews.

1½ cups: 385 cal., 16g fat (3g sat. fat), 0 chol., 671mg sod., 56g carb. (15g sugars, 6g fiber), 9g pro.

HOMEMADE RICOTTA GNOCCHI WITH SPINACH & GORGONZOLA

Gnocchi are thick, soft dumplings made from potatoes that you eat like pasta. In this special dish, the tender little pillows are treated to a creamy white sauce that features butternut squash, spinach and Gorgonzola cheese.

—Brud Holland, Watkins Glen, NY

- -

Prep: 2 hours • **Cook:** 10 min.
Makes: 8 servings

    3   large potatoes
    3   cups reduced-fat ricotta cheese
    ¼   cup grated Romano cheese
    2   Tbsp. olive oil
    1   Tbsp. kosher salt
    6   large eggs
    4½ cups cake flour
    4   qt. water
SAUCE
    2⅔ cups cubed peeled butternut squash
    ⅓   cup thinly sliced fresh basil leaves
    ⅓   cup water
    2   Tbsp. plus 2 tsp. olive oil
    2   garlic cloves, peeled and thinly sliced
    1¼ tsp. kosher salt
    ¾   tsp. pepper
    1⅓ cups heavy whipping cream
    ⅔   cup crumbled Gorgonzola cheese
    1½ lbs. fresh spinach, coarsely chopped

1. Scrub and pierce potatoes. Bake at 400° for 50-55 minutes or until tender. Peel potatoes; press through a potato ricer or strainer into a large bowl. Cool slightly.

2. Add ricotta and Romano cheeses, oil and salt to potato pulp; beat on low speed until smooth. Beat in eggs, one at a time. Add flour; mix well. On a lightly floured surface, knead 10-12 times, forming a soft dough.

3. Divide dough into 16 portions. On a floured surface, roll each portion into a ½-in.-thick rope; cut into ¾-in. pieces. Press and roll each piece with a lightly floured fork.

4. In a Dutch oven, bring water to a boil. Cook the gnocchi in batches until they float, 30-60 seconds. Remove with a slotted spoon and keep warm.

5. In a large saucepan, combine the squash, basil, water, oil, garlic, salt and pepper. Bring to a boil. Cover and cook until the squash is tender, 4-6 minutes.

6. Stir in cream and Gorgonzola. Bring to a boil. Reduce heat; simmer, uncovered, for 2 minutes. Add spinach; cook until spinach is wilted. Serve with gnocchi.

1½ cups gnocchi with ¾ cup spinach mixture: 833 cal., 35g fat (17g sat. fat), 248mg chol., 1420mg sod., 101g carb. (10g sugars, 7g fiber), 29g pro.

CHEESY BLACK BEAN NACHOS

We're trying to go meatless once a week, and this dish helps make those meals fun, quick and super delicious. It's also a smart way to use up beans and canned tomatoes from your pantry.
—*Cynthia Nelson, Saskatoon, SK*

Takes: 20 min. • **Makes:** 4 servings

- 1 can (15 oz.) black beans, rinsed and drained
- 1 can (14½ oz.) diced tomatoes, well drained
- 3 to 4 jalapeno peppers, seeded and sliced
- 4 cups multigrain tortilla chips
- 1 cup shredded cheddar cheese
  Optional toppings: Sour cream, chopped fresh cilantro and additional jalapeno slices

1. Preheat oven to 350°. Mix beans, tomatoes and jalapenos. Arrange chips in an even layer in a 15x10x1-in. pan. Top with bean mixture and cheese.

2. Bake, uncovered, until cheese is melted, 10-12 minutes. Serve nachos immediately with toppings as desired.

Note: Wear disposable gloves when cutting hot peppers; the oils can burn skin. Avoid touching your face.

1 serving: 371 cal., 17g fat (6g sat. fat), 28mg chol., 672mg sod., 42g carb. (6g sugars, 7g fiber), 15g pro.

TEST KITCHEN TIP

Spreading out the ingredients in a large pan helps the chips stay crunchy and evenly coated with toppings.

❄ ⏱ EASY CHANA MASALA

I love this quick, healthy Indian-inspired dish so much I always make sure to have the ingredients stocked in my pantry. It makes weeknight dinners feel a little more special.
—*Janeen Judah, Houston, TX*

- -

Takes: 30 min. • **Makes:** 4 servings

- 1 Tbsp. canola oil
- ½ cup finely chopped onion
- 1 Tbsp. minced fresh gingerroot
- 2 garlic cloves, minced
- 1 jalapeno pepper, seeded and finely chopped, optional
- ½ tsp. salt
- 1 tsp. garam masala
- ½ tsp. ground coriander
- ½ tsp. ground cumin
- 1 can (15 oz.) diced tomatoes, undrained
- 1 can (15 oz.) chickpeas or garbanzo beans, rinsed and drained
- 3 cups hot cooked brown rice
- ¼ cup plain yogurt
  Minced fresh cilantro

1. In a large skillet, heat oil over medium heat. Add onion, ginger, garlic and, if desired, the jalapeno; cook and stir until onion is softened and lightly browned, 4-5 minutes. Add salt and spices; cook and stir 1 minute.

2. Stir in tomatoes and chickpeas; bring to a boil. Reduce heat; simmer, covered, until flavors are blended, 12-15 minutes, stirring occasionally. Serve with rice. Top with yogurt and cilantro.

Freeze option: Freeze the cooled chickpea mixture in freezer containers. To use, partially thaw in refrigerator overnight. Heat through in a saucepan, stirring occasionally and adding a little water if necessary.

¾ cup chickpea mixture with ¾ cup rice: 359 cal., 8g fat (1g sat. fat), 2mg chol., 616mg sod., 64g carb. (8g sugars, 9g fiber), 10g pro.

TEST KITCHEN TIP

This is a quick version of a popular Indian and Pakistani dish. Chana refers to the chickpeas, masala the spices.

BLACK BEAN & RICE ENCHILADAS

I love Mexican food, and I'm always looking for ways to make it more healthy. I renovated a dish that I have enjoyed in restaurants to suit my taste and lifestyle.
—*Christie Ladd, Mechanicsburg, PA*

Prep: 40 min. • **Bake:** 30 min.
Makes: 8 servings

- 1 Tbsp. olive oil
- 1 green pepper, chopped
- 1 medium onion, chopped
- 3 garlic cloves, minced
- 1 can (15 oz.) black beans, rinsed and drained
- 1 can (14½ oz.) diced tomatoes and green chiles
- ¼ cup picante sauce
- 1 Tbsp. chili powder
- 1 tsp. ground cumin
- ¼ tsp. crushed red pepper flakes
- 2 cups cooked brown rice
- 8 flour tortillas (6 in.), warmed
- 1 cup salsa
- 1 cup shredded reduced-fat cheddar cheese
- 3 Tbsp. chopped fresh cilantro leaves

1. Preheat oven to 350°. In a large nonstick skillet, heat oil over medium heat. Add green pepper, onion and garlic; saute until tender. Add the next 6 ingredients; bring to a boil. Reduce heat; simmer, uncovered, until heated through. Add rice; cook 5 minutes longer.

2. Spoon a rounded ½ cup of rice mixture down center of each tortilla. Fold sides over filling and roll up. Place seam side down in a 13x9-in. baking dish coated with cooking spray. Spoon remaining rice mixture along sides of dish. Top tortillas with salsa. Bake, covered, for 25 minutes. Uncover; sprinkle with cheese. Bake until cheese is melted, 2-3 minutes longer. Sprinkle with cilantro before serving.

1 enchilada: 279 cal., 8g fat (2g sat. fat), 10mg chol., 807mg sod., 39g carb. (4g sugars, 5g fiber), 11g pro. **Diabetic exchanges:** 2½ starch, 1 lean meat, 1 vegetable.

GRILLED CHILES RELLENOS

Here's a lighter version of one of my favorite Mexican dishes. The grilled peppers go great with Spanish rice, gazpacho or a refreshing salad with jicama and citrus.

—*Lori Nelson, Austin, TX*

Prep: 45 min. • **Grill:** 10 min.
Makes: 4 servings

1	**cup sour cream**
2	**Tbsp. lime juice**
½	**cup minced fresh cilantro, divided**
1	**small onion, finely chopped**
1	**Tbsp. butter**
1	**large portobello mushroom cap, finely chopped**
1	**small yellow summer squash, finely chopped**
1	**small zucchini, finely chopped**
1	**jalapeno pepper, seeded and finely chopped**
1	**garlic clove, minced**
1	**can (15 oz.) black beans, rinsed and drained**
2	**cups shredded Mexican cheese blend, divided**
1	**cup frozen corn, thawed**
1	**tsp. ground cumin**
½	**tsp. salt**
¼	**tsp. pepper**
4	**large poblano peppers, halved and seeded**

1. In a small bowl, combine the sour cream, lime juice and ¼ cup cilantro. Cover and refrigerate until serving.

2. In a large skillet, saute onion in butter until tender. Add the mushroom, yellow squash, zucchini, jalapeno and garlic; saute 3-5 minutes longer or until vegetables are crisp-tender.

3. Stir in the beans, 1½ cups cheese, corn, cumin, salt, pepper and remaining cilantro. Remove from the heat. Spoon into poblano halves; sprinkle with remaining cheese.

4. Grill the peppers, covered, over indirect medium heat for about 10-14 minutes or until tender. Serve with sour cream sauce.

Note: Wear disposable gloves when cutting hot peppers; the oils can burn skin. Avoid touching your face.

2 stuffed pepper halves: 552 cal., 32g fat (21g sat. fat), 98mg chol., 964mg sod., 42g carb. (10g sugars, 10g fiber), 23g pro.

ITALIAN HERB-LENTIL PATTIES WITH MOZZARELLA

My family has requested this meatless recipe over and over again. It's simple to prepare and even meat lovers like it.

—*Geraldine Lucas, Oldsmar, FL*

Prep: 50 min. • **Cook:** 10 min./batch
Makes: 10 servings

- 3 cups dried lentils, rinsed
- 3 large eggs, lightly beaten
- 1 Tbsp. dried minced onion
- 1 Tbsp. dried parsley flakes
- 1 tsp. dried basil
- 1 tsp. salt
- ½ tsp. dried thyme
- ¼ tsp. pepper
- 8 packets instant plain oatmeal (about 2 cups)
- 2 Tbsp. canola oil
- 10 slices part-skim mozzarella cheese or provolone cheese
  Marinara sauce, warmed, optional

1. Cook lentils according to the package directions; drain and cool slightly.
2. In a large bowl, combine the eggs and the seasonings; stir in cooked lentils and oatmeal. Shape into ten ¾-in.-thick patties.
3. In a large nonstick skillet, heat 1 Tbsp. oil over medium heat. Cook patties in batches until golden brown and a thermometer reads 160°, for 4-6 minutes on each side, adding additional oil as needed. Top with cheese; cook 1-2 minutes longer or until cheese is melted. If desired, serve with marinara sauce.
1 patty: 416 cal., 12g fat (4g sat. fat), 74mg chol., 517mg sod., 54g carb. (2g sugars, 9g fiber), 26g pro.

HEARTY CHICKPEA POTPIE

This veggie potpie is so savory and satisfying! The spring veggies, easy prep and impressive presentation make this a perfect addition to Easter or other family dinners.

—*Deanna McDonald, Muskegon, MI*

Prep: 35 min. • **Cook:** 25 min.
Makes: 6 servings

- 1 pkg. (14.1 oz.) refrigerated pie crust
- 3 Tbsp. butter
- 1 cup diced onions
- 1 cup diced celery
- 1 cup diced carrots
- 1 cup diced potatoes
- 1 cup (4 oz.) frozen peas, thawed
- ¼ cup all-purpose flour
- 1 tsp. poultry seasoning
- ½ tsp. ground turmeric
- ¼ tsp. salt
- ¼ tsp. pepper
- 2 cups vegetable broth
- 1 can (15 oz.) chickpeas or garbanzo beans, rinsed and drained

1. Preheat oven to 400°. Unroll 1 crust into a 9-in. pie plate; trim even with rim. Line unpricked crust with parchment. Fill with pie weights or dried beans. Bake on a lower oven rack until the edges are light golden brown, 15-20 minutes. Remove the parchment and weights; bake until bottom is golden brown, 3-6 minutes longer. Cool on a wire rack.

2. Meanwhile, in a large skillet, melt butter over medium heat. Add onions, celery and carrots; cook and stir until the onions are translucent, about 5 minutes. Stir in potatoes and peas, cooking until vegetables are tender, for 5-7 minutes. Whisk in next 5 ingredients. Increase the heat to medium-high; gradually whisk in the vegetable broth. Bring to a boil; cook, stirring the mixture constantly, until thickened, for 4-6 minutes. Stir in chickpeas. Remove from the heat.

3. Spoon vegetable filling over bottom crust. Unroll remaining crust; place over filling. Trim; cut slits in top.

4. Bake until the top crust is golden, about 15 minutes. Cool 5 minutes before serving.

1 serving: 496 cal., 25g fat (11g sat. fat), 28mg chol., 760mg sod., 61g carb. (8g sugars, 6g fiber), 8g pro.

RICOTTA-STUFFED PORTOBELLO MUSHROOMS

These mushrooms are rich, creamy and bright-tasting at the same time because of the fresh herbs and tomato. I especially like to serve them with grilled asparagus.

—*Tre Balchowsky, Sausalito, CA*

Takes: 30 min. • **Makes:** 6 servings

- ¾ cup reduced-fat ricotta cheese
- ¾ cup grated Parmesan cheese, divided
- ½ cup shredded part-skim mozzarella cheese
- 2 Tbsp. minced fresh parsley
- ⅛ tsp. pepper
- 6 large portobello mushrooms
- 6 slices large tomato
- ¾ cup fresh basil leaves
- 3 Tbsp. slivered almonds or pine nuts, toasted
- 1 small garlic clove
- 2 Tbsp. olive oil
- 2 to 3 tsp. water

1. In a small bowl, mix ricotta cheese, ¼ cup Parmesan cheese, mozzarella cheese, parsley and pepper. Remove and discard stems from the mushrooms; with a spoon, scrape and remove gills. Fill caps with the ricotta mixture. Top with tomato slices.

2. Grill caps, covered, over medium heat until mushrooms are tender, about 8-10 minutes. Remove from grill with a metal spatula.

3. Meanwhile, place the basil, almonds and garlic in a small food processor; pulse until chopped. Add remaining Parmesan cheese; pulse just until blended. While processing, gradually add oil and enough water to reach desired consistency. Spoon over stuffed mushrooms before serving.

Note: To toast nuts, bake in a shallow pan in a 350° oven for 5-10 minutes or cook in a skillet over low heat until lightly browned, stirring the nuts occasionally.

1 stuffed mushroom: 201 cal., 13g fat (4g sat. fat), 22mg chol., 238mg sod., 9g carb. (5g sugars, 2g fiber), 12g pro. **Diabetic exchanges:** 1½ fat, 1 medium-fat meat, 1 vegetable.

READER RAVE

"Very good! Used cottage cheese instead of ricotta because I always have that on hand and still very good! Used my own homemade pesto that I keep frozen to speed up prep."

—RJBEERY75, TASTEOFHOME.COM

APPLE, WHITE CHEDDAR & ARUGULA TARTS

These tarts reminds me of fall in Michigan, where I grew up. Add meat if you like or keep it light. I always like to garnish it with a bit of frizzled prosciutto for the meat lovers.
—*Maria Davis, Hermosa Beach, CA*

Takes: 30 min. • **Makes:** 4 servings

- 1 sheet frozen puff pastry, thawed
- 1 cup shredded white cheddar cheese
- 2 medium apples, thinly sliced
- 2 Tbsp. olive oil
- 1 Tbsp. lemon juice
- 3 cups fresh arugula or baby spinach

1. Preheat oven to 400°. On a lightly floured surface, unfold puff pastry; roll into a 12-in. square. Cut pastry into 4 squares; place on a parchment-lined baking sheet.
2. Sprinkle half of each square with cheese to within ¼ in. of edges; top with apples. Fold pastry over filling. Press the edges with a fork to seal. Bake the tarts until golden brown, 16-18 minutes .
3. In a bowl, whisk oil and lemon juice until blended; add arugula and toss to coat. Serve with tarts.
1 tart: 518 cal., 33g fat (10g sat. fat), 29mg chol., 389mg sod., 46g carb. (8g sugars, 7g fiber), 12g pro.

ASPARAGUS TOFU STIR-FRY

With its flavorful ginger sauce and fresh vegetables, this tasty dish gets rave reviews every time I serve it. And it doesn't bother my husband's food allergies. Asparagus and yellow squash have nice color contrast.

—*Phyllis Smith, Chimacum, WA*

Prep: 15 min. • **Cook:** 20 min.
Makes: 4 servings

- 1   Tbsp. cornstarch
- ½   tsp. sugar
- 1¼ cups vegetable broth
- 4   tsp. reduced-sodium soy sauce
- 2   tsp. minced fresh gingerroot, divided
- 3   tsp. canola oil, divided
- 1   lb. fresh asparagus, trimmed and cut into 1-in. pieces
- 1   medium yellow summer squash, halved and sliced
- 2   green onions, thinly sliced
- 1   pkg. (14 oz.) extra-firm tofu, drained and cut into ½-in. cubes
- ¼   tsp. salt
- ¼   tsp. pepper
- 2   cups hot cooked brown rice
- 2   Tbsp. sliced almonds, toasted

1. Combine cornstarch, sugar, broth and soy sauce until smooth; set aside.
2. In a large nonstick skillet or wok, stir-fry 1 tsp. ginger in 1 tsp. oil for 1 minute. Add asparagus; stir-fry for 2 minutes. Add squash; stir-fry 2 minutes longer. Add onions; stir-fry 1 minute longer or until the vegetables are crisp-tender. Remove and keep warm.
3. In the same pan, stir-fry tofu, salt, pepper and remaining ginger in the remaining oil for 7-9 minutes or until lightly browned. Remove and keep warm.
4. Stir the cornstarch mixture and add to the pan. Bring to a boil; cook and stir for 2 minutes or until thickened. Add asparagus mixture and tofu; heat through. Serve with rice; sprinkle with almonds.
1 serving: 278 cal., 11g fat (1g sat. fat), 0 chol., 682mg sod., 34g carb. (4g sugars, 4g fiber), 14g pro. **Diabetic exchanges:** 2 starch, 1 lean meat, 1 vegetable, 1 fat.

AFRICAN PEANUT SWEET POTATO STEW

When I was in college, my mom made an addicting sweet potato stew. I shared it with friends, and now all of us serve it to our own kids. They all love it, too, of course.

—*Alexis Scatchell, Niles, IL*

Prep: 20 min. • **Cook:** 6 hours
Makes: 8 servings (2½ qt.)

- 1   can (28 oz.) diced tomatoes, undrained
- 1   cup fresh cilantro leaves
- ½   cup chunky peanut butter
- 3   garlic cloves, halved
- 2   tsp. ground cumin
- 1   tsp. salt
- ½   tsp. ground cinnamon
- ¼   tsp. smoked paprika
- 3   lbs. sweet potatoes (about 6 medium), peeled and cut into 1-in. pieces
- 1   can (15 oz.) chickpeas or garbanzo beans, rinsed and drained
- 1   cup water
- 8   cups chopped fresh kale
       Chopped peanuts and additional cilantro leaves, optional

1. Place the first 8 ingredients in a food processor; process until pureed. Transfer to a 5-qt. slow cooker; stir in the sweet potatoes, beans and water.
2. Cook, covered, on low 6-8 hours or until potatoes are tender, adding kale during the last 30 minutes. If desired, top each serving with chopped peanuts and additional cilantro.
1¼ cups: 349 cal., 9g fat (1g sat. fat), 0 chol., 624mg sod., 60g carb. (23g sugars, 11g fiber), 10g pro.

VEGGIE TACOS

These vegetarian tacos are stuffed with a blend of sauteed cabbage, peppers and black beans that is as filling as any meat. Top with avocado, cheese or a dollop of sour cream.

—Taste of Home *Test Kitchen*

Takes: 30 min. • **Makes:** 4 servings

- 2   Tbsp. canola oil
- 3   cups shredded cabbage
- 1   medium sweet red pepper, julienned
- 1   medium onion, halved and sliced
- 2   tsp. sugar
- 1   can (15 oz.) black beans, rinsed and drained
- 1   cup salsa
- 1   can (4 oz.) chopped green chiles
- 1   tsp. minced garlic
- 1   tsp. chili powder
- ¼   tsp. ground cumin
- 8   taco shells, warmed
- ½   cup shredded cheddar cheese
- 1   medium ripe avocado, peeled and sliced

1. In a large skillet, heat oil over medium-high heat; saute cabbage, pepper and onion until crisp-tender, for about 5 minutes. Sprinkle with sugar.
2. Stir in beans, salsa, chiles, garlic, chili powder and cumin; bring to a boil. Reduce heat; simmer, covered, until the flavors are blended, about 5 minutes.
3. Serve in taco shells. Top with cheese and avocado.
2 tacos: 430 cal., 22g fat (5g sat. fat), 14mg chol., 770mg sod., 47g carb. (8g sugars, 10g fiber), 12g pro.

REFRIED BEAN TOSTADAS

Your family won't miss the meat in tasty tostadas topped with refried beans, corn, zucchini and salsa.

—Taste of Home *Test Kitchen*

Takes: 30 min. • **Makes:** 6 servings

6	flour tortillas (8 in.)
½	lb. sliced fresh mushrooms
1	cup diced zucchini
2	Tbsp. canola oil
1	jar (16 oz.) chunky salsa
1	can (7 oz.) white or shoepeg corn, drained
1	can (16 oz.) vegetarian refried beans, warmed
1½	cups shredded lettuce
1½	cups shredded cheddar cheese
2	medium ripe avocados, peeled and sliced
1½	cups chopped tomatoes
6	Tbsp. sour cream

1. In a large ungreased skillet, cook tortillas for 1-2 minutes on each side or until lightly browned. Remove and set aside.

2. In the same skillet, saute mushrooms and zucchini in oil until crisp-tender. Add salsa and corn; cook for 2-3 minutes or until mixture is heated through.

3. Spread refried beans over each tortilla; top with lettuce, salsa mixture, cheese, avocados, tomatoes and sour cream.

1 tostada: 588 cal., 31g fat (10g sat. fat), 40mg chol., 1250mg sod., 60g carb. (9g sugars, 12g fiber), 19g pro.

QUICKPEA CURRY

This colorful curry is a nice change of pace for a busy weeknight. I like to use fresh peas instead of frozen when they're in season.
—*Beth Fleming, Downers Grove, IL*

Prep: 15 min. • **Cook:** 35 min.
Makes: 6 servings

1   **Tbsp. canola oil**
1   **medium onion, finely chopped**
2   **garlic cloves, minced**
1   **Tbsp. curry powder**
2   **cans (14½ oz. each) diced tomatoes, undrained**
2   **cans (15 oz. each) chickpeas or garbanzo beans, rinsed and drained**
2   **cups cubed peeled sweet potato (about 1 medium)**
1   **cup light coconut milk**
2   **tsp. sugar**
¼   **tsp. crushed red pepper flakes**
1   **cup uncooked whole wheat pearl (Israeli) couscous**
1½   **cups frozen peas (about 6 oz.)**
¼   **tsp. salt**
    Chopped fresh parsley
    Plain yogurt, optional

MEAT LOVER OPTION PAGE 320

1. In a large skillet, heat oil over medium heat; saute the onion and garlic with curry powder until tender, 3-4 minutes. Stir in tomatoes, chickpeas, sweet potato, coconut milk, sugar and pepper flakes; bring to a boil. Reduce the heat; simmer, uncovered, until the mixture is thickened and potatoes are tender, for about 25-30 minutes, stirring occasionally.
2. Meanwhile, prepare couscous and peas separately according to package directions. Stir salt into peas.
3. To serve, divide couscous among 6 bowls. Top with chickpea mixture, peas, parsley and, if desired, yogurt.

1 serving: 390 cal., 8g fat (2g sat. fat), 0 chol., 561mg sod., 68g carb. (14g sugars, 13g fiber), 13g pro.

TEST KITCHEN TIP

If you don't have pearl couscous on hand, you can substitute regular couscous.

GRILLED GARDEN
VEGGIE PIZZA, PAGE 83

PIZZA & PASTA FAVORITES

Dig in to deep-dish Chicago pizza, gingery Asian noodles, homey mac & cheese, and all the Italian standbys you love. The entire family will welcome these comfort food classics to the dinner table!

TOMATO BAGUETTE PIZZA

When my tomatoes ripen all at once, I use them up in simple recipes like this one. Cheesy baguette pizzas, served with a salad, are ideal for lunch—and they make standout appetizers, too.

—*Lorraine Caland, Shuniah, ON*

Prep: 25 min. • **Bake:** 10 min.
Makes: 6 servings

- 2 tsp. olive oil
- 8 oz. sliced fresh mushrooms
- 2 medium onions, halved and sliced
- 2 garlic cloves, minced
- ½ tsp. Italian seasoning
- ¼ tsp. salt
  Dash pepper
- 1 French bread baguette (10½ oz.), halved lengthwise
- 1½ cups shredded part-skim mozzarella cheese
- ¾ cup thinly sliced fresh basil leaves, divided
- 3 medium tomatoes, sliced

1. Preheat oven to 400°. In a large skillet, heat oil over medium-high heat; saute mushrooms and onions until tender. Add garlic and seasonings; cook and stir 1 minute.

2. Place baguette halves on a baking sheet, cut side up; sprinkle with half the cheese and ½ cup basil. Top with mushroom mixture, tomatoes and remaining cheese.

3. Bake until cheese is melted, 10-15 minutes. Sprinkle with remaining basil. Cut each half into 3 portions.

1 piece: 260 cal., 7g fat (4g sat. fat), 18mg chol., 614mg sod., 36g carb. (5g sugars, 3g fiber), 13g pro. **Diabetic exchanges:** 2 starch, 1 vegetable, 1 medium-fat meat.

FETTUCCINE WITH BLACK BEAN SAUCE

When my husband needed to go on a heart-smart diet, I had to come up with new ways to get more vegetables into our daily menus. This meatless spaghetti sauce is a winner; it's especially delicious over spinach fettuccine.

—*Marianne Neuman, East Troy, WI*

Takes: 30 min. • **Makes:** 5 servings

- 6 oz. uncooked fettuccine
- 1 small green pepper, chopped
- 1 small onion, chopped
- 1 Tbsp. olive oil
- 2 cups garden-style pasta sauce
- 1 can (15 oz.) black beans, rinsed and drained
- 2 Tbsp. minced fresh basil or 2 tsp. dried basil
- 1 tsp. dried oregano
- ½ tsp. fennel seed
- ¼ tsp. garlic salt
- 1 cup shredded part-skim mozzarella cheese
  Additional chopped fresh basil, optional

1. Cook fettuccine according to package directions. Meanwhile, in a large saucepan, saute green pepper and onion in oil until tender. Stir in the pasta sauce, black beans and seasonings.

2. Bring to a boil. Reduce heat; simmer, uncovered, for 5 minutes. Drain fettuccine. Top with sauce and sprinkle with cheese. If desired, top with chopped fresh basil.

Note: This recipe was tested with Ragu Super Vegetable Primavera pasta sauce.

¾ cup sauce with ¾ cup pasta: 350 cal., 10g fat (3g sat. fat), 17mg chol., 761mg sod., 51g carb. (12g sugars, 8g fiber), 16g pro. **Diabetic exchanges:** 2½ starch, 2 vegetable, 1 lean meat, 1 fat.

Health tip: As long as you're eating a healthy dinner, switch up your noodle game, too. Try this dish with whole wheat, buckwheat, quinoa, chickpea or multigrain pasta.

THE BEST MARINARA SAUCE

I developed this recipe with a friend to make the most of a bumper crop of tomatoes. Now we like to make huge batches—we're talking 220 pounds of tomatoes huge—and then give jars along with a pound of pasta as gifts around the holidays. Knowing this sauce is made from the heart with the best possible ingredients makes me feel good about giving it to my family and friends.
—*Shannon Norris, Cudahy, WI*

Prep: 1 hour + simmering • **Process:** 40 min.
Makes: 9 cups

-   3 Tbsp. olive oil
-   1 cup chopped onion
-   ⅓ cup minced garlic, divided
-   12 lbs. plum tomatoes, quartered
-   2 cups water
-   1¼ cups minced fresh basil, divided
-   ¼ cup minced fresh oregano
-   ¼ cup tomato paste
-   2 tsp. kosher salt
-   1 tsp. coarsely ground pepper
-   ¼ cup plus 1½ tsp. lemon juice

1. In a stockpot, heat oil over medium heat. Add onion; cook and stir until softened, 3-4 minutes. Add 2 Tbsp. garlic; cook 1 minute longer. Add tomatoes, water and ½ cup basil; bring to a boil. Reduce heat; simmer, covered, until tomatoes are completely broken down and soft, about 1 hour, stirring occasionally.

2. Press tomato mixture through a food mill into a large bowl; discard skins and seeds. Return tomato mixture to stockpot; add ½ cup of remaining basil, oregano and remaining garlic. Bring to a boil. Reduce heat; simmer, uncovered, until thickened, 3½-4 hours, stirring occasionally. Add tomato paste and remaining ¼ cup of basil; season with salt and pepper.

3. Add 1 Tbsp. plus 1½ tsp. lemon juice to each of 3 hot 1½-pint jars. Ladle hot mixture into jars, leaving ½-in. headspace. Remove air bubbles and adjust headspace, if necessary, by adding hot mixture. Wipe rims. Center lids on jars; screw on bands until fingertip tight.

4. Place jars into canner with simmering water, ensuring that they are completely covered with water. Bring to a boil; process for 40 minutes. Remove jars and cool.

¾ cup: 131 cal., 4g fat (1g sat. fat), 0 chol., 348mg sod., 22g carb. (13g sugars, 6g fiber), 5g pro. **Diabetic exchanges:** 1½ starch, 1 fat.

TEST KITCHEN TIP

This is one of the very few times bottled lemon juice is preferred over fresh. Bottled juice has a standard pH that is more reliable for canning than that of juice from fresh lemons.

HOW-TO

Quickly Separate and Peel Garlic Cloves

- **SMASH** Place the head of garlic in a bowl and smash with the bottom of a similar-sized bowl. You can also smash between 2 cutting boards.
- **SHAKE** Put the whole crushed bulb in a hard-sided bowl with a similar-sized bowl over the top. Metal is best, but you can use glass or even a firm plastic food storage container with a lid. A jar works, too, but it takes longer to shake. Shake vigorously for 10-15 seconds to separate the papery outer layer from the garlic cloves.
- **DONE** The cloves are peeled and the skins can be easily discarded.

MEATLESS CHILI MAC

I came across this recipe in a newspaper years ago, and it's been a real hit at our house ever since. It's fast and flavorful, and it appeals to all ages.

—*Cindy Ragan, North Huntingdon, PA*

Prep: 15 min. • **Cook:** 25 min.
Makes: 8 servings

- 1 **large onion, chopped**
- 1 **medium green pepper, chopped**
- 1 **Tbsp. olive oil**
- 1 **garlic clove, minced**
- 2 **cups water**
- 1½ **cups uncooked elbow macaroni**
- 1 **can (16 oz.) mild chili beans, undrained**
- 1 **can (15½ oz.) great northern beans, rinsed and drained**
- 1 **can (14½ oz.) diced tomatoes, undrained**
- 1 **can (8 oz.) tomato sauce**
- 4 **tsp. chili powder**
- ½ **tsp. salt**
- 1 **tsp. ground cumin**
- ½ **cup fat-free sour cream**

1. In a Dutch oven, saute onion and green pepper in oil until tender. Add garlic; cook 1 minute longer. Stir in the water, macaroni, beans, tomatoes, tomato sauce, chili powder, salt and cumin.
2. Bring to a boil. Reduce heat; cover and simmer for 15-20 minutes or until macaroni is tender. Top each serving with 1 Tbsp. sour cream.
1¼ cups: 214 cal., 3g fat (1g sat. fat), 3mg chol., 710mg sod., 37g carb. (5g sugars, 8g fiber), 10g pro. **Diabetic exchanges:** 2 starch, 1 lean meat, 1 vegetable.

MEAT LOVER OPTION PAGE 320

FAVORITE DEEP-DISH PIZZA

My kids love to get pizza delivered, but it's expensive and not very healthy. I came up with a one-bowl pizza that is healthier than delivery and lets the kids add toppings of their choice. Now everyone's happy.

—*Sara Lafountain, Rockville, MD*

Prep: 20 min. • **Bake:** 20 min.
Makes: 8 servings

- 1¾ **cups whole wheat flour**
- 1¾ **cups all-purpose flour**
- 2 **pkg. (¼ oz. each) quick-rise yeast**
- 4 **tsp. sugar**
- 1 **tsp. salt**
- 1½ **cups warm water (120° to 130°)**
- ¼ **cup olive oil**
- 1 **can (8 oz.) pizza sauce**
- 8 **oz. fresh mozzarella cheese, sliced**
- 2 **cups shredded Italian cheese blend**
- ½ **tsp. dried oregano**
- ½ **tsp. Italian seasoning**
  Optional: Fresh oregano leaves and crushed red pepper flakes

1. In a large bowl, combine wheat flour, 1 cup all-purpose flour, yeast, sugar and salt. Add water and oil; beat until smooth. Stir in enough remaining flour to form a soft dough. Press dough onto the bottom and up the sides of a greased 13x9-in. baking dish.
2. Top with pizza sauce. Place mozzarella slices over sauce. Sprinkle with shredded cheese, oregano and Italian seasoning. Bake at 400° for 20-25 minutes or until golden brown. If desired, top with fresh oregano leaves and crushed red pepper flakes.
1 slice: 449 cal., 20g fat (9g sat. fat), 42mg chol., 646mg sod., 47g carb. (4g sugars, 5g fiber), 19g pro.

TOFU CHOW MEIN

This is an ideal recipe for a tofu beginner, as it's an easy, approachable way to use it. If you have time, one way to prepare it is to cut the tofu block in half and wrap well in a terry kitchen towel. Let it sit in the fridge for at least an hour to absorb excess water. For a complete meal, serve this dish with Chinese soup and egg rolls!
—*Autumn SinClaire, Gold Beach, OR*

- -

Prep: 15 min. + standing • **Cook:** 15 min.
Makes: 4 servings

8	oz. uncooked whole wheat angel hair pasta
3	Tbsp. sesame oil, divided
1	pkg. (16 oz.) extra-firm tofu
2	cups sliced fresh mushrooms
1	medium sweet red pepper, julienned
¼	cup reduced-sodium soy sauce
3	green onions, thinly sliced

1. Cook pasta according to package directions. Drain; rinse with cold water and drain again. Toss with 1 Tbsp. oil; spread onto a baking sheet and let stand about 1 hour.
2. Meanwhile, cut tofu into ½-in. cubes and blot dry. Wrap in a clean kitchen towel; place on a plate and refrigerate until ready to cook.
3. In a large skillet, heat 1 Tbsp. oil over medium heat. Add pasta, spreading evenly; cook until bottom is lightly browned, about 5 minutes. Remove from pan.
4. In same skillet, heat remaining oil over medium-high heat; stir-fry mushrooms, pepper and tofu until mushrooms are tender, 3-4 minutes. Add pasta and soy sauce; toss and heat through. Sprinkle with green onions.
1½ cups: 417 cal., 17g fat (2g sat. fat), 0 chol., 588mg sod., 48g carb. (3g sugars, 8g fiber), 21g pro. **Diabetic exchanges:** 3 fat, 2½ starch, 2 lean meat, 1 vegetable.

SPINACH-STUFFED PIZZA

I had my first stuffed pizza when I attended college near Chicago. I was amazed to see pizza well over an inch thick, with toppings on the inside! When I serve this version to my family, there are never leftovers.
—*Nancy Gilmour, Sumner, IA*

Prep: 30 min. + rising • **Bake:** 30 min.
Makes: 6 servings

- 1 loaf (1 lb.) frozen bread dough, thawed
- 1 pkg. (10 oz.) frozen chopped spinach, thawed and squeezed dry
- 1 cup chopped fresh mushrooms
- ½ cup chopped onion
- ¼ tsp. salt
- ⅛ tsp. pepper
- 2 cups shredded part-skim mozzarella cheese
- ½ cup pizza sauce
- 2 Tbsp. shredded Parmesan cheese

1. Place thawed dough in a greased bowl, turning once to grease the top. Cover with plastic and let rise in a warm place until doubled, about 1 hour.

2. Preheat oven to 400°. In a large bowl, mix spinach, mushrooms, onion, salt and pepper. Punch down dough; divide into thirds. On a lightly floured surface, roll 1 portion of dough to a 10-in. circle. Transfer to a 9-in. springform pan coated with cooking spray; press dough onto bottom and partway up sides of pan.

3. Sprinkle 1 cup mozzarella cheese onto crust. Top with spinach mixture; sprinkle with remaining mozzarella cheese.

4. On a lightly floured surface, roll out a second portion of dough to a 10-in. circle; place over cheese layer. Pinch together top and bottom crusts to seal. (Save remaining dough for another use.)

5. Bake 25-30 minutes or until crust is lightly browned. Spread pizza sauce over top; sprinkle with Parmesan cheese. Bake 5-6 minutes longer or until the cheese is melted. Let stand 5 minutes before cutting.

1 piece: 293 cal., 11g fat (5g sat. fat), 26mg chol., 789mg sod., 32g carb. (5g sugars, 4g fiber), 17g pro.

SKILLET MAC & CHEESE

This creamy mac 'n' cheese is so simple it's almost too easy! Kids really go for the rich cheese flavor, but I've never met an adult who didn't love it just as much.
—*Ann Bowers, Rockport, TX*

- -

Takes: 25 min. • **Makes:** 4 servings

- 2 **cups uncooked elbow macaroni (about 8 oz.)**
- 2 **Tbsp. butter**
- 2 **Tbsp. all-purpose flour**
- 1½ **cups half-and-half cream**
- ¾ **lb. process cheese (Velveeta), cubed**
  Optional toppings: Fresh arugula, halved cherry tomatoes and coarsely ground pepper

1. Cook macaroni according to package directions; drain.
2. Meanwhile, in a large skillet, melt butter over medium heat. Stir in flour until smooth; gradually whisk in cream. Bring to a boil, stirring constantly. Cook and stir until thickened, about 2 minutes. Reduce heat; stir in cheese until melted.
3. Stir in macaroni; heat through. Top as desired.

1½ cups: 600 cal., 37g fat (23g sat. fat), 144mg chol., 1185mg sod., 40g carb. (9g sugars, 1g fiber), 23g pro.

❄ GREEK SALAD RAVIOLI

Turn the fresh flavors of a Greek salad into a warm dish for cold winter nights. I like to make a large batch, freeze it, then simply drop ravioli into simmering water for dinner in five minutes!

—*Carla Mendres, Winnipeg, MB*

Prep: 45 min. • **Cook:** 5 min./batch
Makes: 8 servings

10	oz. (about 12 cups) fresh baby spinach
½	cup finely chopped roasted sweet red peppers
½	cup pitted and finely chopped ripe olives
½	cup crumbled feta cheese
3	Tbsp. snipped fresh dill
2	to 3 tsp. dried oregano
2	Tbsp. butter
3	Tbsp. all-purpose flour
2	cups whole milk
96	pot sticker or gyoza wrappers
	Snipped fresh dill, optional
	Sauce of choice

1. In a large skillet over medium heat, cook and stir spinach in batches until wilted, 3-4 minutes. Drain on paper towels. In a bowl, combine spinach with next 5 ingredients.

2. In a small saucepan, melt butter over medium heat. Stir in flour until smooth; gradually whisk in milk. Bring to a boil, stirring constantly, until sauce thickens and coats a spoon, 2-3 minutes. Stir into spinach mixture.

3. Place 1 Tbsp. spinach mixture in center of a pot sticker wrapper. (Cover remaining wrappers with a damp paper towel until ready to use.) Moisten wrapper edges with water, and place another wrapper on top. Press edges to seal. Repeat with remaining wrappers.

4. Fill a Dutch oven two-thirds full with water; bring to a boil. Reduce heat; drop ravioli in batches into simmering water until cooked through, 3-4 minutes. If desired, sprinkle with additional dill. Serve with sauce of choice.

Freeze option: Cover and freeze uncooked ravioli on waxed paper-lined baking sheets until firm. Transfer to freezer containers; return to freezer. To use, cook as directed, increasing time to 6 minutes.

Note: Wonton wrappers may be substituted for pot sticker or gyoza wrappers. Stack 2 or 3 wonton wrappers on a work surface; cut into circles with a 3½-in. biscuit or round cookie cutter. Fill and wrap as directed.

6 ravioli: 283 cal., 8g fat (4g sat. fat), 22mg chol., 442mg sod., 44g carb. (4g sugars, 2g fiber), 10g pro. **Diabetic exchanges:** 3 starch, 1 high-fat meat, 1 fat.

READER RAVE

"These were wonderful. We used a regular canned Alfredo sauce to top them. Next time, I think I will use the filling recipe to fill cooked manicotti or large pasta shells and then place them on top of the sauce and simply bake until heated through."
—KELLIE KATCHAM, TASTEOFHOME.COM

LACTOSE-FREE VEGGIE-STUFFED SHELLS

I converted a traditional stuffed shells recipe into a saucy, lactose-free and vegan entree to meet the needs of my family. It turned out so delicious, it was hard to believe there wasn't any cheese in it.
—Kimberly Hammond, Kingwood, TX

Prep: 30 min. • **Bake:** 35 min.
Makes: 12 servings

- 1 pkg. (12 oz.) jumbo pasta shells
- ½ lb. sliced fresh mushrooms
- 1 medium onion, chopped
- 1 Tbsp. olive oil
- 4 garlic cloves, minced
- 1 pkg. (12.3 oz.) silken extra-firm tofu
- 3 Tbsp. lemon juice
- 1 pkg. (10 oz.) frozen chopped spinach, thawed and squeezed dry
- 1 can (3.8 oz.) sliced ripe olives, drained
- 3 Tbsp. minced fresh basil
- ½ tsp. salt
- ⅛ tsp. pepper
- 1 jar (24 oz.) meatless spaghetti sauce
- ¼ cup pine nuts

1. Cook pasta according to package directions; drain. Meanwhile, in a large skillet, saute mushrooms and onion in oil until tender. Add garlic; cook 1 minute longer.
2. In a large bowl, mash tofu with lemon juice. Stir in the spinach, olives, basil, salt and pepper. Add to mushroom mixture; heat through. Spoon into shells.
3. Spread 1 cup spaghetti sauce in a 13x9-in. baking dish coated with cooking spray. Arrange shells over sauce; top with the remaining sauce. Sprinkle with pine nuts.
4. Cover and bake at 375° for 30 minutes. Uncover; bake 5-10 minutes longer or until bubbly.
3 stuffed shells: 198 cal., 5g fat (1g sat. fat), 0 chol., 485mg sod., 32g carb. (7g sugars, 4g fiber), 9g pro. **Diabetic exchanges:** 1½ starch, 1 lean meat, 1 vegetable, 1 fat.

SPINACH & ARTICHOKE PIZZA

My from-scratch pizza has a whole wheat crust flavored with beer. Top it with spinach, artichoke hearts, tomatoes and fresh basil.
—Raymonde Bourgeois, Swastika, ON

Prep: 25 min. • **Bake:** 20 min.
Makes: 6 slices

- 1½ to 1¾ cups white whole wheat flour
- 1½ tsp. baking powder
- ¼ tsp. salt
- ¼ tsp. each dried basil, oregano and parsley flakes
- ¾ cup beer or nonalcoholic beer

TOPPINGS
- 1½ tsp. olive oil
- 1 garlic clove, minced
- 2 cups shredded Italian cheese blend
- 2 cups fresh baby spinach
- 1 can (14 oz.) water-packed quartered artichoke hearts, drained and coarsely chopped
- 2 medium tomatoes, seeded and coarsely chopped
- 2 Tbsp. thinly sliced fresh basil

1. Preheat oven to 425°. In a large bowl, whisk 1½ cups flour, baking powder, salt and dried herbs until blended. Stir in beer just until moistened.
2. Turn dough onto a well-floured surface; knead gently 6-8 times, adding more flour if needed. Press dough to fit a greased 12-in. pizza pan. Pinch edge to form a rim. Bake until edge is lightly browned, about 8 minutes.
3. Mix oil and garlic; spread over crust. Sprinkle with ½ cup cheese; layer with spinach, artichoke hearts and tomatoes. Sprinkle with remaining cheese. Bake until crust is golden and cheese is melted, 8-10 minutes. Sprinkle with fresh basil.
1 slice: 290 cal., 10g fat (6g sat. fat), 27mg chol., 654mg sod., 32g carb. (1g sugars, 5g fiber), 14g pro. **Diabetic exchanges:** 2 starch, 1 medium-fat meat, 1 vegetable.

GRILLED EGGPLANT PITA PIZZAS

We grow eggplants in the garden and love to use them for our special pizza. Grilling adds robust flavor to the crust, veggies and garlic. Waiting for the eggplants to grow is the hardest part!

—*Judith Elaine Barrett, Chelsea, AL*

- -

Prep: 20 min. + standing • **Grill:** 20 min.
Makes: 4 pizzas

- 2 **small eggplants**
- 1 **tsp. salt**
- 1 **large sweet red pepper,**
  halved and sliced
- 1 **medium onion, halved and sliced**
- 12 **garlic cloves, halved**
- 3 **Tbsp. olive oil, divided**
- ¼ **tsp. pepper**
- 4 **whole pita breads**
- 1 **large tomato, seeded and chopped**
- 3 **oz. fresh mozzarella**
  cheese, shredded
- ¼ **cup pitted ripe olives,**
  coarsely chopped
- ½ **tsp. crushed red pepper**
  flakes, optional
- 1 **cup loosely packed basil**
  leaves, coarsely chopped

1. Cut eggplants into ¾-in. slices. Place in a colander over a plate; sprinkle with salt and toss. Let stand 30 minutes.

2. Meanwhile, toss red pepper, onion and garlic with 1 Tbsp. oil. Transfer to a grill wok or open grill basket; place on grill rack. Grill, uncovered, over medium-high heat for 8-12 minutes or until vegetables are crisp-tender and slightly charred, stirring frequently.

3. Rinse and drain eggplants; blot dry with paper towels. Brush eggplants with 1 Tbsp. oil; sprinkle with pepper. Grill, covered, over medium heat 4-5 minutes on each side or until tender. Cut each slice into quarters.

4. Brush both sides of pita breads with remaining oil. Grill pitas, covered, over medium-low heat 1-2 minutes or until bottoms are lightly browned.

5. Remove from grill. Layer grilled sides of pitas with grilled vegetables, tomato, cheese and olives. If desired, sprinkle with pepper flakes. Return to grill; cook, covered, for 3-4 minutes or until cheese is melted. Sprinkle with basil.

Note: If you do not have a grill wok or basket, use a disposable foil pan. Poke holes in the bottom of the pan with a meat fork to allow liquid to drain.

1 pizza: 428 cal., 17g fat (5g sat. fat), 17mg chol., 721mg sod., 59g carb. (12g sugars, 12g fiber), 14g pro.

DID YOU KNOW?

You don't have to peel small eggplants—so save yourself some time and leave the nutrient-rich skin intact. Remove the skin on bigger ones, though. It's often tough and bitter.

LINGUINE PRIMAVERA

This colorful pasta dish is the brainchild of my oldest son. The stick-to-your-ribs pasta includes loads of fresh veggies as well as basil and provolone cheese.
—*Jane Bone, Cape Coral, FL*

Takes: 30 min. • **Makes:** 6 servings

- 6 oz. uncooked linguine
- 2 Tbsp. butter
- 1 Tbsp. olive oil
- 2 medium zucchini, thinly sliced
- ½ lb. fresh mushrooms, sliced
- 1 large tomato, chopped
- 2 green onions, chopped
- 1 garlic clove, minced
- ½ tsp. salt
- ¼ tsp. pepper
- 1 cup shredded provolone cheese
- 3 Tbsp. shredded Parmesan cheese
- 2 tsp. minced fresh basil

1. Cook linguine according to package directions. Meanwhile, in a large skillet, heat butter and oil over medium heat. Add zucchini and mushrooms; saute 3-5 minutes. Add the tomato, onions, garlic and seasonings. Reduce heat; simmer, covered, about 3 minutes.
2. Drain linguine; add to vegetable mixture. Sprinkle with cheeses and basil. Toss to coat.
1½ cups: 260 cal., 13g fat (7g sat. fat), 25mg chol., 444mg sod., 26g carb. (3g sugars, 2g fiber), 12g pro. **Diabetic exchanges:** 1½ starch, 1½ fat, 1 medium-fat meat, 1 vegetable.

MEAT
LOVER
OPTION
PAGE 320

PEPPER RICOTTA PASTA

Garlic, peppers and herbs top creamy ricotta cheese in this meatless skillet meal you can make in just 20 minutes.
—*Janet Boulger, Botwood, NL*

Takes: 20 min. • **Makes:** 6 servings

- 1 cup part-skim ricotta cheese
- ½ cup fat-free milk
- 4 tsp. olive oil
- 1 garlic clove, minced
- ½ tsp. crushed red pepper flakes
- 1 medium green pepper, julienned
- 1 medium sweet red pepper, julienned
- 1 medium sweet yellow pepper, julienned
- 1 medium zucchini, sliced
- 1 cup frozen peas, thawed
- ¼ tsp. dried oregano
- ¼ tsp. dried basil
- 6 oz. fettuccine, cooked and drained

1. Whisk together ricotta cheese and milk; set aside. In a large skillet, heat oil over medium heat. Add garlic and pepper flakes; saute 1 minute. Add next 7 ingredients. Cook and stir over medium heat until vegetables are crisp-tender, about 5 minutes.
2. Add cheese mixture to fettuccine; top with vegetables. Toss to coat. Serve immediately.
1 cup: 229 cal., 7g fat (3g sat. fat), 13mg chol., 88mg sod., 31g carb. (6g sugars, 4g fiber), 11g pro. **Diabetic exchanges:** 2 starch, 1 medium-fat meat, ½ fat.

TEST KITCHEN TIP

To punch up the flavor, use fresh herbs in place of dried in this pasta. Sprinkle with Parmesan cheese before serving.

VEGAN MAC & CHEESE

Buttery cashews and nutritional yeast create a rich, savory sauce in this vegan rendition of good ol' mac & cheese.
—*Taste of Home Test Kitchen*

Prep: 20 min. + standing • **Cook:** 10 min.
Makes: 6 servings

- 2 cups raw cashews
- 16 oz. uncooked elbow macaroni
- 1½ cups water
- ⅓ cup nutritional yeast
- 2 tsp. lemon juice
- 2 tsp. salt
- 2 tsp. onion powder
- 1½ tsp. paprika
- 1 tsp. pepper
- ⅛ tsp. cayenne pepper

1. Rinse cashews in cold water. Place in a large bowl; add water to cover by 3 in. Cover and let stand overnight.
2. Cook macaroni according to package directions. Drain and rinse cashews, discarding liquid. Transfer to a food processor. Add 1½ cups water, nutritional yeast, lemon juice and seasonings; cover and process until pureed, 3-4 minutes, scraping down sides as needed.
3. Drain macaroni; return to pan. Stir in cashew mixture. Cook and stir over medium-low heat until heated through. Sprinkle with additional paprika if desired.
1⅔ cups: 497 cal., 18g fat (3g sat. fat), 0 chol., 803mg sod., 67g carb. (5g sugars, 5g fiber), 18g pro.

WHOLE WHEAT VEGGIE PIZZA

A wonderful crust layered with herbed tomato sauce and veggie toppings encourages my family of six to dig right in to this low-fat main course.
—*Denise Warner, Red Lodge, MT*

- -

Prep: 40 min. + rising • **Bake:** 20 min.
Makes: 2 pizzas (6 slices each)

- ½ cup whole wheat flour
- 2 pkg. (¼ oz. each) quick-rise yeast
- 1 tsp. garlic powder
- ½ tsp. salt
- 2½ cups all-purpose flour
- 1 cup water
- 2 Tbsp. olive oil

SAUCE
- 1 can (14½ oz.) diced tomatoes, undrained
- 1 Tbsp. minced fresh parsley
- 1½ tsp. sugar
- 1½ tsp. Italian seasoning
- 1½ tsp. dried basil
- ½ tsp. garlic powder
- ¼ tsp. pepper

TOPPINGS
- 1 tsp. olive oil
- 1 cup chopped zucchini
- 1 cup sliced fresh mushrooms
- ½ cup chopped green or red pepper
- ¼ cup chopped onion
- 1¼ cups shredded part-skim mozzarella cheese

1. In a large bowl, mix first 4 ingredients and 1 cup all-purpose flour. In a small saucepan, heat water and oil to 120°-130°. Add to dry ingredients; beat on medium speed 3 minutes. Stir in enough remaining flour to form a soft dough.

2. Turn onto a floured surface; knead until smooth and elastic, about 5 minutes. Place in a greased bowl, turning once to grease the top. Cover and let rise in a warm place until doubled, about 30 minutes.

3. In a small saucepan, bring the sauce ingredients to a boil. Reduce the heat; simmer, uncovered, until slightly thickened, 15-18 minutes, stirring occasionally. Remove from heat.

4. Preheat oven to 400°. Punch down dough. On a lightly floured surface, divide dough in half and roll each into a 12-in. circle. Place on 2 greased 12-in. pizza pans; prick with a fork. Bake until lightly browned, 8-10 minutes.

5. Meanwhile, in a skillet, heat oil over medium-high heat; saute vegetables until zucchini is crisp-tender. Spread crusts with sauce; top with vegetables and cheese. Bake until cheese is melted, 12-15 minutes.

1 slice: 190 cal., 6g fat (2g sat. fat), 8mg chol., 234mg sod., 28g carb. (3g sugars, 3g fiber), 7g pro. **Diabetic exchanges:** 1½ starch, ½ vegetable, ½ fat.

TEST KITCHEN TIP

No Italian seasoning on hand? No worries. Simply mix an equal amount of basil, thyme, rosemary and oregano to create your own seasoning blend.

🅕 🕐 MUFFIN-TIN LASAGNAS

This is a fun way to serve lasagna and a great idea to surprise everyone at the table. Easy and quick, these little cups can be made with whatever ingredients your family likes best.
—*Sally Kilkenny, Granger, IA*

Takes: 30 min. • **Makes:** 1 dozen

- 1 **large egg, lightly beaten**
- 1 **carton (15 oz.) part-skim ricotta cheese**
- 2 **cups shredded Italian cheese blend, divided**
- 1 **Tbsp. olive oil**
- 24 **wonton wrappers**
- 1 **jar (24 oz.) garden-style pasta sauce**
  Minced fresh parsley, optional

1. Preheat oven to 375°. In a bowl, mix the egg, ricotta cheese and 1¼ cups Italian cheese blend.

2. Generously grease 12 muffin cups with oil; line each with a wonton wrapper. Fill each with 1 Tbsp. ricotta mixture and 1½ Tbsp. pasta sauce. Top each with a second wrapper, rotating corners and pressing down centers. Repeat ricotta and sauce layers. Sprinkle with remaining cheese blend.

3. Bake until cheese is melted, 20-25 minutes. If desired, sprinkle with parsley.

2 mini lasagnas: 414 cal., 19g fat (9g sat. fat), 83mg chol., 970mg sod., 36g carb. (8g sugars, 2g fiber), 22g pro.

TOFU-VEGGIE PAD THAI

Classic flavors of Thailand abound in this fragrant and flavorful dish featuring peanuts, tofu and noodles. Tofu gives the entree its satisfying protein.

—*Sara Landry, Brookline, MA*

Prep: 25 min. • **Cook:** 15 min.
Makes: 6 servings

- 1 pkg. (12 oz.) whole wheat fettuccine
- 5 Tbsp. reduced-sodium soy sauce
- ¼ cup rice vinegar
- 2 Tbsp. brown sugar
- 1 Tbsp. lime juice
  Dash Louisiana-style hot sauce
- 1 pkg. (12 oz.) extra-firm tofu, drained and cut into ½-in. cubes
- 3 tsp. canola oil, divided
- 2 medium carrots, grated
- 2 cups fresh snow peas, halved
- 3 garlic cloves, minced
- 2 large eggs, lightly beaten
- 2 cups bean sprouts
- 3 green onions, chopped
- ½ cup minced fresh cilantro
- ¼ cup unsalted peanuts, chopped

1. Cook fettuccine according to package directions. Meanwhile, in a small bowl, combine the soy sauce, vinegar, brown sugar, lime juice and hot sauce until smooth; set aside.

2. In a large skillet or wok, stir-fry tofu in 2 tsp. oil until golden brown. Remove and keep warm. Stir-fry carrots and snow peas in remaining oil for 1-2 minutes. Add garlic; cook 1 minute longer or until vegetables are crisp-tender. Add eggs; cook and stir until set.

3. Drain fettuccine; add to vegetable mixture. Stir vinegar mixture and add to the skillet. Bring to a boil. Add tofu, bean sprouts and onions; heat through. Sprinkle with cilantro and peanuts.

1⅓ cups: 383 cal., 11g fat (2g sat. fat), 71mg chol., 806mg sod., 61g carb. (11g sugars, 10g fiber), 18g pro.

BUTTERNUT & PORTOBELLO LASAGNA

Lasagna gets fresh flavor and color when you make it with roasted butternut squash, portobello mushrooms, basil and spinach. We feast on this.

—*Edward and Danielle Walker, Traverse City, MI*

- -

Prep: 1 hour • **Bake:** 45 min. + standing
Makes: 12 servings

1   pkg. (10 oz.) frozen cubed
     butternut squash, thawed
2   tsp. olive oil
1   tsp. brown sugar
¼   tsp. salt
⅛   tsp. pepper

MUSHROOMS
4   large portobello mushrooms,
     coarsely chopped
2   tsp. balsamic vinegar
2   tsp. olive oil
¼   tsp. salt
⅛   tsp. pepper

SAUCE
2   cans (28 oz. each) whole
     tomatoes, undrained
2   tsp. olive oil
2   garlic cloves, minced
1   tsp. crushed red pepper flakes
½   cup fresh basil leaves, thinly sliced
¼   tsp. salt
⅛   tsp. pepper

LASAGNA
9   no-cook lasagna noodles
4   oz. fresh baby spinach (about 5 cups)
3   cups part-skim ricotta cheese
1½   cups shredded part-skim
     mozzarella cheese

1. Preheat oven to 350°. In a large bowl, combine the first 5 ingredients. In another bowl, combine ingredients for mushrooms. Transfer vegetables to 2 separate foil-lined 15x10x1-in. baking pans. Roast 14-16 minutes or until tender, stirring occasionally.

2. Meanwhile, for sauce, drain tomatoes, reserving juices; coarsely chop tomatoes. In a large saucepan, heat oil over medium heat. Add garlic and pepper flakes; cook 1 minute longer. Stir in chopped tomatoes, reserved tomato juices, basil, salt and pepper; bring to a boil. Reduce heat; simmer, uncovered, 35-45 minutes or until thickened, stirring occasionally.

3. Spread 1 cup sauce into a greased 13x9-in. baking dish. Layer with 3 noodles, 1 cup sauce, spinach and mushrooms. Continue layering with 3 noodles, 1 cup sauce, ricotta cheese and roasted squash. Top with remaining noodles and sauce. Sprinkle with mozzarella cheese.

4. Bake, covered, 30 minutes. Bake, uncovered, 15-20 minutes longer or until bubbly. Let stand 15 minutes before serving.

1 piece: 252 cal., 10g fat (5g sat. fat), 27mg chol., 508mg sod., 25g carb. (5g sugars, 4g fiber), 15g pro. **Diabetic exchanges:** 2 starch, 1 medium-fat meat, ½ fat.

⏱ LOADED MEXICAN PIZZA

My husband is a picky eater, but he actually looks forward to this healthy pizza with all the Mexican flavors he loves. Leftovers are no problem, because this meal tastes better the next day.
—*Mary Barker, Knoxville, TN*

- -

Takes: 30 min. • **Makes:** 6 slices

- 1   can (15 oz.) black beans, rinsed and drained
- 1   medium red onion, chopped
- 1   small sweet yellow pepper, chopped
- 3   tsp. chili powder
- ¾   tsp. ground cumin
- 3   medium tomatoes, chopped
- 1   jalapeno pepper, seeded and finely chopped
- 1   garlic clove, minced
- 1   prebaked 12-in. thin pizza crust
- 2   cups chopped fresh spinach
- 2   Tbsp. minced fresh cilantro
  Hot pepper sauce to taste
- ½   cup shredded reduced-fat cheddar cheese
- ½   cup shredded pepper jack cheese

1. In a small bowl, mash black beans. Stir in the onion, yellow pepper, chili powder and cumin. In another bowl, combine the tomatoes, jalapeno and garlic.

2. Place crust on an ungreased 12-in. pizza pan; spread with bean mixture. Top with tomato mixture and spinach. Sprinkle with cilantro, pepper sauce and cheeses.

3. Bake at 400° for 12-15 minutes or until cheese is melted.

Note: Wear disposable gloves when cutting hot peppers; the oils can burn skin. Avoid touching your face.

1 slice: 297 cal., 9g fat (4g sat. fat), 17mg chol., 566mg sod., 41g carb. (5g sugars, 6g fiber), 15g pro. **Diabetic exchanges:** 2½ starch, 1 lean meat, 1 vegetable.

🕐 FRESH CORN & TOMATO FETTUCCINE

This recipe combines delicious whole wheat pasta with the best of fresh garden produce. It's tossed with heart-healthy olive oil, and a little feta cheese gives it bite.

—*Angela Spengler, Niceville, FL*

Takes: 30 min. • **Makes:** 4 servings

8	oz. uncooked whole wheat fettuccine
2	medium ears sweet corn, husked
2	tsp. plus 2 Tbsp. olive oil, divided
½	cup chopped sweet red pepper
4	green onions, chopped
2	medium tomatoes, chopped
½	tsp. salt
½	tsp. pepper
1	cup crumbled feta cheese
2	Tbsp. minced fresh parsley

1. In a Dutch oven, cook fettuccine according to package directions, adding corn during the last 8 minutes of cooking.

2. Meanwhile, in a small skillet, heat 2 tsp. oil over medium-high heat. Add red pepper and green onions; cook and stir until tender.

3. Drain pasta and corn; transfer pasta to a large bowl. Cool corn slightly; cut corn from cob and add to pasta. Add tomatoes, salt, pepper, remaining oil and the pepper mixture; toss to combine. Sprinkle with feta cheese and parsley.

2 cups: 422 cal., 15g fat (4g sat. fat), 15mg chol., 580mg sod., 56g carb. (6g sugars, 10g fiber), 17g pro.

HOW-TO

Keep Parsley (Almost) Forever

To keep parsley fresh for up to a month, trim the stems and place the bunch in a tumbler with an inch of water. Be sure no leaves are in the water. Tie a produce bag around the tumbler to trap humidity; store in the refrigerator. Each time you use the parsley, change the water and turn the produce bag inside out so any moisture that has built up inside the bag can escape.

CHEESY SPINACH-STUFFED SHELLS

I'm very proud of this recipe because I am a beginner cook and it was the first recipe I created on my own. You can adjust it to your liking by adding more spinach or a meat to it.
—Laci Hooten, McKinney, TX

- -

Prep: 45 min. • **Bake:** 45 min.
Makes: 12 servings

- 1 pkg. (12 oz.) jumbo pasta shells
- 1 Tbsp. butter
- 1 cup sliced mushrooms
- 1 small onion, finely chopped
- 4 garlic cloves, minced
- 2 large eggs, lightly beaten
- 1 carton (15 oz.) part-skim ricotta cheese
- 1 pkg. (10 oz.) frozen chopped spinach, thawed and squeezed dry
- 2 Tbsp. minced fresh basil or 2 tsp. dried basil
- ¼ tsp. pepper
- 1 can (4¼ oz.) chopped ripe olives
- 1½ cups shredded Italian cheese blend, divided
- 1½ cups shredded part-skim mozzarella cheese, divided
- 1 jar (24 oz.) marinara sauce
  Additional minced fresh basil, optional

1. Preheat oven to 375°. Cook pasta shells according to package directions for al dente. Drain; rinse with cold water.
2. Meanwhile, in a small skillet, heat butter over medium-high heat. Add mushrooms and onion; cook and stir until vegetables are tender, 4-6 minutes. Add garlic; cook 1 minute longer. Remove from the heat; cool slightly.
3. In a large bowl, mix eggs, ricotta cheese, spinach, basil and pepper. Stir in olives, mushroom mixture and ¾ cup each cheese blend and mozzarella cheese.
4. Spread 1 cup sauce into a 13x9-in. baking dish coated with cooking spray. Fill pasta shells with cheese mixture; place in baking dish, overlapping ends slightly. Spoon remaining sauce over top.
5. Bake, covered, until heated through, 40-45 minutes. Uncover; sprinkle with remaining cheeses. Bake until cheese is melted, about 5 minutes longer. Let stand 5 minutes before serving. If desired, sprinkle with additional basil.

3 stuffed shells: 313 cal., 13g fat (7g sat. fat), 65mg chol., 642mg sod., 32g carb. (5g sugars, 3g fiber), 18g pro. **Diabetic exchanges:** 2 starch, 2 medium-fat meat, ½ fat.

READER RAVE

"These were so good! The only change I made was omitting the mushrooms. I would love them in this, but my guys not so much. This recipe is a winner. I will make these again."
—ANGELA32, TASTEOFHOME.COM

SUMMER SQUASH FLATBREADS

When you want a meatless meal with Mediterranean style, these flatbreads smothered with squash, hummus and mozzarella deliver the goods.
—*Matthew Hass, Ellison Bay, WI*

Takes: 30 min. • **Makes:** 4 servings

- 3 small yellow summer squash, sliced ¼ in. thick
- 1 Tbsp. olive oil
- ½ tsp. salt
- 2 cups fresh baby spinach, coarsely chopped
- 2 naan flatbreads
- ⅓ cup roasted red pepper hummus
- 1 carton (8 oz.) fresh mozzarella cheese pearls
  Pepper

1. Preheat oven to 425°. Toss squash with oil and salt; spread evenly in a 15x10x1-in. baking pan. Roast until tender, 8-10 minutes. Transfer to a bowl; stir in spinach.
2. Place naan on a baking sheet; spread with hummus. Top with squash mixture and cheese. Bake on a lower oven rack just until the cheese is melted, 4-6 minutes. Sprinkle with pepper.

½ topped flatbread: 332 cal., 20g fat (9g sat. fat), 47mg chol., 737mg sod., 24g carb. (7g sugars, 3g fiber), 15g pro.

LINGUINE WITH BROCCOLI RABE & PEPPERS

Broccoli rabe is one of my favorite veggies. Since it cooks right with the linguine, you can multitask. Before you know it, dinner is served.

—*Gilda Lester, Millsboro, DE*

Takes: 25 min. • **Makes:** 6 servings

- 1 lb. broccoli rabe
- 1 pkg. (16 oz.) linguine
- 3 Tbsp. olive oil
- 2 anchovy fillets, finely chopped, optional
- 3 garlic cloves, minced
- ½ cup sliced roasted sweet red peppers
- ½ cup pitted Greek olives, halved
- ½ tsp. crushed red pepper flakes
- ¼ tsp. pepper
- ⅛ tsp. salt
- ½ cup grated Romano cheese

1. Cut ½ in. off ends of broccoli rabe; trim woody stems. Cut stems and leaves into 2-in. pieces. Cook linguine according to package directions, adding broccoli rabe during the last 5 minutes of cooking. Drain, reserving ½ cup pasta water.

2. Meanwhile, in a large skillet, heat oil over medium-high heat. Add anchovies and garlic; cook and stir 1 minute. Stir in red peppers, olives, pepper flakes, pepper and salt.

3. Add linguine and broccoli rabe to skillet; toss to combine, adding reserved pasta water as desired to moisten. Serve with cheese.

1¼ cups: 429 cal., 15g fat (4g sat. fat), 2mg chol., 487mg sod., 60g carb. (4g sugars, 5g fiber), 17g pro.

PASTA PIZZA

My family often requests this main dish. It's a tempting cross between pizza and spaghetti.

—*Andrea Quick, Columbus, OH*

Prep: 25 min. • **Bake:** 10 min.
Makes: 4 servings

- 8 oz. uncooked angel hair pasta
- 4 tsp. olive oil, divided
- 2 cups sliced fresh mushrooms
- ½ cup chopped green pepper
- ¼ cup chopped onion
- 1 can (15 oz.) pizza sauce
- ¼ cup sliced ripe olives
- ½ cup shredded part-skim mozzarella cheese
- ¼ tsp. Italian seasoning

1. Preheat oven to 400°. Cook pasta according to package directions; drain.

2. In a large cast-iron or other ovenproof skillet, heat 1 tsp. oil over medium heat. Add mushrooms, green pepper and onion; saute until tender. Remove with a slotted spoon and keep warm. Increase heat to medium-high. In same skillet, heat remaining oil. Spread pasta evenly in skillet to form a crust. Cook until lightly browned, 5-7 minutes.

3. Turn crust onto a large plate. Reduce heat to medium; slide crust back into skillet. Top with pizza sauce, sauteed vegetables and olives; sprinkle with cheese and Italian seasoning. Bake until the cheese is melted, 10-12 minutes.

1 serving: 374 cal., 10g fat (3g sat. fat), 9mg chol., 532mg sod., 56g carb. (7g sugars, 5g fiber), 14g pro.

GARDEN-FRESH PIZZA SAUCE

This sauce is so healthy because of all the vegetables in it. I freeze it in 1-cup portions so it's always on hand for quick pizzas.
—Helen Lipko, Martinsburg, PA

Prep: 15 min. • **Cook:** 70 min. • **Makes:** 6 cups

- 1¾ cups sliced fresh mushrooms
- 1 medium onion, chopped
- ¼ cup chopped green pepper
- ¼ cup chopped sweet red pepper
- 1 tsp. olive oil
- 1 can (28 oz.) crushed tomatoes
- 2 cans (6 oz. each) tomato paste
- 1 cup water
- 2 Tbsp. sugar
- 1½ tsp. dried basil
- 1½ tsp. dried oregano
- 1 tsp. garlic powder
- ¼ tsp. salt
- ¼ tsp. coarsely ground pepper

1. In a large nonstick saucepan, saute the mushrooms, onion and peppers in oil until tender. Stir in the tomatoes, tomato paste, water, sugar, basil, oregano, garlic powder and salt. Bring to a boil. Reduce heat; simmer, uncovered, for 1 hour or until sauce reaches desired thickness, stirring occasionally.
2. Stir in pepper; cook 5 minutes longer. Spread desired amount over a pizza crust, or cool and then refrigerate or freeze. Sauce may be frozen for up to 3 months.
3 Tbsp.: 25 cal., 0 fat (0 sat. fat), 0 chol., 60mg sod., 6g carb. (3g sugars, 1g fiber), 1g pro.
Diabetic exchanges: 1 vegetable.

BASIC PIZZA CRUST

I like to double this recipe and keep one baked crust in the freezer for a quick snack or meal later on.
—Beverly Anderson, Sinclairville, NY

Prep: 10 min. + resting • **Bake:** 25 min.
Makes: 1 pizza crust (6 slices)

- 1 pkg. (¼ oz.) active dry yeast
- 1 cup warm water (110° to 115°)
- 2 Tbsp. canola oil
- 1 tsp. sugar
- ¼ tsp. salt
- 2½ to 2¾ cups all-purpose flour
  Cornmeal
  Pizza toppings of your choice

1. In a large bowl, dissolve yeast in warm water. Add the oil, sugar, salt and 1½ cups flour. Beat until smooth. Stir in enough remaining flour to form a firm dough. Turn onto a floured surface; cover and let rest for 10 minutes.
2. Roll into a 13-in. circle. Grease a 12-in. pizza pan and sprinkle with cornmeal. Transfer dough to prepared pan, building up edges slightly. Do not let rise. Bake at 425° for 12-15 minutes or until browned. Add toppings; bake 10-15 minutes longer.
1 slice: 236 cal., 5g fat (1g sat. fat), 0 chol., 100mg sod., 41g carb. (2g sugars, 2g fiber), 6g pro.

CHARD & WHITE BEAN PASTA

I love to prepare gluten-free and dairy-free dishes, and this recipe meets the criteria when you use gluten-free pasta. It's also soy-free, nut-free and vegetarian.
—*Amie Valpone, New York, NY*

Prep: 20 min. • **Cook:** 20 min.
Makes: 8 servings

- 1 pkg. (12 oz.) whole wheat or brown rice penne pasta
- 2 Tbsp. olive oil
- 4 cups sliced leeks (white portion only)
- 1 cup sliced sweet onion
- 4 garlic cloves, sliced
- 1 Tbsp. minced fresh sage or 1 tsp. rubbed sage
- 1 large sweet potato, peeled and cut into ½-in. cubes
- 1 medium bunch Swiss chard (about 1 lb.), cut into 1-in. slices
- 1 can (15½ oz.) great northern beans, rinsed and drained
- ¾ tsp. salt
- ¼ tsp. chili powder
- ¼ tsp. crushed red pepper flakes
- ⅛ tsp. ground nutmeg
- ⅛ tsp. pepper
- ⅓ cup finely chopped fresh basil
- 1 Tbsp. balsamic vinegar
- 2 cups marinara sauce, warmed

1. Cook pasta according to package directions. Drain well, reserving ¾ cup pasta water.
2. In a 6-qt. stockpot, heat oil over medium heat; saute leeks and onion until tender, 5-7 minutes. Add garlic and sage; cook and stir 2 minutes.
3. Add sweet potato and chard; cook, covered, over medium-low heat 5 minutes. Stir in beans, dry seasonings and reserved pasta water; cook, covered, until sweet potato and chard are tender, about 5 minutes. Add pasta, basil and vinegar; heat through. Serve with sauce.
1⅓ cups pasta with ½ cup sauce: 369 cal., 6g fat (1g sat. fat), 1mg chol., 801mg sod., 67g carb. (13g sugars, 13g fiber), 14g pro.

GRILLED GARDEN VEGGIE PIZZA

Pile on the veggies—this crisp, grilled crust can take it! The colorful, healthy pizza looks as fresh as it tastes.

—*Diane Halferty, Corpus Christi, TX*

Takes: 30 min. • **Makes:** 6 servings

- 1 medium red onion, cut crosswise into ½-in. slices
- 1 large sweet red pepper, halved, stemmed and seeded
- 1 small zucchini, cut lengthwise into ½-in. slices
- 1 yellow summer squash, cut lengthwise into ½-in. slices
- 2 Tbsp. olive oil
- ½ tsp. salt
- ¼ tsp. pepper
- 1 prebaked 12-in. thin whole wheat pizza crust
- 3 Tbsp. jarred roasted minced garlic
- 2 cups shredded part-skim mozzarella cheese, divided
- ⅓ cup torn fresh basil

1. Brush vegetables with oil; sprinkle with salt and pepper. Grill, covered, over medium heat until tender, 4-5 minutes per side for onion and pepper, 3-4 minutes per side for zucchini and squash.
2. Separate onion into rings; cut pepper into strips. Spread pizza crust with garlic; sprinkle with 1 cup cheese. Top with grilled vegetables, then remaining cheese.
3. Grill pizza, covered, over medium heat until bottom is golden brown and cheese is melted, 5-7 minutes. Top with basil.
1 slice: 324 cal., 15g fat (6g sat. fat), 24mg chol., 704mg sod., 30g carb. (5g sugars, 5g fiber), 16g pro. **Diabetic exchanges:** 2 starch, 2 medium-fat meat, 1 fat.

MEAT LOVER OPTION
PAGE 320

PEANUT GINGER PASTA

To get the luscious taste of Thai takeout at home, combine ginger, basil, lime and peanut butter in a sauce for whole wheat pasta. It's so good, we never have leftovers.

—*Allil Binder, Spokane, WA*

Takes: 30 min. • **Makes:** 4 servings

- 2½ tsp. grated lime zest
- ¼ cup lime juice
- 2 Tbsp. reduced-sodium soy sauce
- 2 tsp. water
- 1 tsp. sesame oil
- ⅓ cup creamy peanut butter
- 2½ tsp. minced fresh gingerroot
- 2 garlic cloves, minced
- ¼ tsp. salt
- ¼ tsp. pepper
- 8 oz. uncooked whole wheat linguine
- 2 cups small fresh broccoli florets
- 2 medium carrots, grated
- 1 medium sweet red pepper, julienned
- 2 green onions, chopped
- 2 Tbsp. minced fresh basil

1. Place the first 10 ingredients in a blender; cover and process until blended. Cook linguine according to package directions, adding broccoli during the last 5 minutes of cooking; drain.
2. Transfer linguine and broccoli to a large bowl. Add remaining ingredients. Add peanut butter mixture and toss to combine.
2 cups: 365 cal., 13g fat (2g sat. fat), 0 chol., 567mg sod., 57g carb. (6g sugars, 10g fiber), 14g pro.

EASY EGG PAD THAI

Here's my simple version of pad thai loaded with crisp, colorful vegetables and zesty flavor. Give fresh and simple a twirl.
—*Colleen Doucette, Truro, NS*

Takes: 30 min. • **Makes:** 4 servings

- 6 oz. uncooked thick rice noodles
- 2 Tbsp. packed brown sugar
- 3 Tbsp. reduced-sodium soy sauce
- 4 tsp. rice vinegar
- 2 tsp. lime juice
- 2 tsp. olive oil
- 3 medium carrots, shredded
- 1 medium sweet red pepper, cut into thin strips
- 4 green onions, chopped
- 3 garlic cloves, minced
- 4 large eggs, lightly beaten
- 2 cups bean sprouts
- ⅓ cup chopped fresh cilantro
   Chopped peanuts, optional
   Lime wedges

1. Prepare noodles according to package directions. Drain; rinse well and drain again. In a small bowl, mix together brown sugar, soy sauce, vinegar and lime juice.
2. In a large nonstick skillet, heat oil over medium-high heat; stir-fry carrots and pepper until crisp-tender, 3-4 minutes. Add green onions and garlic; cook and stir 2 minutes. Remove from pan.
3. Reduce heat to medium. Pour eggs into same pan; cook and stir until no liquid egg remains. Stir in carrot mixture, noodles and sauce mixture; heat through. Add bean sprouts; toss to combine. Top with cilantro and, if desired, peanuts. Serve with lime.
1¼ cups: 339 cal., 8g fat (2g sat. fat), 186mg chol., 701mg sod., 55g carb. (15g sugars, 4g fiber), 12g pro.

FONTINA & SWEET POTATO PIZZA

This recipe came about mainly thanks to my husband, who's a real pizza fan. And it gets nutrient-rich sweet potatoes, which I love, into a meal.
—*Elizabeth Godecke, Chicago, IL*

Prep: 20 min. • **Bake:** 15 min.
Makes: 6 servings

- 1 medium sweet potato (about 10 oz.)
- 2 Tbsp. water
- ¼ tsp. salt
- ⅛ tsp. coarsely ground pepper
- 1 tube (13.8 oz.) refrigerated pizza crust
- 1 cup shredded part-skim mozzarella cheese
- 1 cup shredded fontina cheese
- 2 Tbsp. olive oil, divided
- 1 tsp. minced fresh rosemary or ¼ tsp. dried rosemary, crushed
- 1 tsp. minced fresh thyme or ¼ tsp. dried thyme
- ¼ cup grated Parmesan cheese

1. Preheat oven to 450°. Peel and cut sweet potato into ¼-in. slices. Cut each slice into ½-in.-wide strips; place in a microwave-safe dish. Add water. Microwave, covered, on high 3-4 minutes or until potato is almost tender. Drain; sprinkle with salt and pepper.
2. Unroll and press dough onto a greased 12-in. pizza pan. If desired, pinch edge to form a rim. Sprinkle with mozzarella and fontina cheeses; drizzle with 1 Tbsp. oil.
3. Top with sweet potato; sprinkle with herbs. Drizzle with remaining oil; sprinkle with Parmesan cheese. Bake on lowest oven rack 12-15 minutes or until crust is golden and cheese is melted.
1 slice: 374 cal., 16g fat (7g sat. fat), 35mg chol., 819mg sod., 39g carb. (7g sugars, 2g fiber), 17g pro.

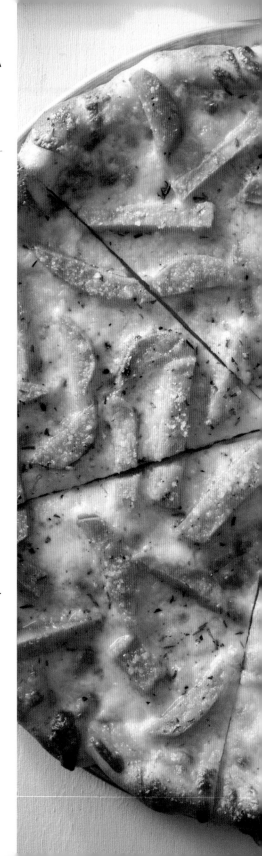

SPINACH FETA TURNOVERS

These quick and easy turnovers are a favorite with my wife, who says they are delicious and melt in your mouth.
—*David Baruch, Weston, FL*

Takes: 30 min. • **Makes:** 4 servings

- 2 large eggs
- 1 pkg. (10 oz.) frozen leaf spinach, thawed, squeezed dry and chopped
- ¾ cup crumbled feta cheese
- 2 garlic cloves, minced
- ¼ tsp. pepper
- 1 tube (13.8 oz.) refrigerated pizza crust
  Refrigerated tzatziki sauce, optional

1. In a bowl, whisk eggs; set aside 1 Tbsp. of eggs. Combine the spinach, feta cheese, garlic, pepper and remaining beaten eggs.
2. Unroll pizza crust; roll into a 12-in. square. Cut into four 6-in. squares. Top each square with about ⅓ cup spinach mixture. Fold into a triangle and pinch edges to seal. Cut slits in top; brush with reserved egg.
3. Place on a greased baking sheet. Bake at 425° until golden brown, 10-12 minutes. If desired, serve with tzatziki sauce.
1 turnover: 361 cal., 9g fat (4g sat. fat), 104mg chol., 936mg sod., 51g carb. (7g sugars, 4g fiber), 17g pro.

EGGPLANT & MUSHROOM
MONTE CRISTO, PAGE 109

BURGERS, SANDWICHES & WRAPS

Say yes to magnificent burgers, great grilled cheese and handy on-the-go wraps. There's no need to compromise satisfaction and taste when these handhelds are on the menu.

CHILES RELLENOS SANDWICHES

Even since my early days of cooking, one thing hasn't changed: I still love to make these zippy grilled sandwiches stuffed with green chiles and cheese.
—*Gladys Hill, Qulin, MO*

Takes: 25 min. • **Makes:** 3 servings

- 1 can (4 oz.) chopped green chiles, drained
- 6 slices white bread
- 3 slices Monterey Jack cheese
- 2 large eggs
- 1 cup 2% milk
- 3 Tbsp. butter
  Salsa, optional

1. Mash green chiles with a fork; spread over 3 slices of bread. Top with cheese and remaining bread. In a shallow bowl, whisk eggs and milk until blended.

2. In a large skillet, heat 1 Tbsp. butter over medium heat. Dip both sides of sandwich in egg mixture. Place in skillet; toast 2-3 minutes on each side or until golden brown and cheese is melted. Repeat with remaining butter and sandwiches. If desired, serve with salsa.

1 sandwich: 388 cal., 22g fat (12g sat. fat), 194mg chol., 713mg sod., 31g carb. (6g sugars, 2g fiber), 16g pro.

⏱ INDIAN SPICED CHICKPEA WRAPS

Raita, an Indian condiment made with yogurt, elevates this vegetarian dish into a satisfying gourmet wrap. I sometimes substitute diced mango or cucumber for the pineapple and add fresh herbs like cilantro or mint.
—*Jennifer Beckman, Falls Church, VA*

- -

Takes: 30 min. • **Makes:** 4 servings

 1 cup (8 oz.) reduced-fat plain yogurt
 ½ cup unsweetened pineapple tidbits
 ¼ tsp. salt
 ¼ tsp. ground cumin
WRAPS
 2 tsp. canola oil
 1 small onion, chopped
 1 Tbsp. minced fresh gingerroot
 2 garlic cloves, minced
 ½ tsp. curry powder
 ¼ tsp. salt
 ¼ tsp. ground coriander
 ¼ tsp. ground cumin
 ¼ tsp. cayenne pepper, optional
 1 can (15 oz.) chickpeas, rinsed and drained
 1 cup canned crushed tomatoes
 3 cups fresh baby spinach
 4 whole wheat tortillas (8 in.), warmed

1. For pineapple raita, mix first 4 ingredients.
2. For wraps, in a large nonstick skillet, heat oil over medium-high heat; saute onion until tender. Add ginger, garlic and seasonings; cook and stir until fragrant, about 1 minute. Stir in chickpeas and tomatoes; bring to a boil. Reduce heat; simmer, uncovered, until slightly thickened, 5-8 minutes, stirring occasionally.
3. To serve, place spinach and chickpea mixture on tortillas. Top with raita and roll up.
1 wrap: 321 cal., 7g fat (1g sat. fat), 3mg chol., 734mg sod., 55g carb. (15g sugars, 10g fiber), 13g pro.

⏱ HEARTY VEGGIE SANDWICHES

This vegetarian delight is not only healthy, it tastes amazing, too. Any way you slice it, this is one refreshing, flavor-filled sandwich!
—*Micki Sannar, Highland, UT*

- -

Takes: 20 min. • **Makes:** 2 servings

 2 tsp. mayonnaise
 2 tsp. prepared mustard
 4 slices whole wheat bread
 4 slices cheddar cheese (¾ oz. each)
 2 slices red onion
 ¼ cup sliced ripe olives, drained
 1 small tomato, sliced
 1 medium ripe avocado, peeled and sliced
 ⅛ tsp. pepper
 4 Tbsp. Italian salad dressing
 2 lettuce leaves

1. Spread mayonnaise and mustard over 2 slices of bread; layer with the cheese, onion, olives, tomato and avocado. Sprinkle with pepper.
2. Drizzle each sandwich with 1 Tbsp. of dressing. Top with lettuce. Drizzle remaining dressing over remaining bread slices; place over sandwiches.
1 sandwich: 479 cal., 29g fat (8g sat. fat), 27mg chol., 1259mg sod., 42g carb. (8g sugars, 10g fiber), 22g pro.

GRILLED BEAN BURGERS

These juicy veggie patties have major flavor from cumin, garlic and chili powder. They can hold their own against any veggie burger you'd buy at the supermarket.

—Marguerite Shaeffer, Sewell, NJ

Prep: 25 min. • **Grill:** 10 min.
Makes: 8 servings

- 1 Tbsp. olive oil
- 1 large onion, finely chopped
- 4 garlic cloves, minced
- 1 medium carrot, shredded
- 1 to 2 tsp. chili powder
- 1 tsp. ground cumin
- ¼ tsp. pepper
- 1 can (15 oz.) pinto beans, rinsed and drained
- 1 can (15 oz.) black beans, rinsed and drained
- 2 Tbsp. Dijon mustard
- 2 Tbsp. reduced-sodium soy sauce
- 1 Tbsp. ketchup
- 1½ cups quick-cooking oats
- 8 whole wheat hamburger buns, split
- 8 lettuce leaves
- ½ cup salsa

1. In a large nonstick skillet, heat oil over medium-high heat; saute onion 2 minutes. Add garlic; cook and stir 1 minute. Stir in carrot and spices; cook and stir until carrot is tender, 2-3 minutes. Remove from heat.
2. In a large bowl, mash pinto and black beans using a potato masher. Stir in mustard, soy sauce, ketchup and carrot mixture. Add oats, mixing well. Shape into eight 3½-in. patties. Place burgers on an oiled grill rack over medium heat or on a greased rack of a broiler pan. Grill, covered, or broil 4 in. from heat until lightly browned and heated through, 4-5 minutes per side. Serve on buns with lettuce and salsa.

Note: Our recipes often give a range on certain herbs and spices to accommodate different tastes. If you like the heat of chili powder, use 2 tsp. in your Grilled Bean Burgers; for a milder version, use 1 tsp.

1 burger: 305 cal., 5g fat (1g sat. fat), 0 chol., 736mg sod., 54g carb. (8g sugars, 10g fiber), 12g pro. **Diabetic exchanges:** 3½ starch, 1 lean meat.

ITALIAN CHEESE LOAF

Here's a deliciously different sandwich. It's yummy warm from the oven or off the grill at a cookout. The cheese in the filling with garden-fresh ingredients nestles delightfully inside the crusty bread. I usually serve it with a salad and onion rings.

—Mary Ann Marino, West Pittsburgh, PA

Prep: 15 min. • **Bake:** 25 min.
Makes: 12 servings

- 1 loaf (1 lb.) French bread
- 2 cups diced fresh tomatoes
- 1 cup shredded part-skim mozzarella cheese
- 1 cup shredded cheddar cheese
- 1 medium onion, finely chopped
- ¼ cup grated Romano cheese
- ¼ cup chopped ripe olives
- ¼ cup Italian salad dressing
- 1 tsp. chopped fresh basil or ¼ tsp. dried basil
- 1 tsp. chopped fresh oregano or ¼ tsp. dried oregano

1. Preheat oven to 350°. Cut top half off loaf of bread. Carefully hollow out both halves of loaf, leaving a ½-in. shell (discard removed bread or save for another use).
2. Combine remaining ingredients. Spoon into bottom half of bread, mounding as necessary; replace top. Wrap in foil. Bake until cheese is melted, about 25 minutes. Slice and serve warm.

1 piece: 204 cal., 8g fat (4g sat. fat), 18mg chol., 478mg sod., 23g carb. (3g sugars, 2g fiber), 9g pro.

PEAR WALDORF PITAS

Here's a guaranteed table-brightener for a brunch, luncheon or party. Just stand back and watch them disappear! I tuck each one into a colorful paper napkin to create an eye-catching presentation.

—*Roxann Parker, Dover, DE*

Prep: 20 min. + chilling
Makes: 20 mini pitas halves

- 2 medium ripe pears, diced
- ½ cup thinly sliced celery
- ½ cup halved seedless red grapes
- 2 Tbsp. finely chopped walnuts
- 2 Tbsp. lemon yogurt
- 2 Tbsp. mayonnaise
- ⅛ tsp. poppy seeds
- 20 miniature pita pocket halves
  Lettuce leaves

1. In a large bowl, combine pears, celery, grapes and walnuts. In another bowl, whisk yogurt, mayonnaise and poppy seeds. Add to pear mixture; toss to coat. Refrigerate for 1 hour or overnight.

2. Line pita halves with lettuce; fill each with 2 Tbsp. pear mixture.

1 pita half: 67 cal., 2g fat (0 sat. fat), 0 chol., 86mg sod., 12g carb. (3g sugars, 1g fiber), 2g pro. **Diabetic exchanges:** 1 starch.

MEAT LOVER OPTION
PAGE 320

CHICKPEA & RED ONION BURGERS

When the grill fills up with other goodies, I bake a batch of chickpea veggie burgers. Even die-hard meat eaters can't resist them.
—*Lily Julow, Lawrenceville, GA*

Takes: 30 min. • **Makes:** 6 servings

- 1 large red onion, thinly sliced
- ¼ cup fat-free red wine vinaigrette
- 2 cans (15 oz. each) chickpeas and garbanzo beans, rinsed and drained
- ⅓ cup chopped walnuts
- ¼ cup toasted wheat germ or dry bread crumbs
- ¼ cup packed fresh parsley sprigs
- 2 large eggs
- 1 tsp. curry powder
- ½ tsp. pepper
- ⅓ cup fat-free mayonnaise
- 2 tsp. Dijon mustard
- 6 hamburger buns, split and toasted
- 6 lettuce leaves
- 3 Tbsp. thinly sliced fresh basil leaves

1. Preheat oven to 375°. In a small bowl, mix onion and vinaigrette. Place chickpeas, walnuts, wheat germ and parsley in a food processor; pulse until blended. Add eggs, curry and pepper; process until smooth.

2. Shape into 6 patties. Place on a baking sheet coated with cooking spray. Bake until a thermometer reads 160°, 10-15 minutes.

3. In a small bowl, mix the mayonnaise and mustard; spread over buns. Serve patties on buns with lettuce, basil and onion mixture.

1 burger: 386 cal., 12g fat (2g sat. fat), 72mg chol., 732mg sod., 54g carb. (10g sugars, 9g fiber), 16g pro.

FRESH MOZZARELLA BASIL SANDWICHES

We love this fast, fresh sandwich, especially when it's too warm to turn on the oven. I like to pair it with a fruity white wine and pasta salad or fancy potato chips. We often add avocado to the sandwiches. In the summer, we use fresh Walla Walla onions!
—*Stacey Johnson, Tacoma, WA*

Takes: 15 min. • **Makes:** 4 servings

- 8   slices sourdough bread, toasted
- ¼   cup wasabi mayonnaise
- ½   lb. fresh mozzarella cheese, sliced
- 2   medium tomatoes, sliced
- 4   thin slices sweet onion
- 8   fresh basil leaves

Spread toast with mayonnaise. On 4 slices, layer cheese, tomatoes, onion and basil; top with remaining toast.

1 serving: 466 cal., 24g fat (10g sat. fat), 50mg chol., 576mg sod., 42g carb. (5g sugars, 3g fiber), 18g pro.

CUCUMBER SANDWICHES

I was introduced to a similar sandwich by a friend many years ago, and I now have made my own version. For a change of pace, I sometimes add thinly sliced onions on top.
—*Karen Schriefer, Stevensville, MD*

Takes: 15 min. • **Makes:** 6 servings

- 1   carton (8 oz.) spreadable cream cheese
- 2   tsp. ranch salad dressing mix
- 12 slices pumpernickel or rye bread
- 2   to 3 medium cucumbers

In a large bowl, combine cream cheese and dressing mix. Spread on 1 side of each slice of bread. Peel cucumbers if desired; thinly slice and place on 6 slices of bread. Top with remaining bread. Serve immediately.

1 sandwich: 244 cal., 10g fat (6g sat. fat), 24mg chol., 672mg sod., 31g carb. (3g sugars, 4g fiber), 8g pro.

GRILLED EGGPLANT SANDWICHES

This eggplant, tomato and goat cheese sandwich, grilled to perfection, makes a delicious meatless meal.
—*Jennifer Jaras, Corona, CA*

Takes: 25 min. • **Makes:** 2 servings

- 2   Tbsp. olive oil
- 1   garlic clove, minced
- 2   ciabatta rolls, split
- 4   slices eggplant (½ in. thick)
- 1   medium heirloom tomato, cut into ½-in. slices
- ¼   tsp. salt
- ⅛   tsp. pepper
- 2   oz. fresh goat cheese, softened
- 6   fresh basil leaves

1. Mix oil and garlic; brush onto cut sides of rolls and both sides of vegetables. Sprinkle vegetables with salt and pepper.

2. Grill eggplant, covered, over medium heat until tender, 4-5 minutes per side. Grill tomato, covered, until lightly browned, 1-2 minutes per side. Grill rolls, cut side down, until toasted, 1-2 minutes.

3. Spread roll bottoms with goat cheese. Top with basil, eggplant and tomato; close sandwiches.

1 sandwich: 538 cal., 21g fat (5g sat. fat), 19mg chol., 958mg sod., 81g carb. (10g sugars, 7g fiber), 15g pro.

Health tip: Make this hearty sandwich into a lower-calorie lunch or dinner by serving it open-faced and using a knife and fork. You'll save more than 150 calories per serving (and bring sodium below 700 milligrams).

THE ULTIMATE GRILLED CHEESE

These gooey grilled cheese sandwiches, subtly seasoned with garlic, are perfect for lunch with sliced apples. And they're really fast to whip up, too. To save time, I soften the cream cheese in the microwave, then blend it with the rest of the ingredients in the same bowl. That makes cleanup a breeze.
—*Kathy Norris, Streator, IL*

Takes: 15 min. • **Makes:** 5 servings

- 3 oz. cream cheese, softened
- ¾ cup mayonnaise
- 1 cup shredded part-skim mozzarella cheese
- 1 cup shredded cheddar cheese
- ½ tsp. garlic powder
- ⅛ tsp. seasoned salt
- 10 slices Italian bread (½ in. thick)
- 2 Tbsp. butter, softened

1. In a large bowl, beat cream cheese and mayonnaise until smooth. Stir in cheeses, garlic powder and seasoned salt. Spread 5 slices of bread with cheese mixture, about ⅓ cup on each. Top with remaining bread.
2. Butter the outsides of sandwiches. In a skillet over medium heat, toast sandwiches for 4-5 minutes on each side or until bread is lightly browned and cheese is melted.
1 serving: 646 cal., 50g fat (18g sat. fat), 84mg chol., 885mg sod., 32g carb. (3g sugars, 2g fiber), 16g pro.

DID YOU KNOW?

Sharp cheddar cheese has been aged longer than regular cheddar. As cheese ages, its flavor becomes increasingly pronounced. Using aged cheese in a recipe can add complexity and rich flavor, even to humble favorites like grilled cheese or mac 'n' cheese.

SMOKED GOUDA VEGGIE MELT

After a long day of teaching, I like to make these cheesy open-faced sandwiches. My 8-year-old daughter is a big fan, too.
—*Charlie Herzog, West Brookfield, VT*

Takes: 25 min. • **Makes:** 4 servings

- 1 cup chopped fresh mushrooms
- 1 cup chopped fresh broccoli
- 1 medium sweet red pepper, chopped
- 1 small onion, chopped
- 2 Tbsp. olive oil
- 8 slices Italian bread (½ in. thick)
- ½ cup mayonnaise
- 1 garlic clove, minced
- 1 cup shredded smoked Gouda cheese

1. Preheat oven to 425°. Place mushrooms, broccoli, pepper and onion in a greased 15x10x1-in. baking pan. Drizzle with oil; toss to coat. Roast 10-12 minutes or until tender.
2. Meanwhile, place bread slices on a baking sheet. Mix mayonnaise and garlic; spread over bread.
3. Change oven setting to broil. Spoon vegetables over bread slices; sprinkle with cheese. Broil 3-4 in. from heat 2-3 minutes or until cheese is melted.
2 open-faced sandwiches: 523 cal., 37g fat (9g sat. fat), 34mg chol., 695mg sod., 35g carb. (5g sugars, 3g fiber), 14g pro.

READER RAVE

"Very good! Substituted creamy avocado for the mayo and they were gone in no time."
—HAPPYJAN, TASTEOFHOME.COM

GREEK SANDWICH BITES

This tiny sandwich tastes just like traditional spanakopita, but it is easier to make.
—*Lynn Scully, Rancho Santa Fe, CA*

Takes: 25 min. • **Makes:** 16 appetizers

- 1 medium onion, finely chopped
- 1 Tbsp. olive oil
- 2 garlic cloves, minced
- 1 lb. fresh baby spinach
- 1 cup (4 oz.) crumbled feta cheese
- ¼ cup pine nuts, toasted
- ¼ tsp. salt
- ¼ tsp. pepper
- ⅛ tsp. ground nutmeg
- 8 slices Italian bread (½ in. thick)
- 4 tsp. butter, softened

1. In a large nonstick skillet, saute onion in oil until tender. Add garlic; cook 1 minute longer. Stir in the spinach; cook and stir until wilted. Drain. Stir in the feta, pine nuts, salt, pepper and nutmeg.
2. Spread over 4 bread slices; top with remaining bread. Spread outsides of sandwiches with butter. Grill, uncovered, over medium heat until bread is browned and cheese is melted, turning once, 3-4 minutes. Cut each sandwich into quarters.
1 appetizer: 87 cal., 5g fat (2g sat. fat), 6mg chol., 200mg sod., 8g carb. (1g sugars, 1g fiber), 4g pro. **Diabetic exchanges:** 1 fat, ½ starch.

GREAT GRAIN BURGERS

I've experimented with many combinations of ingredients to make a good meatless burger, and this is our favorite. The patties cook up golden brown and crispy, making delicious sandwiches.

—Pat Whitaker, Alsea, OR

- -

Prep: 45 min. + chilling • **Cook:** 30 min.
Makes: 12 servings

- ½ cup uncooked brown rice
- ½ cup uncooked bulgur
- 1 Tbsp. salt-free seasoning blend
- ¼ tsp. poultry seasoning
- 2 cups water
- ¼ cup egg substitute
- ½ cup fat-free cottage cheese
- 2 cups finely chopped
     fresh mushrooms
- ¾ cup old-fashioned oats
- ⅓ cup finely chopped onion
- 2 Tbsp. minced fresh parsley
- 1 tsp. salt
- ½ tsp. dried basil
- ⅛ tsp. celery seed
- 1 cup shredded part-skim
     mozzarella cheese
- ¼ cup shredded reduced-fat
     cheddar cheese
- 3 tsp. canola oil, divided
- 12 sandwich rolls
     Optional toppings: Watercress,
     tomato, red onion and avocado

1. Place the first 5 ingredients in a large saucepan; bring to a boil. Reduce heat; simmer, covered, until rice is tender, about 30 minutes. Remove to a bowl; cool slightly. Refrigerate, covered, until cold.

2. Place egg substitute and cottage cheese in a blender; cover and process until smooth. Transfer to a large bowl. Stir in mushrooms, oats, onion, parsley and seasonings. Add mozzarella cheese, cheddar cheese and rice mixture; mix well. Refrigerate, covered, 2 hours or overnight before shaping.

3. Shape ½ cupfuls of mixture into patties, pressing to adhere. In a large nonstick skillet, heat 1 tsp. oil over medium heat; cook 4 patties until lightly browned, about 5 minutes per side. Repeat with remaining patties and oil. Serve on rolls, with toppings as desired.

1 burger: 335 cal., 9g fat (3g sat. fat), 8mg chol., 701mg sod., 51g carb. (6g sugars, 3g fiber), 14g pro.

MINT-CUCUMBER TOMATO SANDWICHES

I jazzed up the quintessential tea-time cucumber sandwich to suit my family's tastes. This is my absolute go-to sandwich in the heat of summer.
—*Namrata Telugu, Terre Haute, IN*

Takes: 15 min. • **Makes:** 4 sandwiches

- 3 Tbsp. butter, softened
- 8 slices sourdough bread
- 1 large cucumber, thinly sliced
- 2 medium tomatoes, thinly sliced
- ¼ tsp. salt
- ⅛ tsp. pepper
- ¼ cup fresh mint leaves

Spread butter over 4 slices of bread. Layer with cucumber and tomatoes; sprinkle with salt, pepper and mint. Top with remaining bread. If desired, cut each sandwich into quarters.

1 sandwich: 286 cal., 10g fat (6g sat. fat), 23mg chol., 631mg sod., 42g carb. (5g sugars, 3g fiber), 9g pro.

⏱ GRILLED CHEESE & PEPPER SANDWICHES

This is a tasty and wholesome sandwich to make for one or two. It's a nice twist on traditional grilled cheese. It's very tasty and filling and especially good with rye bread!
—*Arline Hofland, Deer Lodge, MT*

Takes: 20 min. • **Makes:** 2 servings

- 1 Tbsp. olive oil
- ½ cup chopped onion
- ½ cup chopped green pepper
- ½ cup chopped sweet red pepper
- 2 tsp. chopped seeded jalapeno pepper
- 4 slices rye bread with caraway seeds
- ¾ cup shredded Monterey Jack cheese
- 1 Tbsp. butter, softened

1. In a skillet, heat oil over medium-high heat; saute onion and peppers until tender. Divide between 2 bread slices. Top with cheese and remaining bread. Spread outsides of sandwiches with butter.

2. In a large skillet, toast sandwiches over medium heat until golden brown and cheese is melted, 2-3 minutes per side.

Note: Wear disposable gloves when cutting hot peppers; the oils can burn skin. Avoid touching your face.

1 sandwich: 470 cal., 28g fat (13g sat. fat), 53mg chol., 690mg sod., 39g carb. (7g sugars, 6g fiber), 17g pro.

⏱ ZIPPY EGG SALAD

Egg salad is a refreshing, tasty change from peanut butter sandwiches. The touch of mustard and lemon juice gives this recipe extra zip.

—*Annemarie Pietila, Farmington Hills, MI*

Takes: 10 min. • **Makes:** 2 servings

3	Tbsp. mayonnaise
1½	tsp. prepared mustard
⅛	tsp. salt
⅛	tsp. pepper
⅛	tsp. lemon juice
3	hard-boiled large eggs, coarsely chopped
1	Tbsp. minced green onion
2	slices bread
	Diced tomato, optional

Mix the first 5 ingredients. Stir in eggs and green onion. Serve on bread. If desired, top with tomato.

1 open-faced sandwich: 332 cal., 24g fat (5g sat. fat), 281mg chol., 530mg sod., 16g carb. (3g sugars, 1g fiber), 12g pro.

HOW-TO

Hard-Boil Eggs in a Pressure Cooker

- **PREP** Place trivet insert and 1 cup water in a 6-qt. electric pressure cooker. Set up to 12 eggs on trivet.
- **COOK** Lock lid; close pressure-release valve. Adjust to pressure-cook on high for 5 minutes (for large eggs).
- **COOL** Let pressure release naturally for 5 minutes; quick-release any remaining pressure. Immediately place eggs in ice water to cool. Peel when ready to use.

🕐 PORTOBELLO MELTS

We're always looking for satisfying vegetarian meals, and this one tops the list. These melts are especially delicious in the summer when we have tons of homegrown tomatoes.
—*Amy Smalley, Morehead, KY*

- -

Takes: 20 min. • **Makes:** 2 servings

- 2 **large portobello mushrooms (4 oz. each), stems removed**
- ¼ **cup olive oil**
- 2 **Tbsp. balsamic vinegar**
- ½ **tsp. salt**
- ½ **tsp. dried basil**
- 4 **tomato slices**
- 2 **slices mozzarella cheese**
- 2 **slices Italian bread (1 in. thick)**
  Chopped fresh basil

1. Preheat broiler. Place mushrooms in a shallow bowl. Mix oil, vinegar, salt and dried basil; brush onto both sides of mushrooms. Let stand 5 minutes. Reserve remaining marinade.
2. Place mushrooms on a greased rack of a broiler pan, stem side down. Broil mushrooms 4 in. from heat until tender, 3-4 minutes per side. Top stem sides with tomato and cheese. Broil until cheese is melted, about 1 minute.
3. Place bread on a baking sheet; brush with reserved marinade. Broil 4 in. from heat until lightly toasted, 45-60 seconds. Top with mushrooms. Sprinkle with chopped basil.

1 open-faced sandwich: 460 cal., 35g fat (7g sat. fat), 22mg chol., 934mg sod., 26g carb. (8g sugars, 3g fiber), 12g pro.

Health tip: If you skip the bread to make this low-carb, you can use half the vinaigrette, saving almost 15 grams of fat and 400 milligrams of sodium per serving.

HUMMUS & VEGGIE WRAP-UP

I had a sandwich similar to this once when I stopped at a diner while on a long and arduous walk. I enjoyed it so much that I modified it to my own taste and now have it for lunch on a regular basis. Everyone at work wants to know how to make it.
—*Michael Steffens, Indianapolis, IN*

Takes: 15 min. • **Makes:** 1 serving

2	Tbsp. hummus
1	whole wheat tortilla (8 in.)
¼	cup torn mixed salad greens
2	Tbsp. finely chopped sweet onion
2	Tbsp. thinly sliced cucumber
2	Tbsp. alfalfa sprouts
2	Tbsp. shredded carrot
1	Tbsp. balsamic vinaigrette

Spread hummus over tortilla. Layer with salad greens, onion, cucumber, sprouts and carrot. Drizzle with vinaigrette. Roll up tightly.

1 wrap: 235 cal., 8g fat (1g sat. fat), 0 chol., 415mg sod., 32g carb. (4g sugars, 5g fiber), 7g pro. **Diabetic exchanges:** 2 starch, 1 fat.

BROCCOLI CHEESEBURGERS WITH SPICY SWEET POTATOES

These faux burgers are so packed with flavor that nobody notices they're also packed with protein, fiber and vitamins.
—*Pamela Vachon, Astoria, NY*

Prep: 10 min. • **Cook:** 35 min.
Makes: 4 servings

2	medium sweet potatoes, cut into 12 wedges each
	Cooking spray
1	tsp. salt-free spicy seasoning blend or reduced-sodium Creole seasoning
4	tsp. extra virgin olive oil, divided
1	shallot, minced
1	cup fresh broccoli florets, cut into ¾-in. pieces
1	large egg, beaten
1	cup canned cannellini beans, rinsed and drained
1	cup ready-to-serve quinoa
¾	cup shredded reduced-fat cheddar cheese
4	whole wheat hamburger buns, split
	Optional toppings: Lettuce leaves, tomato slices, ketchup, mustard and reduced-fat mayonnaise

1. Preheat oven to 450°. Spritz sweet potato wedges with cooking spray until lightly coated. Sprinkle with seasoning mix; toss to coat. Arrange in a single layer on a 15x10x1-in. baking sheet. Bake, turning wedges halfway through cooking, until tender and lightly spotted, 30-35 minutes.

2. Meanwhile, in a large nonstick skillet, heat 2 tsp. olive oil over medium heat. Add shallot; cook until translucent, about 2 minutes. Add broccoli; cook just until it turns bright green, about 3 minutes longer.

3. Transfer broccoli mixture to a food processor. Add egg and beans; pulse until ingredients are blended but not pureed. Pour mixture into a large bowl. Add quinoa and cheddar cheese; mix lightly but thoroughly. Shape into four ½-in.-thick patties.

4. In a large nonstick skillet, heat remaining oil over medium-high heat. Add burger patties to skillet; cook until golden and heated through, about 3 minutes on each side.

5. Serve burgers immediately on whole wheat buns with sweet potato wedges. Add toppings as desired.

1 burger with 6 sweet potato wedges:
457 cal., 14g fat (4g sat. fat), 62mg chol., 550mg sod., 65g carb. (14g sugars, 11g fiber), 18g pro.

5i ⓛ PEANUT BUTTER, APPLE & RAISIN SANDWICH

Tart, sweet and crunchy, these open-faced sammies are a perfect after-school (or after-work) snack.

—*James Schend, Pleasant Prairie, WI*

Takes: 5 min. • **Makes:** 1 serving

- 1 Tbsp. creamy peanut butter
- 1 slice crusty white bread
- ¼ medium apple, thinly sliced
- 1 Tbsp. golden raisins
   Ground cinnamon

Spread peanut butter over bread. Top with apple and raisins; sprinkle with cinnamon.
1 open-faced sandwich: 220 cal., 9g fat (2g sat. fat), 0 chol., 212mg sod., 30g carb. (13g sugars, 3g fiber), 7g pro.

VEGGIE BEAN BURGERS

Even though the preparation for this meal seems time-consuming on a busy night, it's so worth it. The recipe will leave you with plenty of leftovers so you won't have to do any cooking the next night. These also beat the veggie burgers from the freezer section.
—*Amber Massey, Argyle, TX*

Prep: 45 min. • **Broil:** 15 min.
Makes: 8 servings

- ½ cup uncooked long grain brown rice
- 1 cup water
- 2 cans (15 oz. each) black beans, rinsed and drained
- 2 large eggs, lightly beaten
- 2 tsp. hot pepper sauce
- 3 tsp. ground cumin
- 3 tsp. chili powder
- 1½ tsp. garlic powder
- ¾ tsp. salt
- 1½ cups Fiber One bran cereal
- 1 medium green pepper, coarsely chopped
- 1 medium onion, quartered
- ¾ cup sliced fresh mushrooms
- 6 garlic cloves, minced
- ¾ cup shredded part-skim mozzarella cheese
- 8 whole wheat hamburger buns, split and warmed
  Optional toppings: Lettuce leaves, tomato slices and onion slices

1. Preheat broiler. In a small saucepan, combine rice and water; bring to a boil. Reduce heat; simmer, covered, until liquid is absorbed and rice is tender, 30-40 minutes.
2. In a large bowl, mash beans until almost smooth; stir in eggs, pepper sauce and seasonings. Pulse bran cereal in a food processor until finely ground; remove to a small bowl. Pulse vegetables and garlic in food processor until finely chopped; add to bean mixture. Add cheese and rice to food processor; pulse to blend, then add to bean mixture. Stir in ground cereal.
3. Shape mixture into eight ½-in.-thick patties; place on a greased foil-lined baking sheet. Broil 4-6 in. from heat until browned, 6-8 minutes per side. Serve in buns. If desired, top with lettuce, tomato and onion.

Note: To bake the patties, preheat oven to 375°. Lightly oil a baking sheet; place patties on baking sheet and bake about 10 minutes on each side.

1 burger: 334 cal., 6g fat (2g sat. fat), 53mg chol., 814mg sod., 60g carb. (6g sugars, 15g fiber), 16g pro.

MEXICAN GRILLED CHEESE SANDWICHES

A little salsa goes a long way in these no-fuss sandwiches. Perked up with sweet peppers, they're flavorful, fun and ideal on busy weeknights.

—Taste of Home *Test Kitchen*

Takes: 25 min. • **Makes:** 4 servings

- 1   medium sweet yellow pepper, chopped
- 1   medium green pepper, chopped
- 2   tsp. olive oil
- 8   slices rye bread
- 2   Tbsp. mayonnaise
- 1   cup fresh salsa, well drained
- ¾   cup shredded Mexican cheese blend
- 2   Tbsp. butter, softened

1. In a small skillet, saute peppers in oil until tender. Spread 4 bread slices with mayonnaise. Layer with peppers, salsa and cheese. Top with remaining bread. Butter outsides of sandwiches.

2. In a small skillet over medium heat, toast sandwiches for 2-4 minutes on each side or until cheese is melted.

1 sandwich: 402 cal., 22g fat (10g sat. fat), 36mg chol., 892mg sod., 39g carb. (6g sugars, 4g fiber), 11g pro.

HEAVENLY EARTH BURGERS

These burgers are packed with nutrition. Fresh parsley and carrot add flecks of color, and sunflower seeds lend an irresistible bit of crunch.

—*Wendy McGowan, Fontana, CA*

Prep: 25 min. • **Cook:** 10 min.
Makes: 6 servings

- 1½   cups cooked brown rice
- ½   cup finely chopped onion
- ¼   cup sunflower kernels
- ¼   cup seasoned bread crumbs
- ½   cup shredded carrot
- 3   Tbsp. minced fresh parsley
- 2   Tbsp. reduced-sodium soy sauce
- ½   tsp. dried thyme
- 1   large egg
- 1   large egg white
- 1   cup canned garbanzo beans or chickpeas, rinsed and drained
- 1½   tsp. canola oil
- 6   whole wheat hamburger buns, split
- 6   lettuce leaves
- 6   slices tomato
- 6   slices onion

1. In a large bowl, combine the first 8 ingredients. In a food processor, combine the egg, egg white and garbanzo beans; cover and process until smooth. Stir into rice mixture. Shape into 6 patties.

2. In a nonstick skillet, cook patties in oil for 5-6 minutes on each side or until lightly browned and crisp. Serve on buns with lettuce, tomato and onion.

1 serving: 320 cal., 9g fat (1g sat. fat), 35mg chol., 634mg sod., 49g carb. (8g sugars, 6g fiber), 11g pro. **Diabetic exchanges:** 3 starch, 1 fat.

🕐 FRESH VEGGIE POCKETS

One summer I worked at a health food store that sold sandwiches. We were close to a college campus, so I made lots of these fresh-filled pitas for the students. With veggies and nutty sunflower kernels, they're a fast-to-fix meal when you're on the go.
—*Linda Reeves, Cloverdale, IN*

Takes: 15 min. • **Makes:** 4 servings

- 1 carton (8 oz.) spreadable cream cheese
- ¼ cup sunflower kernels
- 1 tsp. seasoned salt or salt-free seasoning blend
- 4 whole wheat pita breads (6 in.), halved
- 1 medium tomato, thinly sliced
- 1 medium cucumber, thinly sliced
- 1 cup sliced fresh mushrooms
- 1 ripe avocado, peeled and sliced

In a large bowl, combine the cream cheese, sunflower kernels and seasoned salt; spread about 2 Tbsp. on the inside of each pita half. Layer with the tomato, cucumber, mushrooms and avocado.

2 filled pita halves: 434 cal., 23g fat (9g sat. fat), 37mg chol., 571mg sod., 48g carb. (6g sugars, 8g fiber), 14g pro.

Health tip: If you're looking for more protein, just add garbanzo beans or chopped hard-boiled eggs.

♥ MEAT LOVER OPTION PAGE 320

🕐 CREAMY EGG SALAD

I love this egg salad's versatility—serve it on a nest of mixed greens, tucked into a sandwich or with your favorite crisp crackers.
—*Cynthia Kolberg, Syracuse, IN*

Takes: 10 min. • **Makes:** 3 cups

- 3 oz. cream cheese, softened
- ¼ cup mayonnaise
- ½ tsp. salt
- ⅛ tsp. pepper
- ¼ cup finely chopped green or sweet red pepper
- ¼ cup finely chopped celery
- ¼ cup sweet pickle relish
- 2 Tbsp. minced fresh parsley
- 8 hard-boiled large eggs, chopped

In a bowl, mix cream cheese, mayonnaise, salt and pepper until smooth. Stir in green pepper, celery, relish and parsley. Fold in eggs. Refrigerate, covered, until serving.

½ cup: 228 cal., 19g fat (6g sat. fat), 264mg chol., 456mg sod., 6g carb. (4g sugars, 0 fiber), 9g pro.

TEST KITCHEN TIP

Freshen this recipe from your summer garden by using dill instead of (or in addition to) the parsley. Remember, dill packs quite a punch, so 2 tsp. instead of 2 Tbsp. ought to do it.

EGGPLANT & MUSHROOM MONTE CRISTO

As a child, I wouldn't eat veggies. As a parent, I try to include them in creative ways. I'm proud to say this eggplant sandwich is a hit with my son.

—*Macey Allen, Green Forest, AR*

Takes: 30 min. • **Makes:** 4 servings

- 5 Tbsp. olive oil, divided
- 6 slices eggplant (½ in. thick), halved
- 2½ cups sliced fresh shiitake or baby portobello mushrooms (about 6 oz.)
- 1 large garlic clove, minced
- ½ tsp. salt
- ¼ tsp. pepper
- 2 large eggs
- 2 Tbsp. 2% milk
- ½ cup garlic-herb spreadable cheese (about 3 oz.)
- 8 slices wide-loaf white bread

1. In a large nonstick skillet, heat 1 Tbsp. oil over medium heat. Add eggplant; cook 2-3 minutes on each side or until tender and lightly browned. Remove from pan.

2. In the same pan, heat 2 Tbsp. oil over medium heat. Add mushrooms; cook and stir 2-3 minutes or until tender. Add garlic, salt and pepper; cook 1 minute longer. Remove from pan; wipe skillet clean.

3. In a shallow bowl, whisk eggs and milk until blended. Spread 1 Tbsp. herb cheese over each bread slice. Layer 4 slices with eggplant and mushrooms; top with the remaining bread.

4. In same pan, heat 1 Tbsp. oil over medium heat. Carefully dip both sides of sandwiches in egg mixture, allowing each side to soak 5 seconds. Place 2 sandwiches in skillet; toast 2-3 minutes on each side or until golden brown. Repeat with remaining oil and sandwiches.

1 sandwich: 573 cal., 36g fat (13g sat. fat), 129mg chol., 939mg sod., 52g carb. (9g sugars, 6g fiber), 15g pro.

GRILLED VEGETABLE SANDWICH

Wow! Meat lovers won't even miss the meat, instead they will rave about the simply fabulous flavor of this hearty grilled veggie sandwich. It's wonderful with the crispy crust and light, airy texture of fresh ciabatta bread.
—*Diana Tseperkas, Hamden, CT*

Prep: 20 min. + marinating • **Grill:** 10 min.
Makes: 4 servings

- 1 medium zucchini, thinly sliced lengthwise into ribbons
- 1 medium sweet red pepper, quartered
- 1 small red onion, cut into ½-in. slices
- ¼ cup prepared Italian salad dressing
- 1 loaf ciabatta bread (14 oz.), split
- 2 Tbsp. olive oil
- ¼ cup reduced-fat mayonnaise
- 1 Tbsp. lemon juice
- 2 tsp. grated lemon zest
- 1 tsp. minced garlic
- ½ cup crumbled feta cheese

1. In a bowl or shallow dish, combine the zucchini, pepper, onion and salad dressing. Cover and turn to coat; refrigerate for at least 1 hour. Drain and discard marinade.
2. Brush cut sides of bread with oil; set aside. Place vegetables on grill rack. Grill, covered, over medium heat for 4-5 minutes on each side or until crisp-tender. Remove and keep warm. Grill bread, oil side down, over medium heat for 30-60 seconds or until toasted.
3. In a small bowl, combine the mayonnaise, lemon juice, zest and garlic. Spread over cut side of bread bottom; sprinkle with cheese. Top with vegetables and remaining bread. Cut into 4 slices.
1 serving: 484 cal., 20g fat (4g sat. fat), 13mg chol., 862mg sod., 69g carb. (8g sugars, 5g fiber), 13g pro.

BLACK BEAN CHIP & DIP BURGERS

I tried to create a healthy veggie burger that wasn't dry, crumbly or boring. These amazing burgers taste just like chips and salsa—and even my grandkids prefer them over regular burgers made with meat!
—*KT Rehrig, Allentown, PA*

Prep: 30 min. • **Grill:** 10 min.
Makes: 8 servings

- ⅔ cup water
- ⅓ cup quinoa, rinsed
- 1 can (15 oz.) black beans, rinsed and drained
- 1 jar (16 oz.) salsa, divided
- 1 cup crushed baked tortilla chip scoops
- 2 Tbsp. reduced-sodium taco seasoning
- 8 whole wheat hamburger buns, split
- 8 lettuce leaves
- 8 slices tomato
- 8 slices red onion

1. In a small saucepan, bring water to a boil. Add quinoa. Reduce heat; simmer, covered, 12-15 minutes or until liquid is absorbed. Remove from heat; fluff with a fork.
2. In a large bowl, mash black beans. Add 1 cup salsa, tortilla chips, taco seasoning and cooked quinoa; mix well. Shape into eight ¼-in.-thick patties.
3. Grill, covered, over medium heat for 5-6 minutes on each side or until heated through. Serve on buns with lettuce, tomato, onion and remaining salsa.
Note: To bake the patties, preheat oven to 350°. Place patties on a baking sheet coated with cooking spray. Bake 25-30 minutes or until heated through, turning once.
1 burger: 247 cal., 3g fat (1g sat. fat), 0 chol., 700mg sod., 47g carb. (8g sugars, 7g fiber), 8g pro.

5i ⏱ SOUTHERN PEANUT BUTTER MAYO SANDWICH

Yep, Southerners love the combo of peanut butter and mayo. The mayonnaise flavor disappears into the peanut butter, just making it creamier and more delicious. I add cheddar cheese to mine because, hey, I'm from Wisconsin.

—*James Schend, Pleasant Prairie, WI*

Takes: 5 min. • **Makes:** 1 serving

- 1 **Tbsp. mayonnaise**
- 1 **Tbsp. creamy peanut butter**
- 1 **slice crusty white bread**
- 2 **Tbsp. shredded cheddar cheese**

Combine mayonnaise and peanut butter; spread over bread. Top with cheese.

1 open-faced sandwich: 320 cal., 24g fat (6g sat. fat), 15mg chol., 373mg sod., 18g carb. (3g sugars, 2g fiber), 9g pro.

QUICK TACO WRAPS

I was running late one night, so I shopped in my own fridge and came up with these taco wraps. Everyone at the table was happy.
—*Katie Mitschelen, La Porte, IN*

- -

Takes: 15 min. • **Makes:** 4 servings

- ½ cup cream cheese, softened
- ¼ cup canned chopped green chiles
- ¼ cup sour cream
- 2 Tbsp. taco seasoning
- ½ cup bean dip
- 4 flour tortillas (10 in.)
- ½ cup guacamole dip
- 1 small onion, chopped
- 1 small sweet red pepper, chopped
- ½ cup shredded cheddar cheese
- 1 can (2¼ oz.) sliced ripe olives, drained

1. In a small bowl, beat cream cheese until smooth. Stir in green chiles, sour cream and taco seasoning.
2. Spread bean dip over tortillas to within ½ in. of edges. Layer with guacamole dip, cream cheese mixture, onion, pepper, cheese and olives. Roll up tightly and serve.
1 wrap: 533 cal., 28g fat (13g sat. fat), 51mg chol., 1538mg sod., 48g carb. (3g sugars, 8g fiber), 14g pro.

VEGETARIAN REUBENS

Portobello mushrooms and baby spinach take the place of corned beef in this fresh take on a lunchtime staple.
—Taste of Home *Test Kitchen*

- -

Takes: 20 min. • **Makes:** 4 servings

- 1 pkg. (6 oz.) sliced baby portobello mushrooms
- 2 Tbsp. olive oil, divided
- 1 pkg. (6 oz.) fresh baby spinach
- 8 slices marble rye bread
- ¼ cup prepared Thousand Island salad dressing
- 8 slices process Swiss cheese
- 1 cup sauerkraut, rinsed and well drained
- 2 Tbsp. butter, softened

1. In a large skillet, saute mushrooms in 1 Tbsp. oil until lightly browned; remove with a slotted spoon and set aside. In the same skillet, saute spinach in remaining oil until wilted. Remove from the heat.
2. Spread bread slices with salad dressing and top with a cheese slice. Layer 4 slices with mushrooms, spinach and sauerkraut. Top with remaining bread. Butter outsides of sandwiches.
3. In a small skillet over medium heat, toast sandwiches for 2-3 minutes on each side or until cheese is melted.
1 sandwich: 475 cal., 30g fat (12g sat. fat), 56mg chol., 1446mg sod., 35g carb. (7g sugars, 6g fiber), 18g pro.

ROASTED SWEET POTATO & CHICKPEA PITAS

Here's a hearty take on Mediterranean food, this time with sweet potatoes tucked inside. These unique pockets are delicious for lunch or dinner.
—*Beth Jacobson, Milwaukee, WI*

Takes: 30 min. • **Makes:** 6 servings

- 2 medium sweet potatoes (about 1¼ lbs.), peeled and cubed
- 2 cans (15 oz. each) chickpeas or garbanzo beans, rinsed and drained
- 1 medium red onion, chopped
- 3 Tbsp. canola oil, divided
- 2 tsp. garam masala
- ½ tsp. salt, divided
- 2 garlic cloves, minced
- 1 cup plain Greek yogurt
- 1 Tbsp. lemon juice
- 1 tsp. ground cumin
- 2 cups arugula or baby spinach
- 12 whole wheat pita pocket halves, warmed
- ¼ cup minced fresh cilantro

1. Preheat oven to 400°. Place potatoes in a large microwave-safe bowl; microwave, covered, on high 5 minutes. Stir in chickpeas and onion; toss with 2 Tbsp. oil, garam masala and ¼ tsp. salt.
2. Spread into a 15x10x1-in. pan. Roast until potatoes are tender, about 15 minutes. Cool slightly.
3. Place garlic and remaining oil in a small microwave-safe bowl; microwave on high until garlic is lightly browned, 1-1½ minutes. Stir in yogurt, lemon juice, cumin and remaining salt.
4. Toss potato mixture with arugula. Spoon into pitas; top with sauce and cilantro.
2 filled pita halves: 462 cal., 15g fat (3g sat. fat), 10mg chol., 662mg sod., 72g carb. (13g sugars, 12g fiber), 14g pro.

DELUXE BLACK BEAN BURGERS

Meatless meals are extra tasty when these hearty bean burgers are on the menu. Guacamole and sour cream make the sandwiches feel decadent.
—*Jill Reichardt, St. Louis, MO*

Takes: 20 min. • **Makes:** 4 servings

- 1 can (15 oz.) black beans, rinsed and drained
- ⅔ cup dry bread crumbs
- 1 small tomato, seeded and finely chopped
- 1 jalapeno pepper, seeded and finely chopped
- 1 large egg
- 1 tsp. minced fresh cilantro
- 1 garlic clove, minced
- 1 Tbsp. olive oil
- 4 whole wheat hamburger buns, split Reduced-fat sour cream and guacamole, optional

1. Place beans in a food processor; cover and process until blended. Transfer to a large bowl. Add the bread crumbs, tomato, jalapeno, egg, cilantro and garlic. Mix until combined. Shape into 4 patties.
2. In a large nonstick skillet, cook patties in oil over medium heat until lightly browned, 4-6 minutes on each side. Serve on buns. If desired, top with sour cream and guacamole.
Note: Wear disposable gloves when cutting hot peppers; the oils can burn skin. Avoid touching your face.
1 burger: 323 cal., 8g fat (1g sat. fat), 53mg chol., 557mg sod., 51g carb. (6g sugars, 9g fiber), 13g pro.

5i TOMATO & AVOCADO SANDWICHES

I'm a vegetarian, and this is a tasty, quick and healthy lunch I could eat for every meal. At my house, we call these sandwiches HATS: hummus, avocado, tomato and shallots. They're ingredients I almost always have on hand.
—*Sarah Jaraha, Moorestown, NJ*

Takes: 10 min. • **Makes:** 2 servings

- ½ medium ripe avocado, peeled and mashed
- 4 slices whole wheat bread, toasted
- 1 medium tomato, sliced
- 2 Tbsp. finely chopped shallot
- ¼ cup hummus

Spread avocado over 2 slices of toast. Top with tomato and shallot. Spread hummus over remaining toast slices; place on top of avocado toast, face down on top of tomato layer.

1 sandwich: 278 cal., 11g fat (2g sat. fat), 0 chol., 379mg sod., 35g carb. (6g sugars, 9g fiber), 11g pro. **Diabetic exchanges:** 2 starch, 2 fat.

ZUCCHINI BURGERS

The patties for this omelet-like veggie burger hold together well while cooking and are hearty enough to serve bunless. I like to make them in summer with fresh-picked zucchini.
—*Kimberly Danek Pinkson, San Anselmo, CA*

Takes: 30 min. • **Makes:** 4 servings

- 2 cups shredded zucchini
- 1 medium onion, finely chopped
- ½ cup dry bread crumbs
- 2 large eggs, lightly beaten
- ⅛ tsp. salt
    Dash cayenne pepper
- 3 hard-boiled large egg whites, chopped
- 2 Tbsp. canola oil
- 4 whole wheat hamburger buns, split
- 4 lettuce leaves
- 4 slices tomato
- 4 slices onion

1. In a sieve or colander, drain zucchini, squeezing to remove excess liquid. Pat dry. In a small bowl, combine the zucchini, onion, bread crumbs, eggs, salt and cayenne. Gently stir in chopped egg whites.
2. Heat 1 Tbsp. oil in a large nonstick skillet over medium-low heat. Drop batter by scant ⅔ cupfuls into oil; press lightly to flatten. Fry in batches until golden brown on both sides, using remaining oil as needed.
3. Serve on buns with lettuce leaves, tomato and onion.

1 burger: 314 cal., 12g fat (2g sat. fat), 106mg chol., 467mg sod., 40g carb. (9g sugars, 6g fiber), 13g pro. **Diabetic exchanges:** 2 starch, 1½ fat, 1 lean meat, 1 vegetable.

MEAT LOVER OPTION PAGE 320

SALSA BEAN BURGERS

I created these based on a turkey burger recipe and wanted to make them even better for you. Use your favorite salsa with just the heat you like to make it your own.
—*Jenny Leighty, West Salem, OH*

Prep: 15 min. + chilling • **Cook:** 10 min.
Makes: 4 servings

- 1 can (15 oz.) black beans, rinsed and drained
- ¾ cup panko bread crumbs
- 1 cup salsa, divided
- 1 large egg, lightly beaten
- 2 Tbsp. minced fresh cilantro
- 1 garlic clove, minced
- 2 tsp. canola oil
- 4 whole wheat hamburger buns, split

1. In a large bowl, mash beans. Mix in bread crumbs, ½ cup salsa, egg, cilantro and garlic. Shape bean mixture into 4 patties; refrigerate 30 minutes.
2. In a large skillet, heat oil over medium heat. Cook burgers 3-5 minutes on each side or until a thermometer reads 160°. Serve on buns with remaining salsa.
1 burger: 299 cal., 6g fat (1g sat. fat), 53mg chol., 696mg sod., 49g carb. (7g sugars, 8g fiber), 12g pro. **Diabetic exchanges:** 3 starch, 1 lean meat, ½ fat.

EASY SOUTHWESTERN VEGGIE WRAPS

I developed this recipe when corn was in the farmers market and big, red, juicy tomatoes were in my garden. To make this wrap light and healthy, I use fat-free sour cream, whole grain tortillas and brown rice. Although it's vegetarian by nature, change it up with a cooked chicken breast, diced small.
—*Cindy Beberman, Orland Park, IL*

Takes: 30 min. • **Makes:** 6 servings

- 1 can (15 oz.) black beans, rinsed and drained
- 2 large tomatoes, seeded and diced
- 1 cup frozen corn, thawed
- 1 cup cooked brown rice, cooled
- ⅓ cup fat-free sour cream
- ¼ cup minced fresh cilantro
- 2 shallots, chopped
- 1 jalapeno pepper, seeded and chopped
- 2 Tbsp. lime juice
- ½ tsp. ground cumin
- ½ tsp. chili powder
- ½ tsp. salt
- 6 romaine leaves
- 6 whole wheat tortillas (8 in.), at room temperature

Place all ingredients except romaine and tortillas in a large bowl; toss to combine. To serve, place romaine on tortillas; top with bean mixture and roll up, securing with toothpicks if desired. Cut in half.
Note: Wear disposable gloves when cutting hot peppers; the oils can burn skin. Avoid touching your face.
2 halves: 295 cal., 4g fat (0 sat. fat), 2mg chol., 525mg sod., 53g carb. (6g sugars, 7g fiber), 11g pro.

APPLE-CINNAMON PUDGY PIE

I remember the first time I tasted a pie-iron pie. My sister buttered up two slices of white bread while I peeled a Macintosh apple. She sliced the apple thin, arranged it on a slice of bread, and poured liberal amounts of white sugar and cinnamon over the top. I couldn't believe the magic that came out of that campfire! We made these with raspberry jam, too. *Mmm.*

— *Monica Kronemeyer DeRegt, Abbotsford, BC*

Takes: 10 min. • **Makes:** 1 serving

- 1 Tbsp. butter, softened
- 2 slices white bread
- 1 small Macintosh apple, thinly sliced
- 2 to 3 tsp. cinnamon sugar

1. Spread butter over bread slices; place 1 slice in a greased sandwich iron, buttered side down. Top with sliced apples, cinnamon sugar and remaining slice, buttered side up. Close iron.

2. Cook over a hot campfire until golden brown, turning occasionally, 5-7 minutes.

1 sandwich: 341 cal., 14g fat (8g sat. fat), 31mg chol., 377mg sod., 51g carb. (22g sugars, 4g fiber), 6g pro.

BETTER THAN EGG SALAD

Tofu takes on the taste and texture of egg salad in this quick-fixing sandwich.
—*Lisa Renshaw, Kansas City, MO*

Takes: 20 min. • **Makes:** 4 servings

- ¼ cup reduced-fat mayonnaise
- ¼ cup chopped celery
- 2 green onions, chopped
- 2 Tbsp. sweet pickle relish
- 1 Tbsp. Dijon mustard
- ¼ tsp. ground turmeric
- ¼ tsp. salt
- ⅛ tsp. cayenne pepper
- 1 pkg. (12.3 oz.) silken firm tofu, cubed
- 8 slices whole wheat bread
- 4 lettuce leaves
  Coarsely ground pepper, optional

Mix first 8 ingredients; stir in tofu. Line 4 slices of bread with lettuce. Top with tofu mixture. If desired, sprinkle with pepper; close sandwiches.

1 sandwich: 266 cal., 9g fat (2g sat. fat), 5mg chol., 692mg sod., 31g carb. (7g sugars, 4g fiber), 14g pro. **Diabetic exchanges:** 2 starch, 1 lean meat, 1 fat.

FRUITY PEANUT BUTTER PITAS

My kids ask for these pita sandwiches all the time. They haven't noticed that as good as they taste, they're also good for them.

—*Kim Holmes, Emerald Park, SK*

- -

Takes: 5 min. • **Makes:** 2 servings

¼	cup peanut butter
⅛	tsp. each ground allspice, cinnamon and nutmeg
2	whole wheat pita pocket halves
½	medium apple, thinly sliced
½	medium firm banana, sliced

In a small bowl, blend the peanut butter, allspice, cinnamon and nutmeg. Spread inside pita bread halves; fill with apple and banana slices.

1 pita half: 324 cal., 17g fat (4g sat. fat), 0 chol., 320mg sod., 36g carb. (13g sugars, 6g fiber), 12g pro. **Diabetic exchanges:** 3 fat, 1 starch, 1 lean meat, 1 fruit.

APPLE-WHITE CHEDDAR GRILLED CHEESE

On rainy days when we need comfort food in a hurry, I toast sandwiches of cinnamon-raisin bread with white cheddar, apple and red onion. They also are tasty made with vegan cheese and olive oil instead of butter!

—Kathy Patalsky, New York, NY

Takes: 20 min. • **Makes:** 2 servings

- 4 slices whole wheat cinnamon-raisin bread
- 4 slices sharp white cheddar cheese (3 oz.)
- 1 small apple, thinly sliced
- 1 thin slice red onion, separated into rings
- ¼ tsp. crushed red pepper flakes, optional
- 1 Tbsp. butter, softened

1. Layer each of 2 bread slices with 1 slice cheese. Top with apple and onion. If desired, sprinkle with pepper flakes. Top with the remaining cheese and bread. Spread outsides of sandwiches with butter.

2. In a large skillet, toast sandwiches over medium-low heat 3-5 minutes on each side or until golden brown and cheese is melted.

1 sandwich: 456 cal., 27g fat (14g sat. fat), 75mg chol., 616mg sod., 37g carb. (13g sugars, 5g fiber), 20g pro.

OPEN-FACED PIZZA SANDWICHES

This simple pizza sandwich is a hit with my grandchildren. What could be easier for a Saturday lunch? It took me longer to write the recipe down than it does to fix it!

—Dorothy Eriksen, Salem, OR

Takes: 15 min. • **Makes:** 6 servings

- ¼ cup butter, softened
- 6 slices white bread
- 1 can (15 oz.) vegetarian chili, warmed
- ½ tsp. garlic salt
- ¾ cup pizza sauce
- 1 cup shredded part-skim mozzarella cheese
- 1 tsp. Italian seasoning

1. Butter bread on both sides. On a greased griddle, toast bread on 1 side until lightly browned. Turn; spoon about ¼ cup chili on each slice. Sprinkle with garlic salt.

2. Top each with 2 Tbsp. pizza sauce and about 2 Tbsp. cheese. Sprinkle with Italian seasoning. Cook until bottom is golden brown and cheese is melted.

1 serving: 293 cal., 17g fat (9g sat. fat), 46mg chol., 946mg sod., 21g carb. (4g sugars, 2g fiber), 15g pro.

GARBANZO BEAN BURGERS

These meatless burgers are totally awesome. I think I'd rather have one of these than any cheeseburger at a restaurant. They really rock!
—*Berea Rider, East Point, KY*

- -

Prep: 25 min. • **Cook:** 10 min.
Makes: 4 servings

1   **can (15 oz.) garbanzo beans or chickpeas, rinsed and drained**
3   **Tbsp. water**
1   **tsp. lemon juice**
1   **cup dry bread crumbs**
1   **large egg**
1   **tsp. Italian seasoning**
½   **tsp. garlic powder**
½   **tsp. onion powder**
    Dash crushed red pepper flakes
2   **Tbsp. canola oil**
4   **whole wheat or whole grain hamburger buns, split and toasted**
4   **slices reduced-fat American cheese**
    Optional toppings: Dill pickle slices, fat-free mayonnaise, ketchup, sliced red onion, lettuce and sliced tomato

1. Place the beans, water and lemon juice in a food processor; cover and process until blended. Transfer to a large bowl. Add the bread crumbs, egg and seasonings; mix well. Shape into 4 patties.

2. In a large cast-iron or other heavy skillet, cook patties in oil in batches until lightly browned, 3-4 minutes on each side. Serve on buns with cheese. Top as desired.

1 burger: 447 cal., 16g fat (3g sat. fat), 50mg chol., 807mg sod., 60g carb. (10g sugars, 9g fiber), 17g pro.

CHEDDARY MUSHROOM BURGERS

Even the most stubborn meat-and-potatoes people have a change of heart when they bite into of one of these burgers.
—*Denise Hollebeke, Penhold, AB*

Takes: 25 min. • **Makes:** 4 servings

- 2 cups finely chopped fresh mushrooms
- 2 large eggs, lightly beaten
- ½ cup dry bread crumbs
- ½ cup shredded cheddar cheese
- ½ cup finely chopped onion
- ¼ cup all-purpose flour
- ½ tsp. salt
- ¼ tsp. dried thyme
- ¼ tsp. pepper
- 1 Tbsp. canola oil
- 4 whole wheat hamburger buns, split
- 4 lettuce leaves

1. In a large bowl, combine the first 9 ingredients. Shape into four ¾-in.-thick patties.
2. In a large cast-iron or other heavy skillet, heat oil over medium heat. Add burgers; cook until crisp and lightly browned, 3-4 minutes on each side. Serve on buns with lettuce.
1 burger: 330 cal., 13g fat (5g sat. fat), 121mg chol., 736mg sod., 42g carb. (4g sugars, 5g fiber), 14g pro. **Diabetic exchanges:** 3 starch, 1 medium-fat meat, ½ fat.

MUSHROOM PEAR MELTS

I really like mushrooms with cheese. Add pears, broil away, and you have got a scrumptious open-faced sandwich. Serve with a salad and fruity tea.
—*Marla Hyatt, St. Paul, MN*

Takes: 25 min. • **Makes:** 4 servings

- 2 Tbsp. butter
- 4 cups sliced fresh shiitake or baby portobello mushrooms (about 10 oz.)
- ½ tsp. salt
- ¼ tsp. pepper
- 8 slices whole wheat bread, toasted
- 2 large ripe Bosc pears, thinly sliced
- 8 slices provolone cheese

1. Preheat broiler. In a large cast-iron or other heavy skillet, heat butter over medium-high heat. Add mushrooms; cook and stir until tender, 5-7 minutes. Stir in salt and pepper.
2. Place toast slices on a rack of a broiler pan. Top with mushrooms; layer with pears and cheese. Broil 3-4 in. from heat until cheese is lightly browned, 2-3 minutes.
2 open-faced sandwiches: 421 cal., 20g fat (11g sat. fat), 45mg chol., 883mg sod., 46g carb. (15g sugars, 9g fiber), 19g pro.

⏱ ZESTY VEGGIE PITAS

Cilantro adds oomph wherever it goes. That's why I use it with ingredients from the fridge for a zesty, refreshing sandwich combo.
—*Krista Frank, Rhododendron, OR*

- -

Takes: 20 min. • **Makes:** 4 servings

½	cup hummus
4	whole pocketless pita breads or flatbreads, warmed
4	slices pepper jack cheese
1	cup thinly sliced cucumber
1	large tomato, cut into wedges
¼	cup sliced pepperoncini
¼	cup sliced ripe olives
¼	cup fresh cilantro leaves

Spread hummus over pita breads. Top with remaining ingredients; fold pitas to serve.
1 sandwich: 323 cal., 11g fat (4g sat. fat), 23mg chol., 758mg sod., 42g carb. (2g sugars, 4g fiber), 14g pro. **Diabetic exchanges:** 3 starch, 1 medium-fat meat.

GREEK BROWN &
WILD RICE BOWLS
PAGE 146

GRAIN DISHES & BOWLS

Want amazing taste that's great for you, too? Then reach for whole grain dishes and customizable bowls! These recipes satisfy, are packed with healthy ingredients, and are perfect on the go.

FRUIT & NUT BULGUR PILAF

My mother made this nutritious side dish all the time when we were growing up. I enhanced the recipe with a bigger variety of dried fruit to find an interesting balance between the sweet and salty flavors.
—Ninette Holbrook, Orlando, FL

Takes: 30 min. • **Makes:** 10 servings

- 1 Tbsp. canola oil
- 2 cups bulgur
- ¼ tsp. salt
- ¼ tsp. pepper
- 3 cups vegetable broth
- ½ cup slivered almonds, toasted
- ½ cup golden raisins
- ½ cup dried cranberries
- ½ cup dried apricots, chopped

1. In a large saucepan, heat oil over medium-high heat; cook and stir bulgur until toasted. Stir in salt, pepper and broth; bring to a boil. Reduce heat; simmer, covered, until tender and liquid is almost absorbed, 10-12 minutes.
2. Stir in ⅓ cup each of the almonds, raisins, cranberries and apricots. Serve with the remaining almonds and fruit.
Note: To toast nuts, bake in a shallow pan in a 350° oven for 5-10 minutes or cook in a skillet over low heat until lightly browned, stirring occasionally.
⅔ cup: 199 cal., 5g fat (0 sat. fat), 0 chol., 348mg sod., 38g carb. (13g sugars, 5g fiber), 5g pro.

SCENTED RICE IN BAKED PUMPKIN

This easy, delicious and healthy side dish is a showpiece that always delights. You can switch up the grain, squash, fruits and nuts to suit your taste—it's impossible to go wrong!
—Lynn Heisel, Jackson, MO

Prep: 30 min. • **Bake:** 35 min.
Makes: 2 servings

- 1 small pie pumpkin (about 2 lbs.)
- 1 Tbsp. olive oil
- ½ cup uncooked brown rice
- 1 cup water
- ¼ cup coarsely chopped pecans, toasted
- 3 dried apricots, chopped
- 2 Tbsp. raisins
- ¼ tsp. salt
- ¼ tsp. curry powder
- ⅛ tsp. ground cinnamon
- ⅛ tsp. ground cardamom, optional
- ⅛ tsp. ground cumin

1. Wash pumpkin; cut into 6 wedges. Remove loose fibers and seeds from the inside, and discard seeds or save them for toasting. Brush wedges with oil. Place on an ungreased 15x10x1-in. baking sheet. Bake at 400° for 35-40 minutes or until tender.
2. Meanwhile, in a small saucepan, bring rice and water to a boil. Reduce heat; cover and simmer for 20-25 minutes or until liquid is absorbed and rice is tender. Stir in the pecans, apricots, raisins, salt, curry, cinnamon and, if desired, cardamom.
3. Set 4 pumpkin wedges aside for another use. Sprinkle cumin onto remaining wedges; top with rice mixture.
1 serving: 389 cal., 15g fat (2g sat. fat), 0 chol., 309mg sod., 62g carb. (13g sugars, 5g fiber), 7g pro.

TEST KITCHEN TIP

Use the leftover roasted pie pumpkin any way you would use cooked winter squash: puree and use in soup, mash for a side dish, or cube and stir into stuffing or pilaf.

BLACK BEAN & CORN QUINOA

My daughter's college asked parents for a favorite healthy recipe to use in the dining halls. This quinoa fit the bill.
—*Lindsay McSweeney, Winchester, MA*

Takes: 30 min. • **Makes:** 4 servings

2	Tbsp. canola oil
1	medium onion, finely chopped
1	medium sweet red pepper, finely chopped
1	celery rib, finely chopped
2	tsp. chili powder
¼	tsp. salt
¼	tsp. pepper
2	cups vegetable stock
1	cup frozen corn
1	cup quinoa, rinsed
1	can (15 oz.) black beans, rinsed and drained
⅓	cup plus 2 Tbsp. minced fresh cilantro, divided

1. In a large skillet, heat oil over medium-high heat. Add onion, red pepper, celery and seasonings; cook and stir 5-7 minutes or until vegetables are tender.

2. Stir in stock and corn; bring to a boil. Stir in quinoa. Reduce heat; simmer, covered, for 12-15 minutes or until liquid is absorbed.

3. Add the beans and ⅓ cup cilantro; heat through, stirring occasionally. Sprinkle with remaining cilantro.

Note: Look for quinoa in the cereal, rice or organic food aisle.

1¼ cups: 375 cal., 10g fat (1g sat. fat), 0 chol., 668mg sod., 60g carb. (5g sugars, 10g fiber), 13g pro.

POACHED EGG BUDDHA BOWLS

My husband and I celebrate the arrival of spring with this dish, enjoying it in the backyard. I often include fresh peas and other spring delights.
—Amy McDonough, Carlton, OR

- -

Prep: 5 min. • **Cook:** 65 min.
Makes: 2 servings

- ¾ cup wheat berries
- 3½ cups water, divided
- 2 Tbsp. olive oil
- 2 Tbsp. lemon juice
- 1 Tbsp. thinly sliced fresh mint leaves
- ¼ tsp. salt
- ⅛ tsp. freshly ground pepper
- ½ cup quartered cherry tomatoes
- ½ cup reduced-fat ricotta cheese
- 2 Tbsp. sliced Greek olives
- 2 large eggs
  Additional olive oil and pepper, optional

1. Place wheat berries and 2½ cups water in a large saucepan; bring to a boil. Reduce heat; simmer, covered, until tender, about 1 hour. Drain; transfer to a bowl. Cool slightly.

2. Stir in the oil, lemon juice, mint, salt and pepper; divide between 2 bowls. Top with tomatoes, ricotta cheese and olives.

3. To poach egg, place ½ cup water in a small microwave-safe bowl or glass measuring cup. Break an egg into water. Microwave, covered, on high 1 minute. Microwave in 10-second intervals until white is set and yolk begins to thicken; let stand 1 minute.

4. Using a slotted spoon, transfer egg to 1 of the bowls. Repeat. If desired, drizzle with additional oil and sprinkle with more pepper.

1 serving: 526 cal., 24g fat (5g sat. fat), 201mg chol., 563mg sod., 58g carb. (5g sugars, 10g fiber), 21g pro.

TEST KITCHEN TIP

Wheat berries are whole kernels of wheat. They cook up to a chewy texture with a hint of buttery flavor. Look for them near the other whole grains; they're usually in the baking aisle in small packages.

CONFETTI QUINOA

If you have never tried quinoa, start with my easy side, brimming with colorful veggies. I serve it with orange-glazed chicken.
—*Kim Ciepluch, Kenosha, WI*

Takes: 30 min. • **Makes:** 4 servings

2	**cups water**
1	**cup quinoa, rinsed**
½	**cup chopped fresh broccoli**
½	**cup coarsely chopped zucchini**
¼	**cup shredded carrots**
½	**tsp. salt**
1	**Tbsp. lemon juice**
1	**Tbsp. olive oil**

In a large saucepan, bring water to a boil. Add the next 5 ingredients. Reduce heat; simmer, covered, until liquid is absorbed, 12-15 minutes. Stir in lemon juice and oil; heat through. Remove from heat; fluff with a fork.
Note: Look for quinoa in the cereal, rice or organic food aisle.
⅔ cup: 196 cal., 6g fat (1g sat. fat), 0 chol., 307mg sod., 29g carb. (1g sugars, 4g fiber), 7g pro. **Diabetic exchanges:** 2 starch, ½ fat.

MEAT
LOVER
OPTION
PAGE 320

FIESTA CORN & BEANS

Bursting with southwestern flavors, the zesty veggie medley here can be served as a side dish or a meatless meal-in-one. A dollop of yogurt lends a cool, creamy finishing touch.

—*Gerald Hetrick, Erie, PA*

Prep: 25 min. • **Cook:** 3 hours
Makes: 10 servings

- 1 large onion, chopped
- 1 medium green pepper, cut into 1-in. pieces
- 1 to 2 jalapeno peppers, seeded and sliced
- 1 Tbsp. olive oil
- 1 garlic clove, minced
- 2 cans (16 oz. each) kidney beans, rinsed and drained
- 1 pkg. (16 oz.) frozen corn
- 1 can (14½ oz.) diced tomatoes, undrained
- 1 tsp. chili powder
- ¾ tsp. salt
- ½ tsp. ground cumin
- ½ tsp. pepper
  Optional toppings: Plain yogurt and sliced ripe olives

1. In a large skillet, saute onion and peppers in oil until tender. Add garlic; cook 1 minute longer. Transfer to a 4-qt. slow cooker. Stir in the beans, corn, tomatoes and seasonings.
2. Cover and cook on low for 3-4 hours or until heated through. Serve with yogurt and olives if desired.
Note: Wear disposable gloves when cutting hot peppers; the oils can burn skin. Avoid touching your face.
¾ cup: 149 cal., 2g fat (0 sat. fat), 0 chol., 380mg sod., 28g carb. (5g sugars, 7g fiber), 8g pro. **Diabetic exchanges:** 1 starch, 1 lean meat, 1 vegetable.

JASMINE RICE WITH COCONUT & CHERRIES

Our favorite rice deserves a bit of color and sweetness. We add cherries, peanuts, orange zest and coconut. That does the trick.

—*Joy Zacharia, Clearwater, FL*

Prep: 10 min. • **Cook:** 20 min. + standing
Makes: 6 servings

- 2½ cups water
- 1 Tbsp. olive oil
- ¾ tsp. salt
- 1½ cups uncooked jasmine rice
- ⅓ cup dried cherries
- ¼ cup chopped salted peanuts
- 1 tsp. grated orange zest
- ¼ cup sweetened shredded coconut, toasted

1. In a large saucepan, bring water, oil and salt to a boil. Stir in rice; return to a boil, stirring once. Reduce heat; simmer, covered, until water is absorbed, 15-17 minutes.
2. Stir in cherries, peanuts and orange zest; let stand, covered, 10 minutes. Sprinkle with the coconut.
Note: To toast coconut, bake in a shallow pan in a 350° oven for 5-10 minutes or cook in a skillet over low heat until golden brown, stirring occasionally.
¾ cup: 291 cal., 7g fat (2g sat. fat), 0 chol., 332mg sod., 50g carb. (8g sugars, 1g fiber), 6g pro.

51 SPINACH RICE

I like to serve this Greek-style rice dish with grilled steaks or mushrooms. The elegant dish is easily doubled for guests.
—*Jeanette Cakouros, Brunswick, ME*

Takes: 20 min. • **Makes:** 2 servings

- 2 Tbsp. olive oil
- ½ cup chopped onion
- ¾ cup water
- 1 Tbsp. dried parsley flakes
- ¼ to ½ tsp. salt
- ⅛ tsp. pepper
- ½ cup uncooked instant rice
- 2 cups fresh baby spinach

1. In a saucepan, heat oil over medium-high heat; saute onion until tender. Stir in water, parsley, salt and pepper; bring to a boil. Stir in rice; top with spinach.

2. Cover; remove from heat. Let stand until rice is tender, 7-10 minutes. Stir to combine.

¾ cup: 235 cal., 14g fat (2g sat. fat), 0 chol., 326mg sod., 25g carb. (2g sugars, 2g fiber), 3g pro. **Diabetic exchanges:** 3 fat, 1½ starch, 1 vegetable.

VEGETABLE COUSCOUS SALAD

This healthy vegetable couscous salad features our homegrown eggplant and bell peppers and the fresh herbs we keep in hanging pots in our small condo. It's a welcome partner for any grilled meat or fish. Feel free to add a little crumbled goat cheese or tangy feta.

—*Patricia Levenson, Santa Ana, CA*

Prep: 35 min. • **Grill:** 10 min.
Makes: 10 servings

- ½   cup olive oil
- ⅓   cup balsamic vinegar
- 4   tsp. capers, drained
- 4   tsp. lemon juice
- 2   garlic cloves, minced
- ¾   tsp. Dijon mustard
- 1¼   tsp. minced fresh rosemary or ½ tsp. dried rosemary, crushed
- 1¼   tsp. minced fresh thyme or ½ tsp. dried thyme
- ⅛   tsp. salt
- ⅛   tsp. pepper

SALAD
- 1   pkg. (10 oz.) uncooked couscous
- 2   medium zucchini or yellow summer squash, halved lengthwise
- 2   medium sweet yellow or red peppers, quartered
- 1   Japanese eggplant, halved lengthwise
- 2   Tbsp. olive oil
- ¼   tsp. salt
- ¼   tsp. pepper
- 1   cup grape tomatoes, halved
- ½   cup Greek olives, pitted and sliced
- 1   Tbsp. minced fresh parsley or 1 tsp. dried parsley flakes
- 1   Tbsp. minced fresh basil or 1 tsp. dried basil

1. In a small bowl, whisk together the first 10 ingredients. Refrigerate until serving.
2. Cook couscous according to package directions. Meanwhile, brush zucchini, sweet peppers and eggplant with oil; sprinkle with salt and pepper. Grill, covered, over medium heat until crisp-tender, 10-12 minutes, turning once.
3. Chop grilled vegetables; place in a large bowl. Add the tomatoes, olives, parsley, basil and couscous. Pour dressing over salad and toss to coat. Serve warm or chilled.

¾ cup: 272 cal., 16g fat (2g sat. fat), 0 chol., 244mg sod., 29g carb. (5g sugars, 3g fiber), 5g pro. **Diabetic exchanges:** 2 fat, 1½ starch, 1 vegetable.

TEST KITCHEN TIP

Since this salad can be served warm or cold, it's a clever make-and-take for potlucks and picnics.

⏱ BLACK BEAN BULGUR SALAD

The only cooking in this easy bulgur salad is heating the broth and bulgur. You can adapt the recipe to your preference; if you want to add chopped cooked chicken, use chicken broth in place of vegetable broth.
—*Carole Resnick, Cleveland, OH*

MEAT LOVER OPTION PAGE 320

Takes: 30 min. • **Makes:** 4 servings

- 1 cup bulgur
- 2 cups vegetable broth
- ¼ cup orange juice
- ¼ cup lime juice
- 1 jalapeno pepper, seeded and minced
- 2 Tbsp. olive oil
- ¼ tsp. ground cumin
- 1 cup shredded carrots
- 3 Tbsp. minced fresh cilantro
- 1 can (15 oz.) black beans, rinsed and drained
- 1 cup frozen corn, thawed
- ¾ cup shredded Monterey Jack cheese
  Sliced jalapeno pepper, optional

1. Place bulgur and broth in a small saucepan; bring to a boil. Reduce heat; simmer, covered, until tender, 12-15 minutes. Transfer to a large bowl; cool slightly.

2. For dressing, whisk together citrus juices, minced jalapeno, oil and cumin. Add ⅓ cup dressing to bulgur; stir in carrots and cilantro.

3. To serve, divide bulgur mixture among 4 bowls. Top with beans, corn, cheese and, if desired, sliced jalapeno. Drizzle with the remaining dressing.

1 serving: 402 cal., 14g fat (5g sat. fat), 19mg chol., 688mg sod., 56g carb. (6g sugars, 10g fiber), 16g pro.

⑤ QUINOA WITH PEAS & ONION

Even picky eaters will love this dish. Though it's delicious with freshly shelled peas, you can easily substitute frozen when they aren't in season.

—*Lori Panarella, Phoenixville, PA*

Prep: 30 min. • **Cook:** 10 min.
Makes: 6 servings

- 2 cups water
- 1 cup quinoa, rinsed
- 1 small onion, chopped
- 1 Tbsp. olive oil
- 1½ cups frozen peas
- ½ tsp. salt
- ¼ tsp. pepper
- 2 Tbsp. chopped walnuts

1. In a large saucepan, bring water to a boil. Add quinoa. Reduce heat; cover and simmer for 12-15 minutes or until water is absorbed. Remove from the heat; fluff with a fork.
2. Meanwhile, in a large skillet, saute onion in oil until tender. Add peas; cook and stir until heated through. Stir in the cooked quinoa, salt and pepper. Sprinkle with walnuts.
Note: Look for quinoa in the cereal, rice or organic food aisle.

⅔ cup: 174 cal., 6g fat (1g sat. fat), 0 chol., 244mg sod., 26g carb. (2g sugars, 4g fiber), 6g pro. **Diabetic exchanges:** 1½ starch, 1 fat.

TEST KITCHEN TIP

Quinoa (pronounced KEEN-wah) is an ancient South American grain. It's often referred to as the perfect grain because, unlike other grains, it offers a complete protein. This makes quinoa an excellent choice for vegetarian and vegan meals, which may tend to be low in protein.

AVOCADO & GARBANZO BEAN QUINOA SALAD

This delicious salad is high in protein and holds well in the fridge for a few days. If you make it ahead, add avocados and tomatoes right before serving.

—*Elizabeth Bennett, Seattle, WA*

Prep: 25 min. • **Cook:** 15 min.
Makes: 6 servings

- 1   cup quinoa, rinsed
- 1   can (15 oz.) garbanzo beans or chickpeas, rinsed and drained
- 2   cups cherry tomatoes, halved
- 1   cup crumbled feta cheese
- ½   medium ripe avocado, peeled and cubed
- 4   green onions, chopped (about ½ cup)

DRESSING

- 3   Tbsp. white wine vinegar
- 1   tsp. Dijon mustard
- ¼   tsp. kosher salt
- ¼   tsp. garlic powder
- ¼   tsp. freshly ground pepper
- ¼   cup olive oil

1. Cook quinoa according to package directions; transfer to a large bowl and cool slightly.

2. Add beans, tomatoes, cheese, avocado and green onions to quinoa; gently stir to combine. In a small bowl, whisk the first 5 dressing ingredients. Gradually whisk in oil until blended. Drizzle over salad; gently toss to coat. Refrigerate leftovers.

Note: Look for quinoa in the cereal, rice or organic food aisle.

1⅓ cups: 328 cal., 17g fat (4g sat. fat), 10mg chol., 378mg sod., 34g carb. (3g sugars, 7g fiber), 11g pro. **Diabetic exchanges:** 3 fat, 2 starch, 1 lean meat.

🕐 CHICKPEA MINT TABBOULEH

You'll love this salad warm or chilled. For variety, add feta cheese or use this as a filling for stuffed tomatoes or mushrooms.

—*Bryan Kennedy, Kaneohe, HI*

Takes: 30 min. • **Makes:** 4 servings

- 1   cup bulgur
- 2   cups water
- 1   cup fresh or frozen peas (about 5 oz.), thawed
- 1   can (15 oz.) chickpeas or garbanzo beans, rinsed and drained
- ½   cup minced fresh parsley
- ¼   cup minced fresh mint
- ¼   cup olive oil
- 2   Tbsp. julienned soft sun-dried tomatoes (not packed in oil)
- 2   Tbsp. lemon juice
- ½   tsp. salt
- ¼   tsp. pepper

1. In a large saucepan, combine bulgur and water; bring to a boil. Reduce heat; simmer, covered, 10 minutes. Stir in fresh or thawed peas; cook, covered, until bulgur and peas are tender, about 5 minutes.

2. Transfer to a large bowl. Stir in remaining ingredients. Serve warm, or refrigerate and serve cold.

Note: This recipe was tested with soft sun-dried tomatoes that do not need to be soaked before use.

1 cup: 380 cal., 16g fat (2g sat. fat), 0 chol., 450mg sod., 51g carb. (6g sugars, 11g fiber), 11g pro. **Diabetic exchanges:** 3 starch, 3 fat, 1 lean meat.

DID YOU KNOW?

Bulgur is made from whole wheat kernels that are boiled, dried and cracked. Since it's made from the whole kernel, it's always a whole grain. It has more fiber than quinoa, oats and corn.

MUSHROOMS MARSALA WITH BARLEY

This satisfying vegetarian recipe is a tasty mashup of chicken Marsala and mushroom barley soup. It's perfect as a main dish, but it can also be served, with or without the barley, as a hearty side.
—*Arlene Erlbach, Morton Grove, IL*

Prep: 20 min. • **Cook:** 4¼ hours
Makes: 6 servings

- 1½ lbs. baby portobello mushrooms, cut into ¾-in. chunks
- 1 cup thinly sliced shallots
- 3 Tbsp. olive oil
- ½ tsp. minced fresh thyme
- ¾ cup Marsala wine, divided
- 3 Tbsp. reduced-fat sour cream
- 2 Tbsp. all-purpose flour
- 1½ tsp. grated lemon zest
- ¼ tsp. salt
- ¼ cup crumbled goat cheese
- ¼ cup minced fresh parsley
- 2½ cups hot cooked barley

1. In a 4- or 5-qt. slow cooker, combine mushrooms, shallots, olive oil and thyme. Add ¼ cup Marsala wine. Cook, covered, on low until vegetables are tender, about 4 hours.

2. Stir in sour cream, flour, lemon zest, salt and remaining Marsala. Cook, covered, on low 15 minutes longer. Sprinkle with goat cheese and parsley. Serve with barley.

¾ cup mushrooms with about ⅓ cup barley: 235 cal., 9g fat (2g sat. fat), 7mg chol., 139mg sod., 31g carb. (6g sugars, 5g fiber), 7g pro. **Diabetic exchanges:** 2 starch, 2 fat, 1 vegetable.

TEST KITCHEN TIP

Marsala is an Italian wine fortified with alcohol. Its distinctive flavor is found in many Italian desserts, entrees and side dishes. You can substitute red or white wine, beer or broth for the Marsala. Be prepared: This will change the flavor dramatically.

CURRIED QUINOA & CHICKPEAS

If you're a fan of curry seasoning and you want to cook with more quinoa, this is a must-try recipe for you. Orange juice and raisins are a wonderful addition to this dish.
—*Suzanne Banfield, Basking Ridge, NJ*

Prep: 15 min. • **Cook:** 25 min.
Makes: 4 servings

1½ cups water
½ cup orange juice
1 can (15 oz.) chickpeas or garbanzo beans, rinsed and drained
2 medium tomatoes, seeded and chopped
1 medium sweet red pepper, julienned
1 cup quinoa, rinsed
1 small red onion, finely chopped
½ cup raisins
1 tsp. curry powder
½ cup minced fresh cilantro

1. In a large saucepan, bring water and orange juice to a boil. Stir in chickpeas, tomatoes, red pepper, quinoa, onion, raisins and curry. Return to a boil. Reduce heat; cover and simmer for 15-20 minutes or until liquid is absorbed.
2. Remove from the heat; fluff with a fork. Sprinkle with cilantro.
1½ cups: 355 cal., 5g fat (0 sat. fat), 0 chol., 155mg sod., 70g carb. (20g sugars, 9g fiber), 12g pro.

MEAT LOVER OPTION PAGE 320

CREAMY POLENTA WITH BALSAMIC GLAZE

This delicious and easy side dish goes incredibly well with braised meat. It makes any meal feel a little more elevated.
—Sarah Vasques, Milford, NH

Prep: 15 min. • **Cook:** 2 hours
Makes: 4 servings

- 4   Tbsp. butter, divided
- 1½ cups half-and-half cream, divided
- 1   cup 2% milk
- ¼   tsp. salt
- ⅓   cup cornmeal
- 1   cup balsamic vinegar
- 1   Tbsp. sugar
- ½   cup grated Parmesan cheese

1. In medium saucepan, melt 2 Tbsp. butter over medium heat. Add 1 cup cream, milk and salt. Bring to a low simmer. Gradually whisk in cornmeal. Cook and stir for 3 minutes.

2. Pour the polenta into a 3-qt. slow cooker coated with cooking spray. Cook, covered, on low for 2 hours, stirring every 30 minutes. Meanwhile, in a small saucepan, bring vinegar and sugar to a boil. Reduce heat; simmer, uncovered, until reduced to ⅓ cup. Just before serving, stir cheese and the remaining cream and butter into polenta. To serve, drizzle with balsamic glaze.

½ cup polenta with 1 Tbsp. glaze: 415 cal., 25g fat (16g sat. fat), 89mg chol., 494mg sod., 37g carb. (25g sugars, 1g fiber), 9g pro.

READER RAVE

"My family loved this alternative to mashed potatoes. The 'mmms' and the 'oohs' around the table were delightful to hear! We'll be having more of this soon!"
—GAYLENE2, TASTEOFHOME.COM

BLACK BEAN & SWEET POTATO RICE BOWLS

With three hungry boys in my house, dinners need to be quick and filling, and it helps to get in some veggies, too. This one is a favorite because it's hearty and easy to tweak with different ingredients.
—Kim Van Dunk, Caldwell, NJ

Takes: 30 min. • **Makes:** 4 servings

- ¾   cup uncooked long grain rice
- ¼   tsp. garlic salt
- 1½ cups water
- 3   Tbsp. olive oil, divided
- 1   large sweet potato, peeled and diced
- 1   medium red onion, finely chopped
- 4   cups chopped fresh kale (tough stems removed)
- 1   can (15 oz.) black beans, rinsed and drained
- 2   Tbsp. sweet chili sauce
      Lime wedges, optional
      Additional sweet chili sauce, optional

1. Place rice, garlic salt and water in a large saucepan; bring to a boil. Reduce heat; simmer, covered, until water is absorbed and rice is tender, 15-20 minutes. Remove from heat; let stand 5 minutes.

2. Meanwhile, in a large skillet, heat 2 Tbsp. oil over medium-high heat; saute sweet potato 8 minutes. Add onion; cook and stir until potato is tender, 4-6 minutes. Add kale; cook and stir until tender, 3-5 minutes. Stir in beans; heat through.

3. Gently stir 2 Tbsp. chili sauce and remaining oil into rice; add to potato mixture. If desired, serve with lime wedges and additional chili sauce.

2 cups: 435 cal., 11g fat (2g sat. fat), 0 chol., 405mg sod., 74g carb. (15g sugars, 8g fiber), 10g pro.

Health tip: Sweet potato + kale + black beans = nearly ⅓ of the daily value for fiber per serving!

🍲 BUTTERNUT SQUASH WITH WHOLE GRAINS

Fresh ingredients shine in this scrumptious slow-cooked side. It's low in fat and good for you.
—Taste of Home *Test Kitchen*

- -

Prep: 15 min. • **Cook:** 4 hours
Makes: 12 servings

- 1   medium butternut squash (about 3 lbs.), cut into ½-in. cubes
- 1   cup uncooked whole grain brown and red rice blend
- 1   medium onion, chopped
- ½   cup water
- 3   garlic cloves, minced
- 2   tsp. minced fresh thyme or ½ tsp. dried thyme
- ½   tsp. salt
- ¼   tsp. pepper
- 1   can (14½ oz.) vegetable broth
- 1   pkg. (6 oz.) fresh baby spinach

1. In a 4-qt. slow cooker, combine the first 8 ingredients. Stir in broth.
2. Cook, covered, on low 4-5 hours or until grains are tender. Stir in spinach.
Note: This recipe was tested with RiceSelect Royal Blend Whole Grain Texmati Brown & Red Rice with Barley and Rye. Look for it in the rice aisle.
¾ cup: 97 cal., 1g fat (0 sat. fat), 0 chol., 252mg sod., 22g carb. (3g sugars, 4g fiber), 3g pro. **Diabetic exchanges:** 1½ starch.

MANGO BARLEY SALAD

I made this fresh, colorful mango salad on the fly and it was a big hit! The bright flavor is perfect for a spring or summer picnic, served right away or chilled.

—*Dan Wellberg, Elk River, MN*

Takes: 25 min. • **Makes:** 6 servings

1¾ cups water
1 cup quick-cooking barley
2 medium limes
¼ cup olive oil
1 Tbsp. Dijon mustard
1 Tbsp. honey
½ tsp. salt
¼ tsp. ground cumin
¼ tsp. pepper
½ cup chopped sweet red pepper
½ cup chopped green pepper
¼ cup chopped red onion
1 medium mango, peeled and chopped
¼ cup minced fresh cilantro

1. In a small saucepan, bring water to a boil. Stir in barley. Reduce heat; simmer, covered, until barley is tender, 10-12 minutes. Remove from heat; let stand 5 minutes.
2. Finely grate enough zest from limes to measure 1 tsp. Cut limes crosswise in half; squeeze juice from limes. In a small bowl, whisk lime juice, lime zest, oil, mustard, honey, salt, cumin and pepper until blended.
3. In a large bowl, combine barley, peppers, onion, mango and cilantro. Add dressing; toss to coat. Refrigerate until serving.
¾ cup: 185 cal., 10g fat (1g sat. fat), 0 chol., 261mg sod., 25g carb. (9g sugars, 5g fiber), 2g pro. **Diabetic exchanges:** 2 fat, 1½ starch.

TEST KITCHEN TIP

Just because we call for barley doesn't mean you can't try this made with quinoa, farro or other grains. It's all going to be delicious!

VEGETABLE BARLEY SAUTE

Here's a wonderful side dish you can easily adjust to suit your tastes. Use broccoli instead of green beans, sweet potato ribbons instead of carrots, and switch up the nuts.

—Taste of Home *Test Kitchen*

Takes: 30 min. • **Makes:** 4 servings

½ cup quick-cooking barley
⅓ cup water
3 Tbsp. reduced-sodium soy sauce
2 tsp. cornstarch
1 garlic clove, minced
1 Tbsp. vegetable oil
2 carrots, thinly sliced
1 cup cut fresh green beans (2-in. pieces)
2 green onions, sliced
½ cup unsalted cashews, optional

1. Prepare barley according to package directions. In a small bowl, combine water, soy sauce and cornstarch until smooth; set aside.
2. In a large skillet or wok, saute garlic in oil for 15 seconds. Add carrots and beans; stir-fry for 2 minutes. Add onions; stir-fry 1 minute longer. Stir soy sauce mixture; stir into skillet. Bring to a boil; cook and stir until thickened, about 1 minute. Add barley; heat through. If desired, stir in cashews.
⅔ cup: 148 cal., 4g fat (1g sat. fat), 0 chol., 458mg sod., 24g carb. (3g sugars, 6g fiber), 5g pro. **Diabetic exchanges:** 1½ starch, 1 fat.

MEAT LOVER OPTION PAGE 320

🕐 GREEK BROWN & WILD RICE BOWLS

This fresh rice dish is short on ingredients but packs in so much flavor. It tastes like the Mediterranean in a bowl! For a handheld version, leave out the rice and tuck the rest of the ingredients into a pita pocket.
—*Darla Andrews, Schertz, TX*

- -

Takes: 15 min. • **Makes:** 2 servings

- 1 pkg. (8½ oz.) ready-to-serve whole grain brown and wild rice medley
- ¼ cup Greek vinaigrette, divided
- ½ medium ripe avocado, peeled and sliced
- ¾ cup cherry tomatoes, halved
- ¼ cup crumbled feta cheese
- ¼ cup pitted Greek olives, sliced
  Minced fresh parsley, optional

♥ MEAT LOVER OPTION PAGE 320

In a microwave-safe bowl, combine rice mix and 2 Tbsp. vinaigrette. Cover and cook on high until heated through, about 2 minutes. Divide between 2 bowls. Top with avocado, tomatoes, cheese, olives, remaining dressing and, if desired, parsley.

1 serving: 433 cal., 25g fat (4g sat. fat), 8mg chol., 1355mg sod., 44g carb. (3g sugars, 6g fiber), 8g pro.

Health tip: These otherwise healthy bowls are high in sodium because of the prepared rice, dressing, feta cheese and Greek olives. Save on sodium by cooking the rice from scratch and using a simple oil and vinegar dressing.

FESTIVE RICE

My mom and I transformed plain rice by adding feta, cranberries, pumpkin seeds and cayenne. We wound up with a sweet and spicy crowd-pleaser.
—*Lisa de Perio, Dallas, TX*

Prep: 20 min. • **Bake:** 30 min.
Makes: 6 servings

2¼ cups water
¼ cup butter, cubed
1 tsp. salt
1 tsp. white vinegar
½ tsp. garlic powder
1 cup uncooked jasmine rice
¼ cup salted pumpkin seeds or pepitas
2 tsp. brown sugar
¼ to ½ tsp. cayenne pepper
¼ cup crumbled feta cheese
¼ cup chopped fresh mint
¼ cup dried cranberries

1. Preheat oven to 325°. In a small saucepan, bring first 5 ingredients to a boil. Remove from heat. Pour over rice in a greased 8-in. square baking dish. Bake, covered, until all liquid is absorbed, 30-35 minutes.
2. Meanwhile, in a small nonstick skillet over medium-high heat, cook pumpkin seeds, brown sugar and cayenne pepper, stirring constantly until sugar melts and cayenne coats pumpkin seeds, 4-5 minutes. Remove from heat; transfer to a plate, spreading out seeds to cool.
3. Sprinkle cooked rice with feta, mint, cranberries and spiced pumpkin seeds.
⅔ cup: 244 cal., 11g fat (6g sat. fat), 23mg chol., 514mg sod., 32g carb. (5g sugars, 1g fiber), 5g pro.

MEDITERRANEAN BULGUR BOWL

You can transform this tasty bowl into an Italian version with mozzarella, pesto, tomatoes, spinach and basil.
—*Renata Smith, Brookline, MA*

Takes: 30 min. • **Makes:** 4 servings

1 cup bulgur
½ tsp. ground cumin
¼ tsp. salt
2 cups water
1 can (15 oz.) garbanzo beans or chickpeas, rinsed and drained
6 oz. fresh baby spinach (about 8 cups)
2 cups cherry tomatoes, halved
1 small red onion, halved and thinly sliced
½ cup crumbled feta cheese
¼ cup hummus
2 Tbsp. chopped fresh mint
2 Tbsp. lemon juice

1. In a 6-qt. stockpot, combine the first 4 ingredients; bring to a boil. Reduce heat; simmer, covered, until tender, 10-12 minutes. Stir in garbanzo beans; heat through.
2. Remove from heat; stir in spinach. Let stand, covered, until spinach is wilted, about 5 minutes. Stir in remaining ingredients. Serve warm, or refrigerate and serve cold.
2 cups: 311 cal., 7g fat (2g sat. fat), 8mg chol., 521mg sod., 52g carb. (6g sugars, 12g fiber), 14g pro.

QUINOA TABBOULEH

When my mom and sister developed several food allergies, we had to modify many of our favorite recipes. I substituted quinoa for couscous in this tabbouleh dish, and now we make it all the time.
—*Jennifer Klann, Corbett, OR*

Prep: 35 min. + chilling • **Makes:** 8 servings

- 2   cups water
- 1   cup quinoa, rinsed
- 1   can (15 oz.) black beans, rinsed and drained
- 1   small cucumber, peeled and chopped
- 1   small sweet red pepper, chopped
- ⅓   cup minced fresh parsley
- ¼   cup lemon juice
- 2   Tbsp. olive oil
- ½   tsp. salt
- ½   tsp. pepper

1. In a large saucepan, bring water to a boil. Add quinoa. Reduce heat; cover and simmer until liquid is absorbed, 12-15 minutes. Remove from the heat; fluff with a fork. Transfer to a bowl; cool completely.

2. Add the beans, cucumber, red pepper and parsley. In a small bowl, whisk the remaining ingredients; drizzle over salad and toss to coat. Refrigerate until chilled.

Note: Look for quinoa in the cereal, rice or organic food aisle.

¾ cup: 159 cal., 5g fat (1g sat. fat), 0 chol., 255mg sod., 24g carb. (1g sugars, 4g fiber), 6g pro. **Diabetic exchanges:** 1½ starch, 1 fat.

MEAT LOVER OPTION PAGE 320

SPRING ONION PIMIENTO CHEESE GRITS

Grits were a breakfast staple when I was growing up. Even today, we still have them about three times a week. The trick with grits is the more you whisk, the creamier they'll be.
—*Melissa Pelkey Hass, Waleska, GA*

Prep: 15 min. • **Cook:** 20 min.
Makes: 16 servings

- 2   cups uncooked stone-ground yellow grits
- 1   pkg. (8 oz.) cream cheese, softened
- ½   cup mayonnaise
- 3   cups shredded Monterey Jack cheese
- 1   jar (4 oz.) diced pimientos, drained
- 3   green onions, diced
- 1   tsp. sugar
     Dash cayenne pepper
- ¼   cup butter, softened
     Salt and pepper to taste

1. Prepare grits according to package directions. Keep warm.

2. Meanwhile, using a mixer, beat cream cheese. Add mayonnaise; continue beating until creamy. Add next 5 ingredients, mixing until well blended.

3. Stir butter and pimiento cheese mixture into the warm grits; season to taste. Mix well.

¾ cup: 281 cal., 20g fat (10g sat. fat), 41mg chol., 231mg sod., 19g carb. (1g sugars, 1g fiber), 8g pro.

BLACK BEAN-TOMATO CHILI
PAGE 174

HEARTWARMING SOUPS

Heartwarming soups are the ultimate comfort food, and this chapter is brimming with chili, bisque, stew, pureed vegetable soups and more. You'll find something for all tastes and seasons here.

AUTUMN BISQUE

I like cozy, comforting soups that taste creamy but are dairy-free. This one's full of good stuff like rutabagas, leeks, fresh herbs and almond milk.

—*Merry Graham, Newhall, CA*

Prep: 25 min. • **Cook:** 50 min.
Makes: 12 servings (3 qt.)

¼ cup dairy-free spreadable margarine
2 tsp. minced fresh chives
2 tsp. minced fresh parsley
½ tsp. grated lemon zest
BISQUE
2 Tbsp. olive oil
2 large rutabagas, peeled and cubed (about 9 cups)
1 large celery root, peeled and cubed (about 3 cups)
3 medium leeks (white portion only), chopped (about 2 cups)
1 large carrot, cubed (about ⅔ cup)
3 garlic cloves, minced
7 cups vegetable stock
2 tsp. minced fresh thyme
1½ tsp. minced fresh rosemary
1 tsp. salt
½ tsp. coarsely ground pepper
2 cups almond milk
2 Tbsp. minced fresh chives

1. Mix first 4 ingredients. Using a melon baller or 1-tsp. measuring spoon, shape mixture into 12 balls. Freeze on a waxed paper-lined baking sheet until firm. Transfer to a freezer container; freeze up to 2 months.
2. In a 6-qt. stock pot, heat oil over medium heat; saute rutabagas, celery root, leeks and carrot for 8 minutes. Add garlic; cook and stir for 2 minutes. Stir in stock, herbs, salt and pepper; bring to a boil. Reduce heat; simmer mixture, covered, until vegetables are tender, 30-35 minutes.
3. Puree soup using an immersion blender. Or cool slightly and puree in batches in a blender; return to pan. Stir in milk; heat through. Top servings with chives and herbed margarine.
1 cup: 146 cal., 7g fat (2g sat. fat), 0 chol., 672mg sod., 20g carb. (9g sugars, 5g fiber), 3g pro. **Diabetic exchanges:** 1 starch, 1 fat.

SPINACH & TORTELLINI SOUP

A simple tomato-enhanced broth is perfect for cheese tortellini and fresh spinach. Increase the garlic and add Italian seasoning to suit your taste.

—*Debbie Wilson, Burlington, NC*

Takes: 20 min. • **Makes:** 6 servings (2 qt.)

- 1 tsp. olive oil
- 2 garlic cloves, minced
- 1 can (14½ oz.) no-salt-added diced tomatoes, undrained
- 3 cans (14½ oz. each) vegetable broth
- 2 tsp. Italian seasoning
- 1 pkg. (9 oz.) refrigerated cheese tortellini
- 4 cups fresh baby spinach
  Shredded Parmesan cheese and freshly ground pepper

1. In a large saucepan, heat oil over medium heat. Add garlic; cook and stir 1 minute. Stir in tomatoes, broth and Italian seasoning; bring to a boil. Add tortellini; bring to a gentle boil. Cook, uncovered, just until tortellini are tender, 7-9 minutes.

2. Stir in spinach. Sprinkle servings with cheese and pepper.

1⅓ cups: 164 cal., 5g fat (2g sat. fat), 18mg chol., 799mg sod., 25g carb. (4g sugars, 2g fiber), 7g pro.

CREAMY BUTTERNUT SQUASH & SAGE SOUP

I recently started experimenting with new soup recipes, and I finally created a rich squash version that omits heavy cream altogether, making it a healthier way to curb my creamy-tooth.
—*Nithya Kumar, Davis, CA*

Prep: 20 min. • **Cook:** 50 min.
Makes: 4 servings

- 4 cups cubed peeled butternut squash
- 1 Tbsp. olive oil
- 2 Tbsp. minced fresh sage
- ¼ tsp. salt
- ¼ tsp. pepper

SOUP

- 1 Tbsp. olive oil
- 2 Tbsp. butter, divided
- 1 medium onion, chopped
- 1 garlic clove, minced
- ¾ tsp. salt
- ¼ to ½ tsp. crushed red pepper flakes
- ⅛ tsp. pepper
- 4 cups water
- 1 medium sweet potato, chopped
- 1 medium carrot, chopped

1. Preheat oven to 400°. Place squash in a foil-lined 15x10x1-in. baking pan. Drizzle with oil; sprinkle with sage, salt and pepper. Toss to coat. Roast 30-35 minutes or until tender, stirring occasionally.

2. Meanwhile, in a large saucepan, heat oil and 1 Tbsp. butter over medium heat. Add onion and garlic; cook and stir 3-4 minutes or until softened. Reduce heat to medium-low; cook 30-40 minutes or until deep golden brown, stirring occasionally. Stir in the salt, pepper flakes and pepper.

3. Add water, sweet potato and carrot to saucepan. Bring to a boil. Reduce heat; cook, uncovered, 10-15 minutes or until vegetables are tender. Add squash mixture and the remaining butter to soup. Puree soup using an immersion blender. Or cool soup slightly and puree in batches in a blender; return to pan and heat through.

1½ cups: 255 cal., 13g fat (5g sat. fat), 15mg chol., 659mg sod., 36g carb. (10g sugars, 6g fiber), 3g pro. **Diabetic exchanges:** 3 fat, 2 starch.

FRESH VEGETABLE STEW

Sunny, colorful and brimming with garden flavor, this easy stovetop dish stirs in several different squashes along with other favorite veggies. Why not serve it tonight?
—*Beth Chase, Alexandria, VA*

Prep: 15 min. • **Cook:** 20 min.
Makes: 12 servings (2 qt.)

- 1 large onion, sliced
- 3 garlic cloves, minced
- 1 Tbsp. olive oil
- 1 lb. yellow squash, cut into ½-in. cubes
- 1 lb. pattypan squash, cut into ½-in. cubes
- 2 medium tomatoes, peeled and chopped
- ¾ lb. fresh green beans, cut into 1-in pieces
- 1¼ cups fresh sweet corn
- 1 tsp. salt
- ¼ tsp. pepper

In a Dutch oven, saute onion and garlic in oil until tender. Add squash, tomatoes and beans. Reduce heat; cover and simmer 15 minutes or until squash is tender. Add corn, salt and pepper. Cook for 3 minutes or until corn is tender.

⅔ cup: 59 cal., 2g fat (0 sat. fat), 0 chol., 184mg sod., 11g carb. (0 sugars, 0 fiber), 2g pro. **Diabetic exchanges:** 2 vegetable.

READER RAVE

"For something so simple, it's really tasty. An appreciated recipe for squash season."
—THJADEWOLF, TASTEOFHOME.COM

MEAT LOVER OPTION PAGE 320

TUSCAN PORTOBELLO STEW

Here's a healthy one-skillet meal that's quick and easy to prepare, yet elegant enough for company. I often take this stew to my school's potlucks, where it is devoured by vegetarian teachers and students alike.

—*Jane Siemon, Viroqua, WI*

Prep: 20 min. • **Cook:** 20 min.
Makes: 4 servings

- 2 large portobello mushrooms, coarsely chopped
- 1 medium onion, chopped
- 3 garlic cloves, minced
- 2 Tbsp. olive oil
- ½ cup white wine or vegetable broth
- 1 can (28 oz.) diced tomatoes, undrained
- 2 cups chopped fresh kale
- 1 bay leaf
- 1 tsp. dried thyme
- ½ tsp. dried basil
- ½ tsp. dried rosemary, crushed
- ¼ tsp. salt
- ¼ tsp. pepper
- 2 cans (15 oz. each) cannellini beans, rinsed and drained

1. In a large skillet, saute the mushrooms, onion and garlic in oil until tender. Add the wine. Bring to a boil; cook until liquid is reduced by half. Stir in the tomatoes, kale and seasonings. Bring to a boil. Reduce heat; cover and simmer for 8-10 minutes.
2. Add beans; heat through. Discard bay leaf.
1¼ cups: 309 cal., 8g fat (1g sat. fat), 0 chol., 672mg sod., 46g carb. (9g sugars, 13g fiber), 12g pro. **Diabetic exchanges:** 2 starch, 2 vegetable, 1½ fat, 1 lean meat.

MARKET BASKET SOUP

I use kohlrabi in this soothing veggie soup. The veggie has a mellow broccoli-cabbage flavor and can be served raw, but I like it best in a warm bowl of this.

—*Kellie Foglio, Salem, WI*

Prep: 25 min. • **Cook:** 40 min.
Makes: 11 servings (2¾ qt.)

- 1 Tbsp. olive oil
- 1 large kohlrabi bulb, peeled and chopped
- 4 celery ribs, chopped
- 2 medium onions, chopped
- 2 medium carrots, chopped
- 3 garlic cloves, minced
- 1 tsp. salt
- 1 tsp. coarsely ground pepper
- 6 cups vegetable stock or water
- 2 cans (15½ oz. each) great northern beans, rinsed and drained
- 2 bay leaves
- 2 medium tomatoes, chopped
- 2 Tbsp. minced fresh parsley
- 2 Tbsp. minced fresh tarragon or ¾ tsp. dried tarragon
- 2 Tbsp. minced fresh thyme or ¾ tsp. dried thyme

1. In a stockpot, heat oil over medium-high heat. Stir in kohlrabi, celery, onions and carrots; cook 5 minutes or until onions are softened. Add garlic, salt and pepper; cook and stir 5 minutes.

2. Stir in stock, beans and bay leaves. Bring to a boil over medium-high heat. Reduce heat; simmer, covered, until vegetables are tender, 20-25 minutes. Add remaining ingredients; simmer 5 minutes more. Discard bay leaves.

1 cup: 110 cal., 2g fat (0 sat. fat), 0 chol., 664mg sod., 19g carb. (3g sugars, 6g fiber), 5g pro. **Diabetic exchanges:** 1 starch, 1 vegetable.

VEGAN TORTILLA SOUP

Quinoa may be an unconventional ingredient, but it adds protein to this vegan soup, making it hearty enough for a main dish.

—Taste of Home *Test Kitchen*

Takes: 30 min. • **Makes:** 8 servings (3 qt.)

- 1 Tbsp. olive oil
- 1 medium onion, chopped
- 4 garlic cloves, minced
- 1 jalapeno pepper, seeded and chopped
- 8 cups vegetable broth
- 1 cup quinoa, rinsed
- 2 tsp. chili powder
- ½ tsp. ground cumin
- ½ tsp. salt
- ¼ tsp. pepper
- 1 can (15 oz.) black beans, rinsed and drained
- 3 medium tomatoes, chopped
- 1 cup fresh or frozen corn
- ⅓ cup minced fresh cilantro
  Optional: Cubed avocado, lime wedges and chopped cilantro

Heat oil in a Dutch oven over medium-high heat. Add onion, garlic and jalapeno pepper; cook and stir until tender, 3-5 minutes. Add broth, quinoa and seasonings. Bring to a boil; reduce heat. Simmer, uncovered, until quinoa is tender, about 10 minutes. Add beans, tomatoes, corn, and cilantro; heat through. If desired, serve with optional ingredients.

1½ cups: 182 cal., 4g fat (1g sat. fat), 0 chol., 792mg sod., 31g carb. (5g sugars, 5g fiber), 7g pro. **Diabetic exchanges:** 2 starch, ½ fat.

HEARTY POTATO SOUP

I grew up on a dairy farm in Holland, and now I love my life in Idaho's potato country. My favorite potato soup originally called for heavy cream and bacon fat, but I've trimmed down the recipe.
—*Gladys De Boer, Castleford, ID*

Prep: 20 min. • **Cook:** 30 min.
Makes: 10 servings (about 2½ qt.)

- 6 medium potatoes, peeled and sliced
- 2 carrots, chopped
- 6 celery ribs, chopped
- 8 cups water
- 1 onion, chopped
- 6 Tbsp. butter, cubed
- 6 Tbsp. all-purpose flour
- 1 tsp. salt
- ½ tsp. pepper
- 1½ cups 2% milk

1. In a Dutch oven, cook the potatoes, carrots and celery in water until tender, 15-20 minutes. Drain, reserving liquid and setting vegetables aside.

2. In same pan, saute onion in butter until tender. Stir in flour, salt and pepper; gradually add milk. Bring to a boil; cook and stir until thickened, about 2 minutes. Gently stir in cooked vegetables. Add reserved cooking liquid until soup is desired consistency.

1 cup: 208 cal., 8g fat (5g sat. fat), 21mg chol., 344mg sod., 31g carb. (4g sugars, 4g fiber), 5g pro.

MEAT LOVER OPTION
PAGE 320

❄ CREAMY CAULIFLOWER PAKORA SOUP

My husband and I often crave *pakoras,* deep-fried fritters from India. I wanted to get the same flavors but use a healthier cooking technique, so I made soup using all the classic spices and our favorite veggie, cauliflower!
—*Melody Johnson, Pulaski, WI*

- -

Prep: 20 min. • **Cook:** 20 min.
Makes: 8 servings (3 qt.)

1	large head cauliflower, cut into small florets
5	medium potatoes, peeled and diced
1	large onion, diced
4	medium carrots, peeled and diced
2	celery ribs, diced
1	carton (32 oz.) vegetable stock
1	tsp. garam masala
1	tsp. garlic powder
1	tsp. ground coriander
1	tsp. ground turmeric
1	tsp. ground cumin
1	tsp. pepper
1	tsp. salt
½	tsp. crushed red pepper flakes
	Water or additional vegetable stock
	Fresh cilantro leaves
	Lime wedges, optional

In a Dutch oven over medium-high heat, bring first 14 ingredients to a boil. Cook and stir until vegetables are tender, about 20 minutes. Remove from heat; cool slightly. Process in batches in a blender or food processor until smooth. Adjust consistency as desired with water or additional stock. Sprinkle with fresh cilantro. Serve hot, with lime wedges if desired.

Freeze option: Before adding cilantro, freeze cooled soup in freezer containers. To use, partially thaw in refrigerator overnight. Heat through in a saucepan, stirring occasionally; add water if necessary. Sprinkle with cilantro. If desired, serve with lime wedges.

Note: Look for garam masala in the spice aisle.

1½ cups: 135 cal., 1g fat (0 sat. fat), 0 chol., 645mg sod., 30g carb. (6g sugars, 5g fiber), 4g pro. **Diabetic exchanges:** 1½ starch, 1 vegetable.

CARIBBEAN FRUIT SOUP

This fruit soup is a delicious, refreshing way to begin a warm-weather meal. Jerk seasoning gives each spoonful a little kick of heat.

—Cheryl Perry, Hertford, NC

Prep: 35 min. + chilling
Makes: 12 servings (2 qt.)

- 1 cup each chopped peeled fresh peaches, nectarines, papaya and mango
- 1 cup cubed fresh pineapple
- 1 cup diced cantaloupe
- 1 cup chopped seeded peeled cucumber
- 1 cup chopped sweet red pepper
- ¼ cup thinly sliced green onions
- 2 cups frozen nonalcoholic pina colada mix, thawed
- 1 cup passion fruit or mango nectar
- ¼ cup minced fresh cilantro
- 2 Tbsp. plus 2 tsp. lime juice, divided
- 1 Tbsp. sugar
- 1 Tbsp. Caribbean jerk seasoning
- 1 tsp. salt
- 1 tsp. grated fresh gingerroot
- 1 tsp. minced seeded jalapeno pepper
- 2 medium bananas, sliced
- 1 cup sweetened shredded coconut

1. In a large bowl, combine the peaches, nectarines, papaya, mango, pineapple, cantaloupe, cucumber, red pepper and onions. Place half of fruit mixture in a blender or food processor; cover and process until smooth.

2. Transfer to a large bowl; stir in the remaining fruit mixture, pina colada mix, nectar, cilantro, 2 Tbsp. lime juice, sugar, jerk seasoning, salt, ginger and jalapeno. Cover and refrigerate for 3 hours or until chilled.

3. Toss bananas with remaining lime juice. Garnish soup with bananas and coconut.

⅔ cup: 237 cal., 6g fat (5g sat. fat), 0 chol., 304mg sod., 48g carb. (42g sugars, 3g fiber), 2g pro.

COCONUT CURRY VEGETABLE SOUP

I've been a vegetarian since high school, so modifying recipes to fit my meatless requirements is a challenge I enjoy. This rich and creamy soup is packed with nutrients!

—Carissa Sumner, Washington, DC

Prep: 15 min. • **Cook:** 25 min.
Makes: 6 servings

- 1 Tbsp. canola oil
- 2 celery ribs, chopped
- 2 medium carrots, chopped
- 6 garlic cloves, minced
- 1 Tbsp. minced fresh gingerroot
- 2 tsp. curry powder
- ½ tsp. ground turmeric
- 1 can (14½ oz.) vegetable broth
- 1 can (13.66 oz.) light coconut milk
- 1 medium potato (about 8 oz.), peeled and chopped
- ½ tsp. salt
- 1 pkg. (8.8 oz.) ready-to-serve brown rice
  Lime wedges, optional

1. In a large saucepan, heat oil over medium heat. Add celery and carrots; cook and stir 6-8 minutes or until tender. Add the garlic, ginger, curry powder and turmeric; cook 1 minute longer.

2. Add broth, coconut milk, potato and salt; bring to a boil. Reduce the heat; cook, uncovered, 10-15 minutes or until potato is tender. Meanwhile, heat rice according to package directions.

3. Stir rice into soup. If desired, serve with lime wedges.

¾ cup: 186 cal., 8g fat (4g sat. fat), 0 chol., 502mg sod., 22g carb. (3g sugars, 2g fiber), 3g pro. **Diabetic exchanges:** 1½ starch, 1½ fat.

OVER-THE-RAINBOW MINESTRONE

A rainbow of vegetables are featured in this lovely soup. You can use any multicolored pasta in place of the spirals.

—Crystal Schlueter, Northglenn, CO

Prep: 20 min. • **Cook:** 6 hours 20 minutes
Makes: 10 servings (3¾ qt.)

- 4 large stems Swiss chard (about ½ lb.)
- 2 Tbsp. olive oil
- 1 medium red onion, finely chopped
- 6 cups vegetable broth
- 2 cans (14½ oz. each) fire-roasted diced tomatoes, undrained
- 1 can (16 oz.) kidney beans, rinsed and drained
- 1 can (15 oz.) garbanzo beans or chickpeas, rinsed and drained
- 1 medium yellow summer squash or zucchini, halved and cut into ¼-in. slices
- 1 medium sweet red or yellow pepper, finely chopped
- 1 medium carrot, finely chopped
- 2 garlic cloves, minced
- 1½ cups uncooked spiral pasta
- ¼ cup prepared pesto

1. Cut stems from chard; chop stems and leaves separately. Reserve leaves for adding later. In a large skillet, heat oil over medium heat. Add onion and chard stems; cook and stir 3-5 minutes or until tender. Transfer to a 6-qt. slow cooker.

2. Stir in broth, tomatoes, kidney beans, garbanzo beans, squash, pepper, carrot and garlic. Cook, covered, on low 6-8 hours or until vegetables are tender.

3. Stir in pasta and reserved chard leaves. Cook, covered, on low 20-25 minutes longer or until pasta is tender. Serve with pesto.

1½ cups: 231 cal., 7g fat (1g sat. fat), 2mg chol., 1015mg sod., 34g carb. (7g sugars, 6g fiber), 9g pro.

SLOW-COOKED VEGETABLE WILD RICE SOUP

This thick and hearty soup is packed with colorful vegetables.

—*Thomas Faglon, Somerset, NJ*

Prep: 25 min. • **Cook:** 5 hours
Makes: 12 servings (3 qt.)

- 6 cups reduced-sodium vegetable broth
- 2 cans (14½ oz. each) fire-roasted diced tomatoes
- 2 celery ribs, sliced
- 2 medium carrots, chopped
- 1¾ cups sliced baby portobello mushrooms
- 1 medium onion, chopped
- 1 medium parsnip, peeled and chopped
- 1 medium sweet potato, peeled and cubed
- 1 medium green pepper, chopped
- 1 cup uncooked wild rice
- 2 garlic cloves, minced
- ¾ tsp. salt
- ¼ tsp. pepper
- 2 bay leaves
- 2 fresh thyme sprigs, plus more for topping

Combine all ingredients in a 6- or 7-qt. slow cooker. Cover and cook on high until rice and vegetables are tender, 5-6 hours. Discard bay leaves and thyme sprigs before serving. If desired, remove leaves from remaining thyme sprigs and sprinkle over soup when serving.

1 cup: 117 cal., 0 fat (0 sat. fat), 0 chol., 419mg sod., 25g carb. (7g sugars, 4g fiber), 4g pro.
Diabetic exchanges: 2 vegetable, 1 starch.

TEST KITCHEN TIP

There's a fair amount of chopping for this recipe, but the vegetables can be chopped in advance to reduce the time needed for last-minute prep.

HAZELNUT ASPARAGUS SOUP

My heart is happy when bundles of tender local asparagus start to appear at my grocery store in spring. No one would ever guess this restaurant-quality vegetarian soup can be prepared in less than 30 minutes.
—*Cindy Beberman, Orland Park, IL*

Prep: 20 min. • **Cook:** 15 min.
Makes: 4 servings (3 cups)

- 1 Tbsp. olive oil
- ½ cup chopped sweet onion
- 3 garlic cloves, sliced
  Dash crushed red pepper flakes
- 2½ cups cut fresh asparagus (about 1½ lbs.), trimmed
- 2 cups vegetable broth
- ⅓ cup whole hazelnuts, toasted
- 2 Tbsp. chopped fresh basil
- 2 Tbsp. lemon juice
- ½ cup unsweetened almond milk
- 2 tsp. reduced-sodium tamari soy sauce
- ¼ tsp. salt
  Shaved asparagus, optional

1. In a large saucepan, heat oil over medium heat. Add the onion, garlic and red pepper flakes; cook and stir until onion is softened, 4-5 minutes. Add asparagus and broth; bring to a boil. Reduce heat; simmer, covered, until asparagus is tender, 6-8 minutes. Remove from heat; cool slightly.

2. Place the nuts, basil and lemon juice in a blender. Add asparagus mixture. Process until smooth and creamy. Return to saucepan. Stir in almond milk, tamari sauce and salt. Heat through, taking care not to boil soup. If desired, top with shaved asparagus.

Note: To toast nuts, bake in a shallow pan in a 350° oven for 5-10 minutes or cook in a skillet over low heat until lightly browned, stirring occasionally.

Note: Reduced-sodium soy sauce may be used in place of the tamari soy sauce.

¾ cup: 164 cal., 13g fat (1g sat. fat), 0 chol., 623mg sod., 11g carb. (4g sugars, 4g fiber), 5g pro. **Diabetic exchanges:** 2½ fat, ½ starch.

SATISFYING TOMATO SOUP

After craving tomato soup, I decided to make my own. My sister Joan likes it chunky-style, so she doesn't puree hers. For fun, top the soup with chopped grilled cheese and basil.
—*Marian Brown, Mississauga, ON*

Takes: 30 min. • **Makes:** 4 servings

- 2 tsp. canola oil
- ¼ cup finely chopped onion
- ¼ cup finely chopped celery
- 2 cans (14½ oz. each) diced tomatoes, undrained
- 1½ cups water
- 2 tsp. brown sugar
- ½ tsp. salt
- ½ tsp. dried basil
- ¼ tsp. dried oregano
- ¼ tsp. coarsely ground pepper

1. In a large saucepan, heat oil over medium-high heat. Add onion and celery; cook and stir until tender, 2-4 minutes. Add remaining ingredients. Simmer, uncovered, 10 minutes to allow flavors to blend.

2. Puree soup using an immersion blender. Or cool soup slightly and puree in batches in a blender; return to pan and heat through.

Freeze option: Freeze cooled soup in freezer containers. To use, partially thaw in refrigerator overnight. Heat through in a saucepan, stirring occasionally; add water if necessary.

1¼ cups: 76 cal., 2g fat (0 sat. fat), 0 chol., 627mg sod., 13g carb. (9g sugars, 4g fiber), 2g pro. **Diabetic exchanges:** 2 vegetable, ½ fat.

VEGAN BUTTERNUT SQUASH SOUP

Apple and winter squash are the perfect pair in this cozy vegan soup. For a slightly different flavor that still features classic fall produce, substitute a ripe pear for the apple.
—Taste of Home *Test Kitchen*

Prep: 50 min. • **Cook:** 45 min.
Makes: 8 servings

- 1 large butternut squash (4 to 4½ lbs.)
- 1 medium onion, chopped
- 1 medium tart apple, peeled and coarsely chopped
- 1 Tbsp. olive oil
- 6 garlic cloves, minced
- 4 tsp. minced fresh thyme or 2 tsp. dried thyme
- ½ tsp. dried marjoram
- ¼ tsp. salt
- ¼ tsp. pepper
- 8 cups vegetable broth
- 1 tsp. cider vinegar
  Fresh thyme leaves and cracked black pepper, optional

1. Preheat oven to 400°. Cut squash in half lengthwise; discard seeds. Place squash, cut side down, in a greased 15x10x1-in. baking pan. Bake, uncovered, until tender, 45-60 minutes. Cool slightly. Scoop out flesh; set aside.

2. In a Dutch oven, cook onion and apple in oil until tender. Add garlic; cook 1 minute longer. Stir in the seasonings; cook until fragrant, about 10 seconds. Add broth and squash; bring to a boil. Reduce heat; simmer, uncovered, 15-20 minutes to allow flavors to blend. Cool slightly. In a blender, cover and process soup in batches until smooth.

3. Return pureed mixture to pan; cook and stir until heated through. If desired, garnish with thyme and black pepper.

1½ cups: 148 cal., 2g fat (0 sat. fat), 0 chol., 750mg sod., 33g carb. (10g sugars, 8g fiber), 3g pro.

MEAT LOVER OPTION
PAGE 320

 ## VEGAN CABBAGE SOUP

Comforting soups that simmer all day long are staple dishes for wintry days. For a heartier version, stir in canned cannellini or navy beans.
—Taste of Home *Test Kitchen*

Prep: 15 min. • **Cook:** 6 hours
Makes: 10 servings (2½ qt.)

- 4 cups vegetable stock
- 1 can (14 oz.) Italian diced tomatoes
- 1 can (6 oz.) tomato paste
- 1 small head cabbage (about 1½ lbs.), shredded
- 4 celery ribs, chopped
- 2 large carrots, chopped
- 1 medium onion, chopped
- 2 garlic cloves, minced
- 2 tsp. Italian seasoning
- ½ tsp. salt
  Fresh basil, optional

In a 5- or 6-qt. slow cooker, whisk together stock, diced tomatoes and tomato paste. Stir in vegetables, garlic and seasonings. Cook, covered, on low until vegetables are tender, 6-8 hours. If desired, top with fresh basil.

1 cup: 110 cal., 0 fat (0 sat. fat), 0 chol., 866mg sod., 24g carb. (13g sugars, 6g fiber), 4g pro.

MUSHROOM-BEAN BOURGUIGNON

In our family, boeuf bourguignon has been a staple for generations. And I wanted a meatless alternative. All this dish needs is a French baguette.
—*Sonya Labbe, West Hollywood, CA*

Prep: 15 min. • **Cook:** 1¼ hours
Makes: 10 servings (2½ qt.)

- 4 Tbsp. olive oil, divided
- 5 medium carrots, cut into 1-in. pieces
- 2 medium onions, halved and sliced
- 2 garlic cloves, minced
- 8 large portobello mushrooms, cut into 1-in. pieces
- 1 Tbsp. tomato paste
- 1 bottle (750 ml) dry red wine
- 2 cups mushroom broth or vegetable broth, divided
- 1 tsp. salt
- 1 tsp. minced fresh thyme or ½ tsp. dried thyme
- ½ tsp. pepper
- 2 cans (15½ oz. each) navy beans, rinsed and drained
- 1 pkg. (14.4 oz.) frozen pearl onions
- 3 Tbsp. all-purpose flour

1. In a Dutch oven, heat 2 Tbsp. oil over medium-high heat. Add carrots and onions; cook and stir 8-10 minutes or until onions are tender. Add garlic; cook 1 minute longer. Remove from pan.

2. In the same pan, heat 1 Tbsp. oil over medium-high heat. Add half the mushrooms; cook and stir until lightly browned. Remove from pan; repeat with remaining 1 Tbsp. oil and mushrooms.

3. Return all mushrooms to pan. Add tomato paste; cook and stir 1 minute. Stir in wine, 1½ cups broth, salt, thyme, pepper and carrot mixture; bring to a boil. Reduce heat; simmer, covered, 25 minutes.

4. Add beans and pearl onions; cook 30 minutes longer. In a small bowl, whisk flour and remaining broth until smooth; stir into pan. Bring to a boil; cook and stir until slightly thickened, about 2 minutes.

1 cup: 234 cal., 6g fat (1g sat. fat), 0 chol., 613mg sod., 33g carb. (6g sugars, 7g fiber), 9g pro. **Diabetic exchanges:** 2 starch, 2 vegetable, 1 lean meat, 1 fat.

HOW-TO

Fake a Meaty Flavor with Fond

- Browning tomato paste (as in the Mushroom-Bean Bourguignon recipe) is a classic way to create a rich brown sauce.
- After browning, deglaze with wine or broth and scrape up any browned bits (that's the fond) from the pan.

SO-EASY GAZPACHO

My daughter got this recipe from a friend
a few years ago. Now I serve it often as an
appetizer. It certainly is the talk of any party!
—*Lorna Sirtoli, Cortland, NY*

Prep: 15 min. + chilling • **Makes:** 5 servings

- 2 cups tomato juice
- 4 medium tomatoes, peeled
  and finely chopped
- ½ cup chopped seeded
  peeled cucumber
- ⅓ cup finely chopped onion
- ¼ cup olive oil
- ¼ cup cider vinegar
- 1 tsp. sugar
- 1 garlic clove, minced
- ¼ tsp. salt
- ¼ tsp. pepper

In a large bowl, combine all ingredients. Cover
and refrigerate until chilled, at least 4 hours.
1 cup: 146 cal., 11g fat (2g sat. fat), 0 chol.,
387mg sod., 11g carb. (8g sugars, 2g fiber),
2g pro. **Diabetic exchanges:** 2 vegetable, 2 fat.
Black Bean Zucchini Gazpacho: Substitute
2 large tomatoes for the 4 medium. Add
1 can (15 oz.) drained rinsed black beans,
2 chopped medium zucchini and ¼ tsp.
cayenne pepper.

5i COCONUT CURRY CAULIFLOWER SOUP

When I'm in need of comfort food, I stir up a velvety batch of this Asian-spiced soup. Then I finish it with a sprinkle of cilantro over the top.

—Elizabeth DeHart, West Jordan, UT

- -

Prep: 10 min. • **Cook:** 25 min.
Makes: 10 servings (2½ qt.)

- 2 Tbsp. olive oil
- 1 medium onion, finely chopped
- 3 Tbsp. yellow curry paste
- 2 medium heads cauliflower, broken into florets
- 1 carton (32 oz.) vegetable broth
- 1 cup coconut milk
  Minced fresh cilantro, optional

1. In a large saucepan, heat oil over medium heat. Add onion; cook and stir until softened, 2-3 minutes. Add curry paste; cook until fragrant, 1-2 minutes. Add cauliflower and broth. Increase heat to high; bring to a boil. Reduce heat to medium-low; cook, covered, about 20 minutes.
2. Stir in coconut milk; cook an additional minute. Remove from heat; cool slightly. Puree in batches in a blender or food processor. If desired, top with minced fresh cilantro.
1 cup: 111 cal., 8g fat (5g sat. fat), 0 chol., 532mg sod., 10g carb. (4g sugars, 3g fiber), 3g pro.

GOLDEN BEET & PEACH SOUP WITH TARRAGON

We had a bumper crop of peaches from our two trees this summer, and I've been having fun experimenting with different recipes. After seeing a beet soup recipe in a cookbook, I changed it up a bit to include our homegrown golden beets and to suit my family's tastes.

—*Sue Gronholz, Beaver Dam, WI*

- -

Prep: 20 min. • **Bake:** 40 min. + chilling
Makes: 6 servings

- 2 lbs. fresh golden beets, peeled and cut into 1-in. cubes
- 1 Tbsp. olive oil
- 2 cups white grape-peach juice
- 2 Tbsp. cider vinegar
- ¼ cup plain Greek yogurt
- ¼ tsp. finely chopped fresh tarragon
- 2 medium fresh peaches, peeled and diced
  Additional fresh tarragon sprigs

1. Preheat oven to 400°. Place beets in a 15x10x1-in. baking pan. Drizzle with oil; toss to coat. Roast until tender, 40-45 minutes. Cool slightly.

2. Transfer beets to a blender or food processor. Add juice and vinegar; process until smooth. Refrigerate at least 1 hour. In a small bowl, combine Greek yogurt and tarragon; refrigerate.

3. To serve, divide the beet mixture among individual bowls; place a spoonful of yogurt mixture into each bowl. Top with diced peaches and additional tarragon.

⅔ cup: 159 cal., 4g fat (1g sat. fat), 3mg chol., 129mg sod., 31g carb. (26g sugars, 4g fiber), 3g pro. **Diabetic exchanges:** 2 vegetable, 1 fruit, ½ fat.

TEST KITCHEN TIP

For a whole different taste sensation, substitute ½ tsp. chopped fresh basil, thyme or chives for the tarragon. If you prefer, the herb of your choice may be blended with the beets rather than mixed with the yogurt.

❄ 🍲 PRESSURE-COOKER GREEK-STYLE SOUP

This is a nice warming soup on a chilly day. Lentils are so good for you, too!

—Mary E. Smith, Columbia, MO

Prep: 20 min. • **Cook:** 15 min. + releasing
Makes: 12 servings (3 qt.)

- 4 cups water
- 4 cups vegetable broth
- 2 cups dried lentils, rinsed
- 2 medium carrots, chopped
- 1 small onion, chopped
- 1 celery rib, chopped
- 2 garlic cloves, minced
- 1 tsp. dried oregano
- 1 cup chopped fresh spinach
- ½ cup tomato sauce
- 1 can (2¼ oz.) sliced ripe olives, drained
- 3 Tbsp. red wine vinegar
- ½ tsp. salt
- ¼ tsp. pepper
  Optional toppings: Chopped red onion, chopped parsley and lemon wedges

1. Place water, broth, lentils, carrots, onion, celery, garlic and oregano in a 6-qt. electric pressure cooker. Lock lid; close pressure-release valve. Adjust to pressure cook on high for 15 minutes. Let pressure release naturally for 10 minutes; quick-release any remaining pressure.

2. Stir in spinach, tomato sauce, olives, vinegar, salt and pepper. If desired, serve with red onion, parsley and lemon wedges.

Freeze option: Freeze cooled soup in freezer containers. To use, partially thaw soup in refrigerator overnight. Heat through in a saucepan, stirring occasionally; add broth if necessary.

1 cup: 134 cal., 1g fat (0 sat. fat), 0 chol., 420mg sod., 24g carb. (2g sugars, 4g fiber), 9g pro. **Diabetic exchanges:** 1½ starch, 1 lean meat.

🍲 SPICY LENTIL & CHICKPEA STEW

This recipe came to me from a friend and former co-worker at a health food store. I changed a few things until I found a version that my family loves. My son doesn't like things too spicy, so I make the stew milder for him and add a sprinkle of extra spice in mine. My husband, who farms, works outdoors for long hours at a time and finds this soup hearty enough to keep him satisfied.

—Melanie MacFarlane, Bedeque, PE

Prep: 25 min. • **Cook:** 8 hours
Makes: 8 servings (2¾ qt.)

- 2 tsp. olive oil
- 1 medium onion, thinly sliced
- 1 tsp. dried oregano
- ½ tsp. crushed red pepper flakes
- 2 cans (15 oz. each) chickpeas or garbanzo beans, rinsed and drained
- 1 cup dried lentils, rinsed
- 1 can (2¼ oz.) sliced ripe olives, drained
- 3 tsp. smoked paprika
- 4 cups vegetable broth
- 4 cans (8 oz. each) no-salt-added tomato sauce
- 4 cups fresh baby spinach
- ¾ cup fat-free plain yogurt

1. In a small skillet, heat oil over medium-high heat. Add the onion, oregano and pepper flakes; cook and stir until the onion is tender, 8-10 minutes. Transfer to a 5- or 6-qt. slow cooker.

2. Add chickpeas, lentils, olives and paprika; stir in broth and tomato sauce. Cook, covered, on low 8-10 hours, until lentils are tender. Stir in spinach. Top each serving with yogurt.

1⅓ cups: 266 cal., 4g fat (0 sat. fat), 0 chol., 712mg sod., 45g carb. (11g sugars, 10g fiber), 14g pro. **Diabetic exchanges:** 2 starch, 2 vegetable, 1 lean meat.

FRENCH ONION SOUP FOR 2

I adapted a basic recipe to copy the onion soup served at my favorite restaurant. No matter what my entree, I always ordered the soup. Now I can make it at home. It's a meal in itself or an impressive beginning to a full-course meal.

—Barbara Brunner, Steelton, PA

Prep: 55 min. • **Bake:** 10 min.
Makes: 2 servings

- 2 medium onions, chopped
- 1 tsp. sugar
- 6 Tbsp. butter, divided
- 1 Tbsp. all-purpose flour
- ⅛ tsp. pepper
  Dash ground nutmeg
- 2½ cups reduced-sodium beef or vegetable broth
- 2 Tbsp. grated Parmesan cheese
- 2 slices French bread (1 in. thick)
- 4 slices provolone cheese

1. In a large saucepan, saute onions and sugar in 3 Tbsp. butter until golden brown. Stir in the flour, pepper and nutmeg until blended. Gradually stir in broth. Bring to a boil; cook and stir for 2 minutes. Reduce heat; cover and simmer for 30 minutes. Stir in the Parmesan cheese.

2. Meanwhile, in a large skillet, melt remaining butter; add bread. Cook until golden brown on both sides. Ladle soup into 2 ovenproof bowls. Place a slice of cheese in each bowl; top with bread and remaining cheese. Bake at 375° until the cheese is bubbly, about 10 minutes.

1 serving: 633 cal., 47g fat (30g sat. fat), 131mg chol., 1472mg sod., 34g carb. (9g sugars, 3g fiber), 19g pro.

READER RAVE

"Love this! I tried this French onion soup several years ago, and it's the recipe I keep coming back to. Instead of nutmeg, I use a dash of apple pie spice. I'm certain that's what makes this soup outstanding."

—THISHUNGERING, TASTEOFHOME.COM

🥘 PRESSURE-COOKER LENTIL PUMPKIN SOUP

Plenty of herbs and spices brighten up my hearty pumpkin soup. It's just the thing we need on nippy days and nights.
—*Laura Magee, Houlton, WI*

Prep: 10 min. • **Cook:** 15 min. + releasing
Makes: 6 servings (2¼ qt.)

- 1 lb. medium red potatoes (about 4 medium), cut into ½-in. pieces
- 1 can (15 oz.) canned pumpkin
- 1 cup dried lentils, rinsed
- 1 medium onion, chopped
- 3 garlic cloves, minced
- ½ tsp. ground ginger
- ½ tsp. pepper
- ⅛ tsp. salt
- 2 cans (14½ oz. each) vegetable broth
- 1½ cups water
  Minced fresh cilantro, optional

In a 6-qt. electric pressure cooker, combine the first 10 ingredients. Lock the lid; close pressure-release valve. Adjust to pressure-cook on high for 12 minutes. Let pressure release naturally for 10 minutes; quick-release any remaining pressure. If desired, sprinkle servings with cilantro.

1½ cups: 210 cal., 1g fat (0 sat. fat), 0 chol., 463mg sod., 42g carb. (5g sugars, 7g fiber), 11g pro. **Diabetic exchanges:** 3 starch, 1 lean meat.

Health tip: If lentils aren't in your regular meal rotation, they should be. They're easy on the budget at about $1.50 for a 16-oz. package, and they're packed with fiber, protein, B vitamins and more.

FENNEL CARROT SOUP

This smooth, richly colored soup makes a wonderful first course for a holiday dinner. The fennel seed and curry complement the carrots, apple and sweet potato.

—*Marlene Bursey, Waverly, NS*

Prep: 10 min. • **Cook:** 45 min.
Makes: 8 servings

- 1 Tbsp. butter
- ½ tsp. fennel seed
- 1½ lbs. carrots, sliced
- 1 medium sweet potato, peeled and cubed
- 1 medium apple, peeled and cubed
- 3 cans (14½ oz. each) vegetable broth
- 2 Tbsp. uncooked long grain rice
- 1 bay leaf
- ¼ tsp. curry powder
- 1 Tbsp. lemon juice
- 1 tsp. salt
- ¼ tsp. white pepper
- 2 Tbsp. minced fresh parsley

1. In a large saucepan, melt butter over medium-high heat. Add fennel; cook and stir 2-3 minutes or until lightly toasted. Add carrots, sweet potato and apple; cook and stir 5 minutes longer.
2. Stir in the broth, rice, bay leaf and curry powder; bring to a boil. Reduce heat; simmer, covered, 30 minutes or until vegetables and rice are soft.
3. Remove from heat; cool slightly. Discard bay leaf. Process in batches in a blender until smooth; return to pan. Stir in the lemon juice, salt and pepper. Cook over medium heat 5 minutes or until heated through, stirring occasionally. Sprinkle with parsley.
1 cup: 102 cal., 2g fat (1g sat. fat), 4mg chol., 674mg sod., 20g carb. (9g sugars, 4g fiber), 2g pro. **Diabetic exchanges:** 2 vegetable, 1 starch.

BLACK BEAN-TOMATO CHILI

My daughter Kayla saw a black bean chili while watching a cooking show and called me about it because it looked so good. We messed with our own recipe until we created this easy winner.

—*Lisa Belcastro, Vineyard Haven, MA*

Prep: 10 min. • **Cook:** 35 min.
Makes: 6 servings (2¼ qt.)

- 2 Tbsp. olive oil
- 1 large onion, chopped
- 1 medium green pepper, chopped
- 3 garlic cloves, minced
- 1 tsp. ground cinnamon
- 1 tsp. ground cumin
- 1 tsp. chili powder
- ¼ tsp. pepper
- 3 cans (14½ oz. each) diced tomatoes, undrained
- 2 cans (15 oz. each) black beans, rinsed and drained
- 1 cup orange juice or juice from 3 medium oranges

1. In a Dutch oven, heat oil over medium-high heat. Add onion and green pepper; cook and stir 8-10 minutes or until tender. Add garlic and seasonings; cook 1 minute longer.
2. Stir in the remaining ingredients; bring to a boil. Reduce heat; simmer, covered, 20-25 minutes to allow flavors to blend, stirring chili occasionally.
1½ cups: 232 cal., 5g fat (1g sat. fat), 0 chol., 608mg sod., 39g carb. (13g sugars, 10g fiber), 9g pro. **Diabetic exchanges:** 2 vegetable, 1½ starch, 1 lean meat, 1 fat.

VEGETABLE LENTIL SOUP

Here's a healthy soup that's ideal for vegetarians and those watching their weight. Butternut squash and lentils make it filling, while herbs and other veggies round out the flavor.

—*Mark Morgan, Waterford, WI*

Prep: 15 min. • **Cook:** 4½ hours
Makes: 6 servings (about 2 qt.)

- 3 cups cubed peeled butternut squash
- 1 cup chopped carrots
- 1 cup chopped onion
- 1 cup dried lentils, rinsed
- 2 garlic cloves, minced
- 1 tsp. dried oregano
- 1 tsp. dried basil
- 4 cups vegetable broth
- 1 can (14½ oz.) Italian diced tomatoes, undrained
- 2 cups frozen cut green beans (about 8 oz.)

1. Place the first 8 ingredients in a 5-qt. slow cooker. Cook, covered, on low until lentils are tender, about 4 hours.

2. Stir in tomatoes and beans. Cook, covered, on high until heated through, about 30 minutes.

1⅓ cups: 217 cal., 1g fat (0 sat. fat), 0 chol., 685mg sod., 45g carb. (11g sugars, 8g fiber), 11g pro.

VEGAN CREAM OF MUSHROOM SOUP

I love mushrooms and am learning how to make heartier dishes out of my old favorites. This delicious vegan mushroom soup is low in fat and high in nutrition, and it meets my dietary restrictions.

—Maria Davis, Flower Mound, TX

Prep: 30 min. • **Cook:** 45 min.
Makes: 8 servings

- 1 lb. sliced baby portobello mushrooms
- ½ lb. fresh oyster mushrooms, sliced
- 2 Tbsp. soy sauce
- 4 cups water
- 5 medium carrots, halved
- 5 celery ribs, halved
- 1 medium onion, quartered
- 2 bay leaves
- 2 tsp. dried thyme
- 1 Tbsp. lemon juice
- ¾ tsp. salt
- ¼ tsp. pepper
- ⅛ tsp. cayenne pepper
- 2 cups vegetable broth
- 2 pkg. (1 oz. each) dried shiitake mushrooms
- 1 pkg. (12.3 oz.) silken firm tofu
- 4 green onions, chopped

1. In a large microwave-safe bowl, combine portobello mushrooms, oyster mushrooms and soy sauce. Cover and microwave on high for 5 minutes. Let stand 5 minutes. Strain liquid into a large stockpot, leaving mushrooms in bowl. Add the water, carrots, celery, onion, bay leaves and thyme to stockpot. Bring to a boil over medium-high heat. Reduce heat; simmer, uncovered, 30 minutes. Strain and discard vegetables from stockpot. Return liquid to pot. Stir in lemon juice, salt, pepper and cayenne pepper.

2. In another large microwave-safe bowl, heat 2 cups vegetable broth almost to a boil. Add dried mushrooms and let stand until softened, 2-3 minutes. Strain liquid into stockpot, reserving ½ cup. Combine the reconstituted mushrooms with portobello and oyster mushrooms. Spoon half of mushrooms into stockpot. Spoon the remaining mushrooms into a blender; add tofu and reserved broth. Cover and blend until smooth; stir into stockpot. Cook and stir until heated through. Sprinkle with green onions.

¾ cup: 85 cal., 2g fat (0 sat. fat), 0 chol., 574mg sod., 10g carb. (3g sugars, 3g fiber), 9g pro. **Diabetic exchanges:** 1 lean meat, 1 vegetable.

CHICKPEA TORTILLA SOUP

This vegan tortilla soup recipe is healthy, satisfying and so family-friendly! We love how hearty and flavorful it is. We like to play around with the different toppings we add each time it's served.

—*Julie Peterson, Crofton, MD*

Takes: 30 min. • **Makes:** 8 servings (3 qt.)

- 1 Tbsp. olive oil
- 1 medium red onion, chopped
- 4 garlic cloves, minced
- 1 to 2 jalapeno peppers, seeded and chopped, optional
- ¼ tsp. pepper
- 8 cups vegetable broth
- 1 cup red quinoa, rinsed
- 2 cans (15 oz. each) no-salt-added chickpeas or garbanzo beans, rinsed and drained
- 1 can (15 oz.) no-salt-added black beans, rinsed and drained
- 3 medium tomatoes, chopped
- 1 cup fresh or frozen corn
- ⅓ cup minced fresh cilantro
  Optional ingredients: Crushed tortilla chips, cubed avocado, lime wedges and additional chopped cilantro

Heat oil in a Dutch oven over medium-high heat. Add the red onion, garlic, jalapeno if desired, and pepper; cook and stir until tender, 3-5 minutes. Add the broth and quinoa. Bring to a boil; reduce heat. Simmer, uncovered, until quinoa is tender, about 10 minutes. Add the chickpeas, beans, tomatoes, corn and cilantro; heat through. If desired, serve with optional ingredients.

1½ cups: 289 cal., 5g fat (0 sat. fat), 0 chol., 702mg sod., 48g carb. (5g sugars, 9g fiber), 13g pro.

TEST KITCHEN TIP

You'll love how hearty and filling this is for a meatless soup. Don't skip the lime wedges—the little bit of acid really perks up the flavor of the soup.

CURRIED VEGETABLE SOUP

I created this recipe using frozen veggies to save time. It's easy to scale up for a crowd. I usually prepare enough to make sure there are leftovers. For a buffet, keep this soup warm in a slow cooker and set yogurt out in a separate dish to let guests serve themselves.
—*Heather Demeritte, Scottsdale, AZ*

Prep: 10 min. • **Cook:** 25 min.
Makes: 6 servings (2 qt.)

- 1 Tbsp. canola oil
- 2 garlic cloves, minced
- 1 pkg. (16 oz.) frozen broccoli florets
- 1 pkg. (16 oz.) frozen cauliflower
- 5 cups vegetable broth
- 2 tsp. curry powder
- ½ tsp. salt
- ½ tsp. pepper
- ⅛ tsp. ground nutmeg
  Plain Greek yogurt, optional

1. In a 6-qt. stockpot, heat oil over medium heat. Add garlic; cook and stir 1 minute or until fragrant. Add remaining ingredients except yogurt; bring to a boil. Reduce heat; simmer, covered, 8-10 minutes or until vegetables are tender.
2. Remove soup from heat; cool slightly. Process in batches in a blender until smooth; return to pot and heat through. If desired, top with yogurt to serve.

1⅓ cups: 84 cal., 3g fat (0 sat. fat), 0 chol., 793mg sod., 10g carb. (4g sugars, 4g fiber), 4g pro.

VEGAN CARROT SOUP

Yukon Gold potatoes—instead of cream—make a smooth carrot soup vegan and add a mild sweetness. If you don't have Yukon Golds on hand, russet potatoes will work, too.

—Taste of Home *Test Kitchen*

Takes: 30 min. • **Makes:** 6 servings

- 1   medium onion, chopped
- 2   celery ribs, chopped
- 1   Tbsp. canola oil
- 4   cups vegetable broth
- 1   lb. carrots, sliced
- 2   large Yukon Gold potatoes, peeled and cubed
- 1   tsp. salt
- ¼   tsp. pepper
      Fresh cilantro leaves, optional

1. In a large saucepan, saute onion and celery in oil until tender. Add the broth, carrots and potatoes; bring to a boil. Reduce heat; cover and simmer for 15-20 minutes or until the vegetables are tender. Remove from the heat; cool slightly.
2. Transfer to a blender; cover and process until blended. Return to pan; stir in salt and pepper. Heat through. If desired, sprinkle with cilantro.
1 cup: 176 cal., 3g fat (0 sat. fat), 0 chol., 710mg sod., 35g carb. (7g sugars, 4g fiber), 4g pro. **Diabetic exchanges:** 2 starch, ½ fat.

TEST KITCHEN TIP

Most people think you need to peel carrots before using them, but you don't! Save yourself the extra step and just give them a good scrub as you would any other fresh produce.

MEAT LOVER OPTION PAGE 320

CHUNKY VEGETARIAN CHILI

This robust chili teams rice and beans with a variety of colorful vegetables. The recipe makes a hearty meatless meal.

—Taste of Home *Test Kitchen*

Prep: 20 min. • **Cook:** 25 min.
Makes: 11 servings (2¾ qt.)

- 1   medium green pepper, chopped
- 1   medium onion, chopped
- 3   garlic cloves, minced
- 1   Tbsp. canola oil
- 2   cans (14½ oz. each) Mexican-style stewed tomatoes, undrained
- 1   can (16 oz.) kidney beans, rinsed and drained
- 1   can (15 oz.) pinto beans, rinsed and drained
- 1   can (11 oz.) whole kernel corn, drained
- 2½ cups water
- 1   cup uncooked long grain rice
- 1   to 2 Tbsp. chili powder
- 1½ tsp. ground cumin

In a Dutch oven, saute the green pepper, onion and garlic in oil until tender. Stir in all remaining ingredients; bring to a boil. Reduce heat; cover and simmer until rice is cooked, stirring occasionally, 25-30 minutes. If thinner chili is desired, add more water.
1 cup: 196 cal., 2g fat (0 sat. fat), 0 chol., 424mg sod., 37g carb. (6g sugars, 6g fiber), 7g pro. **Diabetic exchanges:** 2½ starch.

BOW TIE & SPINACH
SALAD, PAGE 202

SIDES & SALADS

Round out any meal with simple weeknight sides, smoky grilled vegetables or a holiday-season casserole. Plus, you'll love the scrumptious salads perfect for warm-weather dining.

⑤ 🕐 SHREDDED GINGERED BRUSSELS SPROUTS

Even people who normally don't care for Brussels sprouts will ask for a second helping of these.
—*James Schend, Pleasant Prairie, WI*

- -

Takes: 25 min. • **Makes:** 6 servings

- 1 lb. fresh Brussels sprouts (about 5½ cups)
- 1 Tbsp. olive oil
- 1 small onion, finely chopped
- 1 Tbsp. minced fresh gingerroot
- 1 garlic clove, minced
- ½ tsp. salt
- 2 Tbsp. water
- ¼ tsp. pepper

1. Trim Brussels sprouts. Cut sprouts lengthwise in half, then cut crosswise into thin slices.

2. Place a large skillet over medium-high heat. Add the Brussels sprouts; cook and stir until sprouts begin to brown lightly, 2-3 minutes. Add oil and toss to coat. Stir in onion, ginger, garlic and salt. Add water; reduce heat to medium and cook, covered, until vegetables are tender, 1-2 minutes. Stir in pepper.

¾ cup: 56 cal., 2g fat (0 sat. fat), 0 chol., 214mg sod., 8g carb. (2g sugars, 3g fiber), 2g pro. **Diabetic exchanges:** 1 vegetable, ½ fat.

Molasses-Sriracha Sprouts: Add 1 Tbsp. molasses and 2 tsp. sriracha to the water and cook as directed.

Sesame-Ginger Sprouts: Substitute toasted sesame oil for the olive oil and proceed as directed. Sprinkle 1 Tbsp. toasted sesame seeds over cooked sprouts before serving.

Cranberry-Pecan Sprouts: Add ¼ cup dried cranberries with the onion and ginger. Cook as directed; sprinkle with 2 Tbsp. chopped toasted pecans before serving.

Curry Sprouts: Add 1 tsp. curry powder with the onion and ginger; cook as directed.

❋ 🍲 SLOW-COOKER POTLUCK BEANS

It was the morning of our family potluck and I still needed something to bring. I threw together this recipe while drinking my morning coffee. By the end of the gathering, the beans were all gone and someone had even washed my crock for me!
—*Mary Anne Thygesen, Portland, OR*

- -

Prep: 10 min. • **Cook:** 4 hours
Makes: 12 servings

- 1 cup brewed coffee
- ½ cup packed brown sugar
- ¼ cup spicy brown mustard
- 2 Tbsp. molasses
- 2 cans (16 oz. each) butter beans
- 2 cans (16 oz. each) kidney beans
- 2 cans (16 oz. each) navy beans

In a greased 3- or 4-qt. slow cooker, mix the first 4 ingredients. Rinse and drain beans; stir into coffee mixture. Cook, covered, on low until flavors are blended, 4-5 hours.

Freeze option: Freeze cooled beans in freezer containers. To use, partially thaw in refrigerator overnight. Heat through in a covered saucepan, stirring occasionally; add water if necessary.

½ cup: 243 cal., 0 fat (0 sat. fat), 0 chol., 538mg sod., 50g carb. (13g sugars, 10g fiber), 14g pro.

🅕 ACORN SQUASH SLICES

Acorn squash is a favorite with my family. This recipe has a sweet maple flavor and an appealing nuttiness from pecans. It's easy, too, because you don't have to peel the squash.
—*Richard Lamb, Williamsburg, IN*

Prep: 15 min. • **Bake:** 40 min.
Makes: 6 servings

- 2 medium acorn squash (about 1½ lbs. each)
- ½ tsp. salt
- ¾ cup maple syrup
- 2 Tbsp. butter, melted
- ⅓ cup chopped pecans, optional

1. Cut squash in half lengthwise; remove and discard seeds and membrane. Cut each half widthwise into ½-in. slices; discard ends.
2. Place slices in a greased 13x9-in. baking dish. Sprinkle with salt. Combine syrup and butter; pour over squash. Sprinkle with pecans if desired.
3. Cover and bake at 350° for 40-45 minutes or until tender.

3 slices: 170 cal., 7g fat (0 sat. fat), 0 chol., 98mg sod., 31g carb. (0 sugars, 0 fiber), 2g pro. **Diabetic exchanges:** 1 starch, 1 fruit, 1 fat.

DID YOU KNOW?

North America's top maple-syrup producer—by far—is the Canadian province of Quebec. Directly north of Vermont, Quebec produces an astounding amount of syrup each year: 7,989,000 gallons. Vermont is runner-up with 890,000 gallons, followed by Canada's Ontario and New York and Maine in the U.S.

MEATLESS TACO SALAD

This colorful salad blends together all your favorite taco ingredients—minus the ground beef. And you won't miss the meat at all! The guacamole dressing is thick and creamy.
—*Kimberly Dray, Pflugerville, TX*

MEAT LOVER OPTION PAGE 320

Takes: 20 min. • **Makes:** 2 servings

- ⅓ cup guacamole
- ¼ cup sour cream
- 2 Tbsp. chopped green pepper
- 1 Tbsp. chopped green onions
- 1 Tbsp. prepared Italian salad dressing
- ¼ tsp. chili powder
- ¼ tsp. pepper
- 3 cups shredded lettuce
- 8 cherry tomatoes, halved
- ½ cup canned kidney beans, rinsed and drained
- ¼ cup sliced ripe olives
- ½ cup crushed corn chips
- ½ cup shredded cheddar cheese

In a small bowl, combine the first 7 ingredients; set aside. In a large bowl, combine the lettuce, tomatoes, beans and olives. Arrange lettuce mixture on a serving plate; top with guacamole mixture. Sprinkle with corn chips and cheese.

1 serving: 486 cal., 33g fat (12g sat. fat), 35mg chol., 849mg sod., 34g carb. (7g sugars, 9g fiber), 16g pro.

HOW-TO

Keep That Guac Green

Yes, you can make your guac ahead of time and keep it nice and green. Just use a thin layer of water to banish browning. Here's how:

- In an airtight container, use a spoon to flatten the surface of the guacamole and remove any air pockets.
- Slowly pour in about ½ in. water to cover the surface, using the spoon to gently disperse the water.
- Refrigerate, covered, up to 2 days. To serve, carefully pour off water, stir guacamole and enjoy.

SIMPLE LEMON PARSLEY POTATOES

For a simply delicious side dish, I often prepare these potatoes. I like that there are only a few ingredients and that it all goes from stove to table in so little time.
—*Dorothy Pritchett, Wills Point, TX*

Takes: 20 min. • **Makes:** 12 servings

> 3 lbs. small new red potatoes, quartered
> ½ cup butter, melted
> 3 Tbsp. lemon juice
> 3 Tbsp. minced fresh parsley

Cook potatoes in boiling salted water until tender, about 15 minutes; drain. Combine butter, lemon juice and parsley; pour over the potatoes and stir gently to coat.
¾ cup: 150 cal., 8g fat (5g sat. fat), 20mg chol., 84mg sod., 18g carb. (1g sugars, 2g fiber), 2g pro.

VEGAN QUINOA SALAD

Toasting the grain before it simmers isn't essential, but it does add a pleasant nuttiness to the flavor of this salad. Mix and match whatever fresh herbs and veggies you have on hand.
—Taste of Home *Test Kitchen*

Takes: 30 min. • **Makes:** 6 cups

- 1½ cups quinoa, rinsed and well drained
- 3 cups water
- ¼ cup plus 2 Tbsp. olive oil
- 1 Tbsp. grated lemon zest
- ¼ cup lemon juice
- 4 garlic cloves, minced
- 6 Tbsp. minced fresh parsley
- 6 Tbsp. minced fresh mint
- 1½ tsp. salt
- 1 cup cherry tomatoes, halved
- 2 mini cucumbers, sliced
- 1 medium sweet red pepper, chopped
- ½ cup chopped red onion

1. In a large saucepan, cook and stir quinoa over medium-high heat 3-5 minutes or until toasted. Add water; bring to a boil. Reduce heat; simmer, covered, 12-15 minutes or until liquid is absorbed. Transfer to a large bowl. Cool slightly.
2. In a small bowl, whisk the oil, lemon zest, lemon juice, garlic, parsley, mint and salt. Add the vegetables to quinoa; drizzle with dressing and toss to combine. Cover and refrigerate until ready to serve.

¾ cup: 227 cal., 12g fat (2g sat. fat), 0 chol., 449mg sod., 25g carb. (3g sugars, 3g fiber), 5g pro. **Diabetic exchanges:** 2 fat, 1½ starch.

SPICY GRILLED BROCCOLI

My kids eat this spiced broccoli without cheese; it's that good. It transports easily to the beach, the park or tailgate parties and also works great on an indoor grill.
—*Kathy Lewis-Martinez, Spring Valley, CA*

Prep: 20 min. + standing • **Grill:** 10 min.
Makes: 6 servings

- 2 bunches broccoli

MARINADE
- ½ cup olive oil
- ¼ cup cider vinegar
- 1 tsp. onion powder
- 1 tsp. garlic powder
- 1 tsp. smoked paprika
- ½ tsp. salt
- ½ tsp. crushed red pepper flakes
- ¼ tsp. pepper

1. Cut each broccoli bunch into 6 pieces. In a 6-qt. stockpot, place a steamer basket over 1 in. of water. Place broccoli in basket. Bring water to a boil. Reduce heat to maintain a simmer; steam, covered, 4-6 minutes or until crisp-tender.
2. In a large bowl, whisk marinade ingredients until blended. Add broccoli; gently toss to coat. Let stand, covered, 15 minutes.
3. Drain broccoli, reserving marinade. Grill broccoli, covered, over medium heat or broil 4 in. from heat 6-8 minutes or until broccoli is tender, turning once. If desired, serve with reserved marinade.

2 pieces : 122 cal., 6g fat (1g sat. fat), 0 chol., 135mg sod., 15g carb. (4g sugars, 6g fiber), 6g pro. **Diabetic exchanges:** 2 vegetable, 1 fat.

🟢🔵 MINTY PEAS & ONIONS

Mother always relied on peas and onions when she was in a hurry and needed a quick side. Besides being easy to prepare, this dish was loved by everyone in our family. It was handed down to my mother by my grandmother.

—Santa D'Addario, Jacksonville, FL

Takes: 20 min. • **Makes:** 8 servings

- 2 large onions, cut into ½-in. wedges
- ½ cup chopped sweet red pepper
- 2 Tbsp. vegetable oil
- 2 pkg. (16 oz. each) frozen peas
- 2 Tbsp. minced fresh mint
  or 2 tsp. dried mint

In a large skillet, saute onions and red pepper in oil until onions just begin to soften. Add peas; cook, uncovered, stirring occasionally, for 10 minutes or until heated through. Stir in mint and cook for 1 minute.

1 serving: 134 cal., 4g fat (1g sat. fat), 0 chol., 128mg sod., 19g carb. (9g sugars, 6g fiber), 6g pro. **Diabetic exchanges:** 1 starch, 1 fat.

VEGAN GREEN BEAN CASSEROLE

Now everyone can enjoy this classic Thanksgiving side. Just a few small tweaks make this a vegan casserole, but no one will know the difference!
—Taste of Home *Test Kitchen*

Prep: 15 min. • **Bake:** 25 min.
Makes: 16 servings

- 8 oz. sliced fresh mushrooms
- 1 medium onion, chopped
- 2 tsp. olive oil
- 3 garlic cloves, minced
- 3 cups dairy-free sour cream
  Browning sauce, optional
- 1 tsp. salt
- ½ tsp. ground black pepper
- 3 pkg. (12 oz. each) frozen cut green beans, thawed
- 4 cups shredded dairy-free cheddar-flavored cheese
- ¼ cup dairy-free buttery spread
- 1 cup crushed Ritz crackers
- 1 cup french-fried onions, coarsely chopped

1. Preheat oven to 350°. In a large skillet, saute mushrooms and onion in oil over medium heat until tender. Add garlic; cook and stir 1 minute. Stir in the sour cream, browning sauce if desired, salt and pepper until blended. Add green beans and cheese; stir to coat. Transfer to a greased 13x9-in. baking dish.
2. In a small bowl, melt buttery spread. Stir in crushed crackers and fried onions; sprinkle over the casserole. Bake until bubbly and top is golden brown, 25-30 minutes.
¾ cup: 327 cal., 23g fat (11g sat. fat), 0 chol., 944mg sod., 26g carb. (2g sugars, 2g fiber), 3g pro.

❄ 🍲 SLOW-COOKER VEGAN BAKED BEANS

This vegan version of baked beans doesn't need an oven. The slow cooker makes it the ultimate hands-off party dish.
—Taste of Home *Test Kitchen*

Prep: 10 min. + soaking • **Cook:** 9 hours
Makes: 8 servings

- 1 lb. dried navy beans
- 2 cups water
- 1 medium onion, chopped
- ½ cup molasses
- ⅓ cup packed brown sugar
- 2 Tbsp. ketchup
- 2 tsp. ground mustard
- ½ tsp. liquid smoke, optional
- ½ tsp. salt
- ½ tsp. pepper
- ¼ tsp. ground nutmeg
- ¼ tsp. ground cloves

1. Sort beans and rinse in cold water. Place beans in a large bowl; add enough water to cover by 2 in. Let stand, covered, overnight.
2. Drain and rinse beans, discarding liquid. Transfer the beans to a greased 3-qt. slow cooker. In a small bowl, combine remaining ingredients. Stir into slow cooker.
3. Cook, covered, on low 9-10 hours or until beans are tender.
Freeze option: Freeze cooled beans in freezer containers. To use, partially thaw in refrigerator overnight. Heat through in a saucepan, stirring occasionally; add water if necessary.
½ cup: 294 cal., 1g fat (0 sat. fat), 0 chol., 161mg sod., 60g carb. (27g sugars, 9g fiber), 13g pro.

CAULIFLOWER CASSEROLE

To dress up cauliflower, my mom used a delightful mixture of a cheesy sauce, bright red and green pepper pieces, and crushed cornflakes. We enjoyed this casserole so much that leftovers were rare.
—*Linda McGinty, Parma, OH*

Prep: 15 min. • **Bake:** 30 min.
Makes: 8 servings

- 1   medium head cauliflower, broken into florets
- 1   cup sour cream
- 1   cup shredded cheddar cheese
- ½   cup crushed cornflakes
- ¼   cup chopped green pepper
- ¼   cup chopped sweet red pepper
- 1   tsp. salt
- ¼   cup grated Parmesan cheese
      Paprika

1. Place 1 in. of water in a saucepan; add cauliflower. Bring to a boil. Reduce heat; cover and simmer until crisp-tender, 5-10 minutes. Drain.
2. In a large bowl, combine the cauliflower, sour cream, cheddar cheese, cornflakes, peppers and salt; transfer to a greased 2-qt. baking dish. Sprinkle with Parmesan cheese and paprika.
3. Bake, uncovered, at 325° until heated through, 30-35 minutes.
1 serving: 162 cal., 10g fat (7g sat. fat), 37mg chol., 503mg sod., 10g carb. (4g sugars, 2g fiber), 7g pro.

VEGGIE NICOISE SALAD

More and more people in my workplace are becoming vegetarians. When we cook or eat together, the focus is on fresh produce. This salad combines some of our favorite ingredients in one dish—and with the hard-boiled eggs and kidney beans, it delivers enough protein to satisfy those who are skeptical of vegetarian fare.
—*Elizabeth Kelley, Chicago, IL*

Prep: 40 min. • **Cook:** 25 min.
Makes: 8 servings

- ⅓   cup olive oil
- ¼   cup lemon juice
- 2   tsp. minced fresh oregano
- 2   tsp. minced fresh thyme
- 1   tsp. Dijon mustard
- 1   garlic clove, minced
- ¼   tsp. coarsely ground pepper
- ⅛   tsp. salt
- 1   can (16 oz.) kidney beans, rinsed and drained
- 1   small red onion, halved and thinly sliced
- 1   lb. small red potatoes (about 9), halved
- 1   lb. fresh asparagus, trimmed
- ½   lb. fresh green beans, trimmed
- 12 cups torn romaine (about 2 small bunches)
- 6   hard-boiled large eggs, quartered
- 1   jar (6½ oz.) marinated quartered artichoke hearts, drained
- ½   cup Nicoise or kalamata olives

READER RAVE

"What a wonderful salad on our table for Easter dinner."
—LERAJEANFOSTER, TASTEOFHOME.COM

1. For vinaigrette, whisk together the first 8 ingredients. In another bowl, toss the kidney beans and onion with 1 Tbsp. vinaigrette. Set aside bean mixture and remaining vinaigrette.
2. Place potatoes in a saucepan and cover with water. Bring to a boil. Reduce heat; simmer, covered, until tender, 10-15 minutes. Drain. While potatoes are warm, toss with 1 Tbsp. vinaigrette; set aside.
3. In a pot of boiling water, cook asparagus just until crisp-tender, 2-4 minutes. Remove with tongs and immediately drop into ice water. Drain and pat dry. In same pot of boiling water, cook green beans until crisp-tender, 3-4 minutes. Remove beans; place in ice water. Drain and pat dry.
4. To serve, toss the asparagus with 1 Tbsp. vinaigrette; toss the green beans with 2 tsp. vinaigrette. Toss the romaine with remaining vinaigrette; place on a platter. Arrange vegetables, kidney bean mixture, eggs, artichoke hearts and olives over top.
1 serving: 329 cal., 19g fat (4g sat. fat), 140mg chol., 422mg sod., 28g carb. (6g sugars, 7g fiber), 12g pro. **Diabetic exchanges:** 3 fat, 2 medium-fat meat, 2 vegetable, 1½ starch.

MEAT
LOVER
OPTION
PAGE 320

⑤ ⏱ ARTICHOKE CAPRESE PLATTER

I dressed up the classic Italian trio of mozzarella, tomatoes and basil with marinated artichokes. It looks so yummy on a pretty platter set out on a buffet. Using fresh mozzarella is the key to this salad's amazing taste.

—*Margaret Wilson, San Bernardino, CA*

Takes: 15 min. • **Makes:** 12 servings

- 2   jars (7½ oz. each) marinated artichoke hearts
- 2   Tbsp. red wine vinegar
- 2   Tbsp. olive oil
- 6   plum tomatoes, sliced
- 1   lb. fresh mozzarella cheese, sliced
- 2   cups loosely packed fresh basil leaves
     Coarsely ground pepper, optional

1. Drain the artichokes, reserving ½ cup marinade. In a small bowl, whisk vinegar, oil and the reserved marinade.

2. On a large serving platter, arrange the artichokes, tomatoes, mozzarella cheese and basil. Drizzle with vinaigrette. If desired, sprinkle with coarsely ground pepper.

½ cup: 192 cal., 16g fat (7g sat. fat), 30mg chol., 179mg sod., 5g carb. (2g sugars, 1g fiber), 7g pro.

5i ⏱ BALSAMIC ZUCCHINI SAUTE

This super fast vegetarian dish is flavorful and uses only a few ingredients, so it's easy to whip up while your entree is cooking.
—*Elizabeth Bramkamp, Gig Harbor, WA*

Takes: 20 min. • **Makes:** 4 servings

- 1 Tbsp. olive oil
- 3 medium zucchini, cut into thin slices
- ½ cup chopped sweet onion
- ½ tsp. salt
- ½ tsp. dried rosemary, crushed
- ¼ tsp. pepper
- 2 Tbsp. balsamic vinegar
- ⅓ cup crumbled feta cheese

In a large skillet, heat oil over medium-high heat; saute zucchini and onion until crisp-tender, 6-8 minutes. Stir in seasonings. Add vinegar; cook and stir 2 minutes. Top with feta cheese.

½ cup: 94 cal., 5g fat (2g sat. fat), 5mg chol., 398mg sod., 9g carb. (6g sugars, 2g fiber), 4g pro. **Diabetic exchanges:** 1 vegetable, 1 fat.

5i ⏱ GRILLED BRUSSELS SPROUTS

During a beach vacation, in an effort to cook our entire meal outside on the grill, I made our not-so-simple veggie choice into a simple grilled side dish. For spicier sprouts, season with red pepper flakes.
—*Tiffany Ihle, Bronx, NY*

Takes: 30 min. • **Makes:** 4 servings

- 16 fresh Brussels sprouts (about 1½-in. diameter), trimmed
- 1 medium sweet red pepper
- 1 medium onion
- ½ tsp. salt
- ½ tsp. garlic powder
- ¼ tsp. coarsely ground pepper
- 1 Tbsp. olive oil

1. In a large saucepan, place a steamer basket over 1 in. of water. Bring water to a boil. Place Brussels sprouts in basket. Reduce heat to maintain a simmer; steam, covered, until crisp-tender, 4-6 minutes. Cool slightly; cut each sprout in half.
2. Cut red pepper and onion into 1½-in. pieces. On 4 metal or soaked wooden skewers, alternately thread Brussels sprouts, red pepper and onion. Mix salt, garlic powder and pepper. Brush vegetables with oil; sprinkle with salt mixture. Grill, covered, over medium heat or broil 4 in. from heat until vegetables are tender, 10-12 minutes, turning occasionally.

1 skewer: 84 cal., 4g fat (1g sat. fat), 0 chol., 316mg sod., 11g carb. (4g sugars, 4g fiber), 3g pro. **Diabetic exchanges:** 1 vegetable, ½ fat.

WHEAT BERRY SALAD

I'm a former junk food fan who discovered the beauty of wheat berries. They're tender yet chewy in this lemony salad that's tossed with cherries and walnuts.

—*Nancy Lange, Phoenix, AZ*

Prep: 20 min. • **Cook:** 1 hour + cooling
Makes: 6 servings

- 1½ cups wheat berries
- 2 celery ribs, finely chopped
- ½ cup dried cherries, chopped
- ½ cup chopped walnuts, toasted
- ¼ cup minced fresh parsley
- 1 green onion, chopped
- 3 Tbsp. olive oil
- 2 Tbsp. lemon juice
- ¼ tsp. salt
- ¼ tsp. pepper
  Mixed salad greens, optional

1. Place wheat berries in a large saucepan; add water to cover by 2 in. Bring to a boil. Reduce heat; simmer, covered, about 1 hour or until tender. Drain; transfer to a large bowl. Cool completely.
2. Add celery, cherries, walnuts, parsley and green onion to wheat berries. In a small bowl, whisk oil, lemon juice, salt and pepper until blended; add to salad and toss to coat. If desired, serve over greens.
¾ cup: 323 cal., 14g fat (2g sat. fat), 0 chol., 112mg sod., 45g carb. (7g sugars, 7g fiber), 8g pro.

🟢 MEXICAN STREET CORN BAKE

We discovered Mexican street corn at a festival. This easy one-pan version saves on prep and cleanup. Every August, I freeze a lot of our own fresh sweet corn, and I use that in this recipe. But store-bought corn would work just as well.

—*Erin Wright, Wallace, KS*

Prep: 10 min. • **Bake:** 35 min.
Makes: 6 servings

- 6 cups frozen corn (about 30 oz.), thawed and drained
- 1 cup mayonnaise
- 1 tsp. ground chipotle pepper
- ¼ tsp. salt
- ¼ tsp. pepper
- 6 Tbsp. chopped green onions, divided
- ½ cup grated Parmesan cheese
  Lime wedges, optional

1. Preheat oven to 350°. Mix the first 5 ingredients and 4 Tbsp. green onions; transfer to a greased 1½-qt. baking dish. Sprinkle with cheese.
2. Bake, covered, 20 minutes. Uncover; bake until bubbly and lightly browned, 15-20 minutes longer. Sprinkle with remaining green onions. If desired, serve with lime wedges.
⅔ cup: 391 cal., 30g fat (5g sat. fat), 8mg chol., 423mg sod., 30g carb. (4g sugars, 3g fiber), 6g pro.

RUTABAGA CARROT CASSEROLE

This pretty side with its sweet, crunchy topping makes a delightful alternative to the traditional sweet potato casserole.
—*Joan Hallford, North Richland Hills, TX*

Prep: 30 min. • **Bake:** 30 min.
Makes: 8 servings

- 1 large rutabaga, peeled and cubed
- 3 large carrots, shredded
- 1 large egg, beaten
- 2 Tbsp. brown sugar
- 1 Tbsp. butter
- ½ tsp. salt
- ¼ tsp. ground nutmeg
  Dash pepper
- 1 cup cooked brown rice
- 1 cup fat-free evaporated milk

TOPPING
- ¼ cup all-purpose flour
- ¼ cup packed brown sugar
- 2 Tbsp. cold butter
- ½ cup chopped pecans

1. Place rutabaga in a Dutch oven and cover with water. Bring to a boil. Cook, uncovered, until tender, 15-20 minutes, adding carrots during the last 5 minutes of cooking; drain.
2. In a large bowl, mash the rutabaga mixture with egg, brown sugar, butter, salt, nutmeg and pepper. Stir in rice and milk. Transfer mixture to an 11x7-in. baking dish coated with cooking spray.
3. For topping, in a small bowl, combine flour and brown sugar; cut in butter until crumbly. Stir in the pecans. Sprinkle over top. Bake, uncovered, at 350° until casserole is bubbly, 30-35 minutes.
½ cup: 249 cal., 11g fat (3g sat. fat), 39mg chol., 267mg sod., 34g carb. (21g sugars, 4g fiber), 6g pro. **Diabetic exchanges:** 2 starch, 2 fat.

🟦 🟤 LEMON GARLIC MUSHROOMS

I baste whole mushrooms with a lemony oil to prepare this simple side dish. Using skewers or a basket makes it easy to turn them as they grill to perfection.
—*Diane Hixon, Niceville, FL*

Takes: 15 min. • **Makes:** 4 servings

- ¼ cup lemon juice
- 3 Tbsp. minced fresh parsley
- 2 Tbsp. olive oil
- 3 garlic cloves, minced
  Pepper to taste
- 1 lb. large fresh mushrooms

1. For dressing, whisk together the first 5 ingredients. Toss mushrooms with 2 Tbsp. of mixture.
2. Grill mushrooms, covered, over medium-high heat until tender, 5-7 minutes per side. Toss with remaining mixture before serving.
1 serving: 94 cal., 7g fat (1g sat. fat), 0 chol., 2mg sod., 6g carb. (0 sugars, 0 fiber), 3g pro. **Diabetic exchanges:** 1½ fat, 1 vegetable.

MEAT
LOVER
OPTION
PAGE 320

HEARTY
ASIAN LETTUCE SALAD

It may sound nutty, but this meatless version of your favorite restaurant salad packs in 13 grams of protein and is bursting with juicy flavor.

—Taste of Home *Test Kitchen*

Takes: 20 min. • **Makes:** 2 servings

- 1 cup ready-to-serve brown rice
- 1 cup frozen shelled edamame
- 3 cups spring mix salad greens
- ¼ cup reduced-fat sesame ginger salad dressing
- 1 medium navel orange, peeled and sectioned
- 4 radishes, sliced
- 2 Tbsp. sliced almonds, toasted

1. Prepare rice and edamame according to package directions.

2. In a large bowl, combine the salad greens, rice and edamame. Drizzle with salad dressing and toss to coat. Divide the salad mixture between 2 plates; top with orange segments, radishes and almonds.

1 serving: 329 cal., 10g fat (1g sat. fat), 0 chol., 430mg sod., 44g carb. (12g sugars, 7g fiber), 13g pro.

CHERRY TOMATO MOZZARELLA SAUTE

This side dish is full of flavor and so quick to put together. The cherry tomatoes and mozzarella are perfect alongside almost any main dish you can think of.

—*Summer Jones, Pleasant Grove, UT*

Takes: 25 min. • **Makes:** 4 servings

- 2 tsp. olive oil
- ¼ cup chopped shallots
- 1 tsp. minced fresh thyme
- 1 garlic clove, minced
- 2½ cups cherry tomatoes, halved
- ¼ tsp. salt
- ¼ tsp. pepper
- 4 oz. fresh mozzarella cheese, cut into ½-in. cubes

In a large skillet, heat oil over medium-high heat; saute shallots with thyme until tender. Add garlic; cook and stir 1 minute. Stir in tomatoes, salt and pepper; heat through. Remove from heat; stir in cheese.

⅔ cup: 127 cal., 9g fat (4g sat. fat), 22mg chol., 194mg sod., 6g carb. (4g sugars, 2g fiber), 6g pro.

GRILLED VEGGIES WITH CAPER BUTTER

We enjoy the tart, peppery taste of capers. No one likes a bland veggie, and caper butter helps peppers, squash and zucchini shine.

—Danyelle Crum, Indian Trail, NC

Prep: 25 min. • **Grill:** 10 min.
Makes: 8 servings

- ¼ cup butter, cubed
- 2 garlic cloves, minced
- 1 Tbsp. lemon juice
- 2 tsp. capers, drained and chopped
- 1 Tbsp. minced fresh parsley
- 2 medium zucchini, cut in half lengthwise
- 2 medium crookneck or yellow summer squash, cut in half lengthwise
- 1 medium sweet yellow or orange pepper, quartered
- 1 medium sweet red pepper, quartered
- 2 large portobello mushrooms, stems removed
- 3 green onions, trimmed
- 2 Tbsp. olive oil
- ½ tsp. salt
- ¼ tsp. pepper

1. In a small saucepan, melt butter over medium-low heat. Add the garlic; cook 2 minutes. Add lemon juice and capers; cook 2 minutes. Stir in parsley.
2. Brush vegetables with oil; sprinkle with salt and pepper.
3. Grill the zucchini, squash and peppers, covered, over medium heat 4-5 minutes on each side or until crisp-tender, basting occasionally with butter mixture. Grill the mushrooms and onions, covered, 1-2 minutes on each side or until tender, basting occasionally with butter mixture.
4. Cut vegetables as desired; transfer to a serving platter. Drizzle with the remaining butter mixture.

1 serving: 117 cal., 10g fat (4g sat. fat), 15mg chol., 219mg sod., 7g carb. (3g sugars, 2g fiber), 2g pro.

⏱ FRIED ONIONS & APPLES

Since a lot of delicious onions are grown in our state, they are always part of my menu. This tangy side dish is perfect in the fall. The inspiration for this unusual combination was a prolific apple tree!
—*Janice Mitchell, Aurora, CO*

Takes: 30 min. • **Makes:** 12 servings

- 3 large yellow onions, sliced
- 3 Tbsp. butter
- 6 large tart red apples, sliced
- ½ cup packed brown sugar
- 1 tsp. salt
- ½ tsp. paprika
- ⅛ tsp. ground nutmeg

1. In a large cast-iron or other heavy skillet, saute onions in butter until tender. Place apples on top of onions. Combine remaining ingredients; sprinkle over apples.
2. Cover and simmer for 10 minutes. Uncover and simmer until apples are tender, 5 minutes longer. Serve with a slotted spoon.
1 cup: 137 cal., 3g fat (2g sat. fat), 8mg chol., 230mg sod., 28g carb. (24g sugars, 4g fiber), 1g pro.

READER RAVE

"I would never have dreamed of combining apples and onions, but the result was delicious. Thank you for sharing your fine recipe."
—MAGGIEWB, TASTEOFHOME.COM

🕔⏱ SIMPLE MAPLE BAKED BEANS

I came up with this recipe in a pinch after running out of baked beans at our oldest daughter's birthday party. I dressed up canned beans with maple syrup and a few other ingredients to produce this sweet, saucy version that tastes like homemade. These are so easy, I rarely make baked beans from scratch anymore.
—*Brenda Tetreault, Newport Center, VT*

Takes: 15 min. • **Makes:** 10 servings

- 1 medium onion, chopped
- 1 to 2 Tbsp. canola oil
- 3 cans (28 oz. each) baked beans
- 1½ tsp. ground mustard
- 1 tsp. garlic salt
- ¾ to 1 cup maple syrup

In a Dutch oven, cook the onion in oil until tender. Add the beans, mustard and garlic salt. Cook over medium heat until bubbly, stirring occasionally. Add maple syrup; heat through, stirring occasionally.
¾ cup: 168 cal., 3g fat (1g sat. fat), 6mg chol., 513mg sod., 34g carb. (21g sugars, 5g fiber), 4g pro.

SAVORY ZUCCHINI BREAD PUDDING

I've been serving this dish for years and always receive compliments on it. If you don't have day-old bread in your pantry, simply slice fresh bread and bake it at 300° for 10 minutes before cubing it.
—*Mary Ann Dell, Phoenixville, PA*

Prep: 25 min. • **Bake:** 40 min.
Makes: 12 servings

- 1 small onion, chopped
- 1 celery rib, chopped
- 3 Tbsp. butter
- 1 cup all-purpose flour
- 2 Tbsp. sugar
- 1 tsp. baking powder
- 1 tsp. salt
- 1 tsp. ground cinnamon
- 1 tsp. poultry seasoning
- ½ cup canned pumpkin
- 2 large eggs
- ⅓ cup 2% milk
- ¼ cup butter, melted
- 4 cups day-old cubed bread
- 3 medium zucchini, chopped
- ½ cup shredded cheddar cheese

1. In a small skillet, saute onion and celery in butter until tender; set aside.

2. In a large bowl, combine the flour, sugar, baking powder, salt, cinnamon and poultry seasoning. In a small bowl, whisk pumpkin, eggs, milk and butter; stir into dry ingredients just until moistened. Fold in the bread cubes, zucchini, cheese and onion mixture.

3. Transfer to a greased 13x9-in. baking dish. Cover and bake at 325° for 30 minutes. Uncover; bake 10-15 minutes longer or until lightly browned.

¾ cup: 182 cal., 10g fat (6g sat. fat), 58mg chol., 408mg sod., 20g carb. (5g sugars, 2g fiber), 5g pro.

BOW TIE & SPINACH SALAD

With pasta salad, it's easy to change up ingredients. We like to add grilled chicken and pine nuts, and sometimes we substitute black beans for the garbanzo beans.
—*Julie Kirkpatrick, Billings, MT*

Takes: 30 min. • **Makes:** 6 servings

- 2 cups uncooked multigrain bow tie pasta
- 1 can (15 oz.) garbanzo beans or chickpeas, rinsed and drained
- 6 cups fresh baby spinach (about 6 oz.)
- 2 cups fresh broccoli florets
- 2 plum tomatoes, chopped
- 1 medium sweet red pepper, chopped
- ½ cup cubed part-skim mozzarella cheese
- ½ cup pitted Greek olives, halved
- ¼ cup minced fresh basil
- ⅓ cup reduced-fat sun-dried tomato salad dressing
- ¼ tsp. salt
- ¼ cup chopped walnuts, toasted

1. Cook pasta according to the package directions. Drain; transfer to a large bowl.

2. Add beans, vegetables, cheese, olives and basil to pasta. Drizzle with dressing and sprinkle with salt; toss to coat. Sprinkle with walnuts.

Note: To toast nuts, bake in a shallow pan in a 350° oven for 5-10 minutes or cook in a skillet over low heat until lightly browned, stirring occasionally.

2 cups: 319 cal., 13g fat (2g sat. fat), 6mg chol., 660mg sod., 39g carb. (6g sugars, 7g fiber), 14g pro. **Diabetic exchanges:** 2 starch, 2 fat, 1 lean meat, 1 vegetable.

🅵 ⏱ ORANGE-GLAZED BEETS

Beets were a popular vegetable in our house when I was growing up, and this recipe is a favorite of ours. It's easy to make, and the orange gives it a delightful citrus flavor.
—*Susan Punzal, Orchard Park, NY*

Takes: 25 min. • **Makes:** 8 servings

- ¾ cup orange marmalade
- 6 Tbsp. orange juice
- ⅓ cup butter, cubed
- ¼ tsp. salt
- ¼ tsp. pepper
- 3 cans (14½ oz. each) sliced beets, drained

In a large skillet, combine first 5 ingredients. Bring to a boil; cook and stir until thickened, 3-4 minutes. Add the beets; cook and stir until most of the liquid is absorbed, 6-8 minutes longer.

½ cup: 194 cal., 8g fat (5g sat. fat), 20mg chol., 443mg sod., 32g carb. (27g sugars, 3g fiber), 2g pro.

MEAT LOVER OPTION PAGE 320

FARMERS MARKET ORZO SALAD

We like to use orzo as a base for veggies, lemony vinaigrette and cheeses such as mozzarella, feta or smoked Gouda.

—*Heather Dezzutto, Raleigh, NC*

Prep: 25 min. • **Grill:** 10 min.
Makes: 8 servings

- 1 pkg. (16 oz.) orzo pasta
- 2 small yellow summer squash, halved lengthwise
- 1 medium zucchini, halved lengthwise
- 1 medium red onion, quartered
- 8 Tbsp. olive oil, divided
- ½ tsp. salt, divided
- ¼ tsp. pepper, divided
- 3 Tbsp. lemon juice
- 8 oz. smoked mozzarella cheese, cut into ¼-in. cubes
- 1½ cups grape tomatoes, halved lengthwise
- ½ cup chopped fresh basil
- ½ cup pine nuts, toasted

1. Cook orzo according to the package directions; drain. Brush yellow squash, zucchini and onion with 2 Tbsp. oil; sprinkle with ¼ tsp. salt and ⅛ tsp. pepper. Grill vegetables, covered, over medium heat or broil 4 in. from heat 10-12 minutes or until lightly charred and tender, turning once. Cool slightly. Cut into 1-in. pieces.
2. In a small bowl, whisk lemon juice and remaining oil until blended. In a large bowl, combine orzo, grilled vegetables, mozzarella, tomatoes, basil and remaining salt and pepper. Add dressing; toss to coat. Sprinkle with pine nuts.

1¼ cups: 291 cal., 27g fat (7g sat. fat), 25mg chol., 274mg sod., 7g carb. (4g sugars, 2g fiber), 9g pro.

🕐 EGGPLANT FRIES

My kids love this snack—and I like that it is healthy. Coated with Italian seasoning, Parmesan cheese and garlic salt, these veggie sticks are broiled, not fried, so there's no guilt when you crunch into them.

—*Mary Murphy, Atwater, CA*

Takes: 20 min. • **Makes:** 6 servings

- 2 large eggs
- ½ cup grated Parmesan cheese
- ½ cup toasted wheat germ
- 1 tsp. Italian seasoning
- ¾ tsp. garlic salt
- 1 medium eggplant (about 1¼ lbs.) Cooking spray
- 1 cup meatless pasta sauce, warmed

1. Preheat broiler. In a shallow bowl, whisk together eggs. In another shallow bowl, mix cheese, wheat germ and seasonings.
2. Trim ends of eggplant; cut eggplant lengthwise into ½-in.-thick slices. Cut slices lengthwise into ½-in. strips. Dip eggplant in eggs, then coat with cheese mixture. Place on a baking sheet coated with cooking spray.
3. Spritz eggplant with additional cooking spray. Broil 4 in. from heat 3 minutes. Turn eggplant; spritz with additional cooking spray. Broil until golden brown, 1-2 minutes. Serve immediately with pasta sauce.

1 serving: 135 cal., 5g fat (2g sat. fat), 68mg chol., 577mg sod., 15g carb. (6g sugars, 4g fiber), 9g pro. **Diabetic exchanges:** 1 medium-fat meat, 1 vegetable, ½ starch.

FESTIVE CORN & BROCCOLI

Try substituting a tablespoon of minced fresh basil for the dried and two to three ears of sweet corn (cut fresh from the cob, about a cup) for the Mexicorn.
—*Lucile Throgmorton, Clovis, NM*

Takes: 15 min. • **Makes:** 5 servings

- 1 pkg. (16 oz.) frozen chopped broccoli, thawed
- 1 can (7 oz.) Mexicorn, drained
- ¼ cup butter, cubed
- 1 tsp. dried basil
- ½ tsp. salt
- ⅛ tsp. garlic powder
- ⅛ tsp. pepper

In a large cast-iron or other heavy skillet, combine the broccoli, corn and butter; cook over medium heat until butter is melted. Stir in the basil, salt, garlic powder and pepper. Cover and cook until vegetables are tender, 8-10 minutes, stirring occasionally.

⅔ cup: 135 cal., 9g fat (6g sat. fat), 24mg chol., 541mg sod., 12g carb. (3g sugars, 4g fiber), 4g pro.

SCORED POTATOES

Here's a fun alternative to plain baked potatoes. It's easy to help yourself to just the amount you want, too, since the potato halves are scored into sections. My mom serves these pretty potatoes alongside any main dish.
—*Barbara Wheeler, Sparks Glencoe, MD*

Prep: 10 min. • **Bake:** 50 min.
Makes: 4 servings

- 4 large baking potatoes
- 2 Tbsp. butter, melted, divided
- ⅛ tsp. paprika
- 1 Tbsp. minced fresh parsley
  Salt and pepper to taste

1. With a sharp knife, cut potatoes in half lengthwise. Slice each half widthwise 6 times, but not all the way through; fan potatoes slightly.

2. Place in a shallow baking dish. Brush potatoes with 1 Tbsp. butter. Sprinkle with paprika, parsley, salt and pepper. Bake, uncovered, at 350° for 50 minutes or until tender. Drizzle with remaining butter.

2 potato halves: 336 cal., 6g fat (4g sat. fat), 15mg chol., 68mg sod., 65g carb. (3g sugars, 8g fiber), 8g pro.

🍲 ITALIAN SPAGHETTI SQUASH

Here's the easiest spaghetti squash recipe I know! Fill the squash with whatever sauce ingredients score big at your house.

—*Melissa Brooks, Sparta, WI*

Prep: 15 min. • **Cook:** 6¼ hours
Makes: 4 servings

- 1   medium spaghetti squash (3 lbs.)
- 1   can (14½ oz.) diced tomatoes, undrained
- 1   cup sliced fresh mushrooms
- ½   tsp. salt
- ½   tsp. dried oregano
- ¼   tsp. pepper
- ¾   cup shredded part-skim mozzarella cheese

1. Halve squash lengthwise; discard seeds. Fill with tomatoes and mushrooms; sprinkle with seasonings. Place in an oval 7-qt. slow cooker, tilting one slightly to fit.

2. Cook, covered, on low until squash is tender, 6-8 hours. Sprinkle with cheese. Cook, covered, on low until cheese is melted, 10-15 minutes. To serve, cut each half into 2 portions.

¾ cup: 195 cal., 6g fat (3g sat. fat), 14mg chol., 661mg sod., 31g carb. (4g sugars, 7g fiber), 9g pro. **Diabetic exchanges:** 2 starch, 1 medium-fat meat.

Health tip: Cup for cup, spaghetti squash is lower in carbs than white pasta, but it's also higher in fiber and vitamin C.

OVERNIGHT MAPLE OATMEAL
PAGE 240

BRUNCH TIME

Find morning specialties here to please every diner on your list. From simple make-aheads that can serve one to magnificient crowd-sized casseroles, you'll love these ways to start the day.

BLACK BEAN & WHITE CHEDDAR FRITTATA

This is one of my favorite comfort foods for breakfast or even a quick dinner. I like to make it with lime salsa. But if you're looking for something with more kick, use hot salsa or add some chipotle pepper.
—Aysha Schurman, Ammon, ID

Prep: 20 min. • **Cook:** 15 min.
Makes: 6 servings

- 6 large eggs
- 3 large egg whites
- ¼ cup salsa
- 1 Tbsp. minced fresh parsley
- ¼ tsp. salt
- ¼ tsp. pepper
- 1 Tbsp. olive oil
- ⅓ cup finely chopped green pepper
- ⅓ cup finely chopped sweet red pepper
- 3 green onions, finely chopped
- 2 garlic cloves, minced
- 1 cup canned black beans, rinsed and drained
- ½ cup shredded white cheddar cheese
  Optional toppings: Minced fresh cilantro, sliced ripe olives and additional salsa

1. Preheat broiler. In a large bowl, whisk the first 6 ingredients until blended.
2. In a 10-in. ovenproof skillet, heat oil over medium-high heat. Add peppers and green onions; cook and stir 3-4 minutes or until peppers are tender. Add garlic; cook 1 minute longer. Stir in beans. Reduce heat to medium; stir in egg mixture. Cook, uncovered, 4-6 minutes or until nearly set. Sprinkle with cheese.
3. Broil 3-4 in. from heat 3-4 minutes or until light golden brown and eggs are completely set. Let stand 5 minutes. Cut into wedges. If desired, serve with toppings.
1 wedge: 183 cal., 10g fat (4g sat. fat), 196mg chol., 378mg sod., 9g carb. (2g sugars, 2g fiber), 13g pro. **Diabetic exchanges:** 2 medium-fat meat, ½ starch, ½ fat.

PRESSURE-COOKER HOMEMADE CHUNKY APPLESAUCE

This applesauce is so easy. My family loves the things I make from scratch, and it's good knowing exactly what I'm putting in it!
—Marilee Cardinal, Burlington, NJ

Prep: 10 min. • **Cook:** 5 min. + releasing
Makes: 5 cups

- 7 medium McIntosh, Empire or other apples (about 3 lbs.)
- ½ cup sugar
- ½ cup water
- 1 Tbsp. lemon juice
- ¼ tsp. almond or vanilla extract

1. Peel, core and cut each apple into 8 wedges. Cut each wedge crosswise in half; place in a 6-qt. electric pressure cooker. Add remaining ingredients.
2. Lock the lid; close the pressure-release valve. Adjust to pressure-cook on high for 3 minutes. Let pressure release naturally. Mash apples with a potato masher or use an immersion blender until desired consistency is reached.
¾ cup: 139 cal., 0 fat (0 sat. fat), 0 chol., 0 sod., 36g carb. (33g sugars, 2g fiber), 0 pro.

❄ SPICED APRICOT BAKED OATMEAL

Eat these spiced oatmeal squares while they're still warm for a cozy morning treat. I freeze mine in single servings so I can grab, go and microwave when I get to work. I'm not too humble to say I have the best breakfast in the office.

—*Ellie Martin Cliffe, Milwaukee, WI*

- -

Prep: 15 min. • **Bake:** 25 min.
Makes: 12 servings

- ¾ cup packed brown sugar
- 3 tsp. pumpkin pie spice
- 2 tsp. baking powder
- ½ tsp. salt
- ¼ tsp. ground cardamom
- 3 cups old-fashioned oats
- ½ cup chopped dried apricots
- ½ cup chopped pecans, toasted
- 3 large eggs, room temperature
- 1½ cups fat-free milk
- ½ cup unsweetened applesauce
- 1½ tsp. vanilla extract
- ¼ cup butter, melted

TOPPINGS

- 3 cups vanilla yogurt
- ½ cup apricot preserves, warmed

1. Preheat oven to 350°. In a large bowl, mix first 5 ingredients; stir in oats, apricots and pecans. In another bowl, whisk together eggs, milk, applesauce and vanilla; gradually whisk in melted butter. Stir into oat mixture.
2. Transfer to a greased 11x7-in. baking dish. Bake, uncovered, 25-30 minutes or until set and edges are lightly browned. Cut into 12 portions; serve with toppings.

Freeze option: Freeze cooled portions of oatmeal in airtight freezer containers. To use, microwave each portion on high for 20-30 seconds or until heated through. Serve with toppings.

Note: To toast nuts, bake in a shallow pan in a 350° oven for 5-10 minutes or cook in a skillet over low heat until lightly browned, stirring occasionally.

1 piece with ¼ cup yogurt and 2 tsp. preserves: 327 cal., 11g fat (4g sat. fat), 60mg chol., 280mg sod., 52g carb. (33g sugars, 3g fiber), 9g pro.

WARM GRAPEFRUIT WITH GINGER-SUGAR

Sweetly broiled grapefruit is a specialty at my bed-and-breakfast. In addition to serving it at breakfast or brunch, try it as a light snack or dessert.
—*Stephanie Levy, Lansing, NY*

Takes: 15 min. • **Makes:** 2 servings

- 1 large red grapefruit
- 2 to 3 tsp. chopped crystallized ginger
- 2 tsp. sugar

1. Preheat broiler. Cut grapefruit crosswise in half. With a small knife, cut around the membrane in the center of each half and discard. Cut around each section to loosen fruit. Place on a baking sheet, cut side up.
2. Mix ginger and sugar; sprinkle over fruit. Broil 4 in. from heat until sugar is melted, about 4 minutes.

½ grapefruit: 85 cal., 0 fat (0 sat. fat), 0 chol., 3mg sod., 22g carb. (17g sugars, 2g fiber), 1g pro. **Diabetic exchanges:** 1 fruit, ½ starch.

51 🕒 RISE & SHINE PARFAIT

Start your day with a smile. This fruit, yogurt and granola parfait is so easy to make. You can also use whatever favorite fresh fruit is in season and looking best at the supermarket.
—*Diana Laskaris, Chicago, IL*

Takes: 15 min. • **Makes:** 4 servings

- 4   **cups fat-free vanilla yogurt**
- 2   **medium peaches, chopped**
- 2   **cups fresh blackberries**
- ½   **cup granola without raisins or Kashi Go Lean Crunch cereal**

Layer half of the yogurt, peaches, blackberries and granola into 4 parfait glasses. Repeat layers.

1 serving: 259 cal., 3g fat (0 sat. fat), 7mg chol., 6mg sod., 48g carb. (27g sugars, 7g fiber), 13g pro.

BAKED CHEDDAR EGGS & POTATOES

I love having breakfast for dinner, especially this combo of eggs, potatoes and cheese. It starts in a skillet on the stovetop and then I pop it into the oven to bake.
—*Nadine Merheb, Tucson, AZ*

Takes: 30 min. • **Makes:** 4 servings

- 3 Tbsp. butter
- 1½ lbs. red potatoes, chopped
- ¼ cup minced fresh parsley
- 2 garlic cloves, minced
- ¾ tsp. kosher salt
- ⅛ tsp. pepper
- 8 large eggs
- ½ cup shredded extra-sharp cheddar cheese

1. Preheat oven to 400°. In a 10-in. cast-iron or other ovenproof skillet, heat butter over medium-high heat. Add potatoes; cook and stir until golden brown and tender. Stir in parsley, garlic, salt and pepper. With the back of a spoon, make 4 wells in the potato mixture; break 2 eggs into each well.
2. Bake until egg whites are completely set and yolks begin to thicken but are not hard, 9-11 minutes. Sprinkle with cheese; bake until cheese is melted, 1 minute.
1 serving: 395 cal., 23g fat (12g sat. fat), 461mg chol., 651mg sod., 29g carb. (3g sugars, 3g fiber), 19g pro.

TROPICAL FRENCH TOAST

Weekends are hectic in my house and we rarely find time to have breakfast together. When I make this special French toast on a Saturday morning, my boys are more than happy to help in the kitchen and eat together!
—*Amie Carlock, Brick, NJ*

Prep: 15 min. + standing
Cook: 10 min./batch • **Makes:** 8 servings

- 1 loaf (1½ lbs.) day-old multigrain bread, unsliced
- 4 large eggs
- 1 can (13.66 oz.) coconut milk
- 2 Tbsp. vanilla extract
- ⅛ tsp. salt
- 4 Tbsp. coconut oil, divided
- 1 cup heavy whipping cream
- 2 Tbsp. sugar
- ¼ tsp. coconut extract
- 1 peeled medium mango, chopped Sweetened shredded coconut, toasted

1. Cut bread into ¾-in. slices; place in a single layer in a 15x10-in. rimmed baking pan. Whisk together eggs, coconut milk, vanilla and salt. Carefully pour egg mixture evenly over bread; let stand 20 minutes.
2. In a large skillet, heat 2 Tbsp. coconut oil over medium heat. Cook bread in batches until golden brown, 3-4 minutes per side, adding remaining coconut oil as necessary. Meanwhile, beat heavy cream until it begins to thicken. Add sugar and coconut extract; beat until soft peaks form.
3. Top the French toast with chopped mango, whipped cream and toasted shredded coconut.
1 serving: 547 cal., 32g fat (22g sat. fat), 127mg chol., 418mg sod., 49g carb. (16g sugars, 7g fiber), 17g pro.

🍲 RASPBERRY-COCONUT FRENCH TOAST

I put the ingredients in the slow-cooker crock the night before, refrigerate it, then pop the crock into the slow cooker in the morning. You can use regular milk or half-and-half, include your favorite jam, and substitute almond extract for the vanilla.

—*Teri Lee Rasey, Cadillac, MI*

Prep: 20 min. + chilling • **Cook:** 2¾ hours
Makes: 12 servings

- 6 **large eggs**
- 1½ **cups refrigerated sweetened coconut milk**
- 1 **tsp. vanilla extract**
- 1 **loaf (1 lb.) French bread, cubed**
- 1 **pkg. (8 oz.) cream cheese, cubed**
- ⅔ **cup seedless raspberry jam**
- ½ **cup sweetened shredded coconut**
  Whipped cream, fresh raspberries and toasted sweetened shredded coconut

1. In a large bowl, whisk eggs, coconut milk and vanilla until blended. Place half of the bread in a greased 5- or 6-qt. slow cooker; layer with half of the cream cheese, jam, coconut and egg mixture. Repeat layers. Refrigerate, covered, overnight.
2. Cook, covered, on low 2¾-3¼ hours or until a knife inserted in the center comes out clean. Serve warm with whipped cream, raspberries and toasted coconut.
1 cup: 280 cal., 12g fat (7g sat. fat), 112mg chol., 338mg sod., 35g carb. (16g sugars, 1g fiber), 9g pro.

TEST KITCHEN TIP

If you like extra crunch, toast the coconut before adding it to the slow cooker. Toasted chopped nuts would be tasty, too.

SOUTHWEST HASH WITH ADOBO-LIME CREMA

Add a splash of white vinegar to the poaching water right before you drop in the eggs. It helps keep them from separating.
—*Brooke Keller, Lexington, KY*

Prep: 20 min. • **Bake:** 25 min.
Makes: 4 servings

- 3 medium sweet potatoes (about 1½ lbs.), cubed
- 1 medium onion, chopped
- 1 medium sweet red pepper, chopped
- 1 Tbsp. canola oil
- 1 tsp. garlic powder
- 1 tsp. smoked paprika
- ¾ tsp. ground chipotle pepper
- ½ tsp. salt
- ¼ tsp. pepper
- ⅔ cup canned black beans
- 4 large eggs
- ½ cup reduced-fat sour cream
- 2 Tbsp. lime juice
- 2 tsp. adobo sauce
- ½ medium ripe avocado, peeled and sliced, optional
- 2 Tbsp. minced fresh cilantro

1. Preheat oven to 400°. Place the sweet potatoes, onion and red pepper in a 15x10x1-in. baking pan coated with cooking spray. Drizzle with oil; sprinkle with seasonings. Toss to coat. Roast until potatoes are tender, 25-30 minutes, adding beans during the last 10 minutes.

2. Place 2-3 in. of water in a large saucepan or skillet with high sides. Bring to a boil; adjust heat to maintain a gentle simmer. Break cold eggs, 1 at a time, into a small bowl; holding bowl close to surface of water, slip each egg into the water.

3. Cook, uncovered, 3-5 minutes or until whites are completely set and yolks begin to thicken but are not hard. Using a slotted spoon, lift eggs out of water.

4. In a small bowl, mix sour cream, lime juice and adobo sauce. Divide the sweet potato mixture among 4 bowls; top each with an egg, the sour cream mixture and, if desired, avocado. Sprinkle with cilantro.

1 serving: 304 cal., 12g fat (3g sat. fat), 222mg chol., 520mg sod., 37g carb. (15g sugars, 6g fiber), 13g pro. **Diabetic exchanges:** 2 starch, 1½ fat, 1 medium-fat meat.

MEAT LOVER OPTION
PAGE 320

FULL GARDEN FRITTATA

I was cooking for a health-conscious friend and wanted to serve a frittata. To brighten it up, I added leftover bruschetta topping and fresh mozzarella. Now *that's* breakfast! It's become a favorite among my friends and family, and a staple in my recipe book.
—*Melissa Rosenthal, Vista, CA*

Prep: 25 min. • **Bake:** 10 min.
Makes: 2 servings

- 4 **large eggs**
- ⅓ **cup 2% milk**
- ¼ **tsp. salt, divided**
- ⅛ **tsp. coarsely ground pepper**
- 2 **tsp. olive oil**
- ½ **medium zucchini, chopped**
- ½ **cup chopped baby portobello mushrooms**
- ¼ **cup chopped onion**
- 1 **garlic clove, minced**
- 2 **Tbsp. minced fresh basil**
- 1 **tsp. minced fresh oregano**
- 1 **tsp. minced fresh parsley**
  Optional toppings: Halved grape tomatoes, small fresh mozzarella cheese balls and thinly sliced fresh basil

1. Preheat oven to 375°. In a bowl, whisk eggs, milk, ⅛ tsp. salt and pepper. In an 8-in. ovenproof skillet, heat oil over medium-high heat. Add zucchini, mushrooms and onion; cook and stir until tender. Add garlic, herbs and remaining salt; cook 1 minute longer. Pour in egg mixture.

2. Bake frittata, uncovered, until eggs are set, 10-15 minutes. Cut into 4 wedges. If desired, serve with toppings.

2 wedges: 227 cal., 15g fat (4g sat. fat), 375mg chol., 463mg sod., 7g carb. (5g sugars, 1g fiber), 15g pro. **Diabetic exchanges:** 2 medium-fat meat, 1 vegetable, 1 fat.

Health tip: The protein in eggs helps power up muscles and their B vitamins are essential for energy and metabolism.

TROPICAL FRUIT SALAD

Add a serving of fruit to breakfast with this delicious medley. Toasted coconut, mango and more bring the flavor of the tropics to any menu.

—*Katie Covington, Blacksburg, SC*

Takes: 25 min. • **Makes:** 8 servings

- 1 medium mango, peeled and cubed
- 1 medium green apple, cubed
- 1 medium red apple, cubed
- 1 medium pear, cubed
- 1 medium navel orange, peeled and chopped
- 2 medium kiwifruit, peeled and chopped
- 10 seedless red grapes, halved
- 2 Tbsp. orange juice
- 1 firm medium banana, sliced
- ¼ cup sweetened shredded coconut, toasted

In a large bowl, gently combine the first 7 ingredients. Drizzle with orange juice; toss gently to coat. Refrigerate until serving. Just before serving, fold in banana and sprinkle with coconut.

¾ cup: 101 cal., 1g fat (1g sat. fat), 0 chol., 10mg sod., 24g carb. (17g sugars, 3g fiber), 1g pro. **Diabetic exchanges:** 1½ fruit.

FRUIT & NUT BAKED OATMEAL

In my part of the Midwest, baked oatmeal is a Mennonite speciality. My grown daughters are always delighted if we have leftovers for them to take home.

—*Fancheon Resler, Albion, IN*

Prep: 15 min. • **Bake:** 35 min.
Makes: 8 servings

- 6 cups quick-cooking oats
- 4 tsp. baking powder
- 1 tsp. ground cinnamon
- 4 large eggs, room temperature
- 2 cups 2% milk
- 1½ cups packed brown sugar
- 1 cup canola oil
- 1 cup shredded apple
- 1 cup dried cranberries
- ½ cup chopped walnuts, toasted
  Additional 2% milk

1. Preheat oven to 400°. Mix oats, baking powder and cinnamon. In another bowl, whisk eggs, milk, brown sugar and oil until blended; stir into oat mixture. Fold in apple, cranberries and walnuts.
2. Transfer to a greased 13x9-in. baking dish. Bake, uncovered, until set and edges are lightly browned, 35-40 minutes. Slice; serve with milk.

Freeze option: Freeze cooled individual pieces on waxed paper-lined baking sheets until firm. Transfer to freezer containers; return to the freezer. To use, microwave each piece on high until heated through, 1-2 minutes.

1 piece: 816 cal., 41g fat (5g sat. fat), 98mg chol., 319mg sod., 106g carb. (61g sugars, 8g fiber), 15g pro.

❄ 🕐 FLUFFY BANANA PANCAKES

I love to make pancakes for my family on Saturday mornings. Since we often have ripe bananas, I decided to add them to a batch of pancake batter. The results were fantastic!
—*Lori Stevens, Riverton, UT*

- -

Takes: 30 min. • **Makes:** 14 pancakes

- 1 cup all-purpose flour
- 1 cup whole wheat flour
- 3 Tbsp. brown sugar
- 1 tsp. baking powder
- 1 tsp. baking soda
- 1 tsp. ground cinnamon
- ½ tsp. salt
- 2 large eggs, room temperature
- 2 cups buttermilk
- 2 Tbsp. canola oil
- 1 tsp. vanilla extract
- 1 ripe medium banana, finely chopped
- ⅓ cup finely chopped walnuts

1. In a large bowl, combine the first 7 ingredients. In another bowl, whisk eggs, buttermilk, oil and vanilla until blended. Add to dry ingredients, stirring just until moistened. Fold in banana and walnuts.

2. Pour the batter by ¼ cupfuls onto a hot griddle coated with cooking spray. Cook until bubbles begin to form on top and bottoms are golden brown. Turn; cook until second side is golden brown.

Freeze option: Freeze cooled pancakes between layers of waxed paper in a freezer container. To use, place pancakes on an ungreased baking sheet, cover with foil and reheat in a preheated 375° oven 5-10 minutes. Or place 2 pancakes on a microwave-safe plate and microwave on high for 40-50 seconds or until heated through.

2 pancakes: 283 cal., 10g fat (2g sat. fat), 63mg chol., 503mg sod., 40g carb. (12g sugars, 4g fiber), 9g pro. **Diabetic exchanges:** 2½ starch, 1½ fat.

Fluffy Strawberry Pancakes: Replace chopped banana with ¾ cup chopped fresh strawberries; proceed as directed.

Fluffy Peach Pancakes: Replace chopped banana with ¾ cup chopped fresh or frozen peaches; proceed as directed.

Fluffy Blueberry Pancakes: Replace chopped banana with ¾ cup chopped fresh or frozen blueberries; proceed as directed.

🔟 🕐 CURRY SCRAMBLE

I have eggs every morning, and this is a great change from the classic scrambled egg meal. I like to add sliced peppers on top if I have them on hand.
—*Valerie Belley, St. Louis, MO*

- -

Takes: 15 min. • **Makes:** 4 servings

8	**large eggs**
¼	**cup fat-free milk**
½	**tsp. curry powder**
¼	**tsp. salt**
⅛	**tsp. pepper**
⅛	**tsp. ground cardamom, optional**
2	**medium tomatoes, sliced or chopped**

1. In a large bowl, whisk the eggs, milk, curry powder, salt, pepper and, if desired, cardamom until blended.

2. Place a lightly greased large nonstick skillet over medium heat. Pour in egg mixture; cook and stir until eggs are thickened and no liquid egg remains. Serve with tomatoes.

1 serving: 160 cal., 10g fat (3g sat. fat), 372mg chol., 299mg sod., 4g carb. (3g sugars, 1g fiber), 14g pro. **Diabetic exchanges:** 2 medium-fat meat.

BLUEBERRY CANTALOUPE SALAD

Add a fresh touch to any meal with these cute cups. The simple citrus dressing really jazzes up the fruit.

—*R. Jean Rand, Edina, MN*

Takes: 10 min. • **Makes:** 4 servings

- ¾ cup orange yogurt
- 1½ tsp. lemon juice
- ¾ tsp. poppy seeds
- ½ tsp. grated orange zest
- 2 cups diced cantaloupe
- 1 cup fresh blueberries

In a small bowl, mix yogurt, lemon juice, poppy seeds and orange zest. To serve, divide cantaloupe and blueberries among 4 dishes; top with yogurt dressing.

¾ cup with 3 Tbsp. dressing: 76 cal., 1g fat (0 sat. fat), 1mg chol., 24mg sod., 17g carb. (15g sugars, 1g fiber), 2g pro. **Diabetic exchanges:** 1 fruit.

🍲 SLOW-COOKER FRITTATA PROVENCAL

This recipe means that a delectable dinner is ready when I walk in the door from work. The meatless slow-cooker meal also makes an elegant brunch for lazy weekend mornings.
—*Connie Eaton, Pittsburgh, PA*

- -

Prep: 30 min. • **Cook:** 3 hours
Makes: 6 servings

- ½ cup water
- 1 Tbsp. olive oil
- 1 medium Yukon Gold potato, peeled and sliced
- 1 small onion, thinly sliced
- ½ tsp. smoked paprika
- 12 large eggs
- 1 tsp. minced fresh thyme or ¼ tsp. dried thyme
- 1 tsp. hot pepper sauce
- ½ tsp. salt
- ¼ tsp. pepper
- 1 log (4 oz.) fresh goat cheese, coarsely crumbled, divided
- ½ cup chopped soft sun-dried tomatoes (not packed in oil)

HOW-TO

Quickly De-Stem Fresh Thyme

Getting all the small leaves off a sprig of thyme can be tricky, so try this simple hack. Thread a stem through a hole in a colander. This will remove every tiny bit of thyme while collecting it all in the basin of the strainer.

1. Layer two 24-in. pieces of aluminum foil; starting with a long side, fold up foil to create a 1-in.-wide strip. Shape strip into a coil to make a rack for bottom of a 6-qt. oval slow cooker. Add water to slow cooker; set foil rack in water.

2. In a large skillet, heat oil over medium-high heat. Add potato and onion; cook and stir until potato is lightly browned, 5-7 minutes. Stir in paprika. Transfer to a greased 1½-qt. baking dish (dish must fit in slow cooker).

3. In a large bowl, whisk eggs, thyme, pepper sauce, salt and pepper; stir in 2 oz. cheese. Pour over potato mixture. Top with tomatoes and remaining goat cheese. Place dish on the foil rack.

4. Cook, covered, on low until eggs are set and a knife inserted in center comes out clean, 3-4 hours.

Note: We tested this recipe with tomatoes that are ready to use without soaking. When using whole sun-dried tomatoes that are not oil-packed, cover with boiling water and let stand until soft. Drain before chopping.

1 wedge: 245 cal., 14g fat (5g sat. fat), 385mg chol., 338mg sod., 12g carb. (4g sugars, 2g fiber), 15g pro. **Diabetic exchanges:** 2 medium-fat meat, 1 starch, ½ fat.

RAINBOW QUICHE

With plenty of veggies and a creamy egg-cheese filling, this tasty quiche gets two thumbs up!

—Lilith Fury, Adena, OH

- -

Prep: 30 min. • **Bake:** 40 min. + standing
Makes: 8 servings

- 1 **sheet refrigerated pie crust**
- 2 **Tbsp. butter**
- 1 **small onion, finely chopped**
- 1 **cup sliced fresh mushrooms**
- 1 **cup small fresh broccoli florets**
- ½ **cup finely chopped sweet orange pepper**
- ½ **cup finely chopped sweet red pepper**
- 3 **large eggs, lightly beaten**
- 1⅓ **cups half-and-half cream**
- ¾ **tsp. salt**
- ½ **tsp. pepper**
- 1 **cup shredded Mexican cheese blend, divided**
- 1 **cup fresh baby spinach**

1. Preheat oven to 425°. Unroll pie crust onto a lightly floured surface, roll to a 12-in. circle. Transfer to a 9-in. deep-dish pie plate, trim and flute edge. Refrigerate while preparing the filling.

2. In a large skillet, heat butter over medium-high heat; saute onion, mushrooms, broccoli and peppers until mushrooms are lightly browned, 6-8 minutes. Cool slightly.

3. Whisk together eggs, cream, salt and pepper. Sprinkle ½ cup cheese over crust; top with spinach and vegetable mixture. Sprinkle with remaining cheese. Pour in the egg mixture.

4. Bake on a lower oven rack 15 minutes. Reduce oven setting to 350°; bake until a knife inserted in the center comes out clean, 25-30 minutes. (Cover edge loosely with foil if necessary to prevent overbrowning.) Let stand 10 minutes before cutting.

1 piece: 347 cal., 25g fat (15g sat. fat), 140mg chol., 537mg sod., 20g carb. (3g sugars, 1g fiber), 10g pro.

Rainbow Quiche for 12: Use the recipe to fill 2 frozen deep-dish pie crusts. Bake quiches for 40-45 minutes. Each quiche serves 6.

MEAT LOVER OPTION
PAGE 320

HEARTY MULTIGRAIN PANCAKES

Oats and whole wheat flour make these tasty pancakes extra hearty. Try them with applesauce spooned on top.

—Jeri Tirmenstein, Apache Junction, AZ

Takes: 20 min. • Makes: 4 pancakes

- ¼ cup all-purpose flour
- ¼ cup whole wheat flour
- ¼ cup quick-cooking oats
- 1 Tbsp. brown sugar
- 1 tsp. baking powder
- ¼ tsp. salt
- ½ cup plus 1 Tbsp. fat-free milk
- 2 Tbsp. egg substitute
- 2 tsp. canola oil
  Optional: Fresh berries, maple syrup and butter

1. In a large bowl, combine the first 6 ingredients. Combine the milk, egg substitute and oil; add to dry ingredients just until moistened.

2. Pour batter by ¼ cupfuls onto a greased hot griddle. Turn when bubbles form on top; cook until the second side is golden brown. If desired, serve with optional toppings.

2 pancakes: 243 cal., 6g fat (1g sat. fat), 1mg chol., 559mg sod., 40g carb. (11g sugars, 3g fiber), 9g pro. **Diabetic exchanges:** 2½ starch, 1 fat.

Vanilla Pancakes: Omit whole wheat flour and oats. Use ¾ cup all-purpose flour. Add ¾ tsp. vanilla extract to milk mixture. Proceed as recipe directs.

ZUCCHINI & GOUDA SKILLET FRITTATA

This is a version of a skillet dish that my mother-in-law, Millie, created to use up all that extra summertime zucchini. The Gouda melts beautifully, but you can make it with Swiss or sharp cheddar, too.

—Susan Marshall, Colorado Springs, CO

Takes: 30 min. • Makes: 6 servings

- 6 large eggs
- 2 Tbsp. 2% milk
- 1 tsp. chopped fresh oregano
- ½ tsp. salt
- ⅛ tsp. pepper
- 2 Tbsp. butter
- 2 medium zucchini (7 to 8 oz. each), thinly sliced
- 1 medium onion, chopped
- 2 Tbsp. olive oil
- 1 medium tomato, diced
- 1 cup shredded Gouda cheese
- 2 Tbsp. minced fresh basil

1. Combine the first 5 ingredients; set aside. In a large nonstick skillet, melt butter over medium heat. Add zucchini and onion. Cook until tender, 6-8 minutes; remove.

2. In same skillet, heat oil over medium heat. Add egg mixture. Cook until set, gently lifting edges of cooked egg to allow liquid to run underneath. Top with zucchini mixture, diced tomato and cheese. Cover and cook until cheese is melted, 2-3 minutes. Sprinkle basil on top.

1 wedge: 238 cal., 19g fat (8g sat. fat), 218mg chol., 462mg sod., 6g carb. (4g sugars, 1g fiber), 12g pro.

PRESSURE-COOKED BROCCOLI EGG CUPS

Serving brunch? This delicious egg mixture is filled with crunchy bites of broccoli and rich, melty Swiss cheese. I promise you'll love it!
—*Edna Hoffman, Hebron, IN*

Takes: 25 min. • **Makes:** 4 servings

7	large eggs
1½	cups half-and-half cream
3	Tbsp. shredded Swiss cheese
2	tsp. minced fresh parsley
1	tsp. minced fresh basil
¼	tsp. salt
⅛	tsp. cayenne pepper
1	to 1½ cups frozen broccoli florets, thawed and coarsely chopped

1. Whisk 3 eggs with next 6 ingredients; pour into 4 greased 1-pint canning jars. Divide broccoli among jars; top each with 1 egg.
2. Place trivet insert and 1 cup water in a 6-qt. electric pressure cooker. Place jars on trivet. Center lids on jars; screw on bands until fingertip tight. Lock lid; close pressure-release valve. Adjust to pressure-cook on high for 6 minutes. Quick-release pressure. Remove lid; using tongs, remove jars. Let stand 3 minutes before serving.
1 serving: 274 cal., 19g fat (10g sat. fat), 375mg chol., 333mg sod., 5g carb. (4g sugars, 1g fiber), 16g pro.

RASPBERRY PEACH PUFF PANCAKE

Here's a simple, satisfying treat that's perfect for when you have company for brunch. It's elegant enough that you can even serve it for dessert at other meals.
—*Taste of Home Test Kitchen*

Prep: 15 min. • **Bake:** 20 min.
Makes: 4 servings

2	medium peaches, peeled and sliced
½	tsp. sugar
½	cup fresh raspberries
1	Tbsp. butter
3	large eggs, room temperature, lightly beaten
½	cup fat-free milk
⅛	tsp. salt
½	cup all-purpose flour
¼	cup vanilla yogurt

1. Preheat oven to 400°. In a small bowl, toss peaches with sugar; gently stir in raspberries.
2. Place butter in a 9-in. pie plate; heat in oven until butter is melted, 2-3 minutes. Meanwhile, in a small bowl, whisk eggs, milk and salt until blended; gradually whisk in flour. Remove pie plate from oven; tilt carefully to coat bottom and sides with butter. Immediately pour in egg mixture.
3. Bake until pancake is puffed and browned, 18-22 minutes. Remove from oven; serve immediately with fruit and yogurt.
1 piece with ½ cup fruit and 1 Tbsp. yogurt: 199 cal., 7g fat (3g sat. fat), 149mg chol., 173mg sod., 25g carb. (11g sugars, 3g fiber), 9g pro. **Diabetic exchanges:** 1 medium-fat meat, 1 fruit, ½ starch, ½ fat.

CAST-IRON SCRAMBLED EGGS

I love these easy eggs, which use fresh ingredients that I usually have on hand. They make a quick and simple breakfast!
—*Bonnie Hawkins, Elkhorn, WI*

Takes: 25 min. • **Makes:** 6 servings

12	large eggs
2	Tbsp. water
¼	tsp. salt
¼	tsp. pepper
⅔	cup finely chopped sweet onion
1	jalapeno pepper, seeded and chopped
2	Tbsp. butter
1	log (4 oz.) fresh goat cheese, crumbled
3	Tbsp. minced chives

1. In a large bowl, whisk the eggs, water, salt and pepper; set aside.
2. Place a 10-in. cast-iron skillet on grill rack over medium-hot heat. In the skillet, saute onion and jalapeno in butter until tender. Add egg mixture; cook and stir until almost set. Add cheese and chives; cook and stir until eggs are completely set.

⅔ cup: 217 cal., 16g fat (7g sat. fat), 446mg chol., 342mg sod., 3g carb. (2g sugars, 0 fiber), 15g pro.

❄ ROASTED VEGETABLE STRATA

With the abundance of zucchini my family has in the fall, this is the perfect dish to use some of what we have. Cheesy and rich, the warm, classic breakfast dish is sure to please!
—*Colleen Doucette, Truro, NS*

Prep: 55 min. + chilling • **Bake:** 40 min.
Makes: 8 servings

- 3 large zucchini, halved lengthwise and cut into ¾-in. slices
- 1 each medium red, yellow and orange peppers, cut into 1-in. pieces
- 2 Tbsp. olive oil
- 1 tsp. dried oregano
- ½ tsp. salt
- ½ tsp. pepper
- ½ tsp. dried basil
- 1 medium tomato, chopped
- 1 loaf (1 lb.) unsliced crusty Italian bread
- ½ cup shredded sharp cheddar cheese
- ½ cup shredded Asiago cheese
- 6 large eggs
- 2 cups fat-free milk

1. Preheat oven to 400°. Toss zucchini and peppers with oil and seasonings; transfer to a 15x10x1-in. pan. Roast until tender, 25-30 minutes, stirring once. Stir in tomato; cool slightly.

2. Trim ends from bread; cut bread into 1-in. slices. In a greased 13x9-in. baking dish, layer half of each of the following: bread, roasted vegetables and cheeses. Repeat layers. Whisk together eggs and milk; pour evenly over top. Refrigerate, covered, 6 hours or overnight.

3. Preheat oven to 375°. Remove casserole from refrigerator while the oven heats. Bake, uncovered, until golden brown, 40-50 minutes. Let stand 5-10 minutes before cutting.

Freeze option: Cover and freeze unbaked casserole. To use, partially thaw in refrigerator overnight. Remove from the refrigerator 30 minutes before baking. Preheat oven to 375°. Bake casserole as directed, increasing time as necessary to heat through and for a thermometer inserted in center to read 165°.

1 piece: 349 cal., 14g fat (5g sat. fat), 154mg chol., 642mg sod., 40g carb. (9g sugars, 4g fiber), 17g pro. **Diabetic exchanges:** 2 starch, 1 medium-fat meat, 1 vegetable, 1 fat.

READER RAVE

"Very good. I added sliced fresh eggplant in place of some of the zucchini."
—JUANNBRAD, TASTEOFHOME.COM

🕔 ⏱ BERRY SMOOTHIE BOWL

We turned one of our favorite smoothies into a smoothie bowl and topped it with even more fresh fruit and a few toasted almonds for a little crunch.
—Taste of Home *Test Kitchen*

Takes: 5 min. • **Makes:** 2 servings

- 1 cup fat-free milk
- 1 cup frozen unsweetened strawberries
- ½ cup frozen unsweetened raspberries
- 3 Tbsp. sugar
- 1 cup ice cubes
  Optional: Sliced fresh strawberries, fresh raspberries, chia seeds, fresh pumpkin seeds, unsweetened shredded coconut and sliced almonds

Place the milk, berries and sugar in a blender; cover and process until smooth. Add ice cubes; cover and process until smooth. Divide mixture between 2 serving bowls. If desired, add optional toppings.

1½ cups: 155 cal., 0 fat (0 sat. fat), 2mg chol., 54mg sod., 35g carb. (30g sugars, 2g fiber), 5g pro.

SHAKSHUKA BREAKFAST PIZZA

I turned traditional shakshuka into a fun brunch pizza. Its sweet, spicy and crunchy ingredients make it perfect for morning, noon or night.

—Phillipe Sobon, Harwood Heights, IL

Prep: 35 min. • **Bake:** 15 min.
Makes: 6 servings

- 1   Tbsp. olive oil
- 1   large onion, thinly sliced
- 1   Tbsp. ground cinnamon
- 1   Tbsp. paprika
- 2   tsp. ground cumin
- 2   garlic cloves, minced
- ⅛   tsp. cayenne pepper
- 1   can (14½ oz.) whole plum tomatoes, undrained
- 1   tsp. hot pepper sauce
- ½   tsp. salt
- ¼   tsp. pepper
- 1   loaf (1 lb.) frozen pizza dough, thawed
- 6   large eggs
- ½   cup crumbled feta cheese

1. Preheat oven to 400°. In a large saucepan, heat oil over medium-high heat. Add onion; cook and stir until tender, 4-5 minutes. Add cinnamon, paprika, cumin, garlic and cayenne; cook 1 minute longer. Stir in the tomatoes, hot sauce, salt and pepper; cook and stir over medium heat until thickened, about 10 minutes.

2. Meanwhile, grease a 12-in. pizza pan. Roll pizza dough to fit pan. Pinch edge to form a rim. Bake until edge is lightly browned, 10-12 minutes.

3. Spread crust with tomato mixture. Using a spoon, make 6 indentations in tomato mixture; carefully break an egg into each. Sprinkle with feta. Bake until egg whites are completely set and yolks begin to thicken but are not hard, 12-15 minutes.

1 serving: 336 cal., 12g fat (3g sat. fat), 191mg chol., 654mg sod., 41g carb. (4g sugars, 5g fiber), 16g pro.

SHIITAKE & MANCHEGO SCRAMBLE

This savory breakfast dish takes everyday scrambled eggs up a few notches. The rich flavor is so satisfying in the morning, and it's even better served with buttery toasted Italian bread.

—Thomas Faglon, Somerset, NJ

Takes: 25 min. • **Makes:** 8 servings

- 2   Tbsp. extra virgin olive oil, divided
- ½   cup diced onion
- ½   cup diced sweet red pepper
- 2   cups thinly sliced fresh shiitake mushrooms (about 4 oz.)
- 1   tsp. prepared horseradish
- 8   large eggs, beaten
- 1   cup heavy whipping cream
- 1   cup shredded Manchego cheese
- 1   tsp. kosher salt
- 1   tsp. coarsely ground pepper

1. In a large nonstick skillet, heat 1 Tbsp. olive oil over medium heat. Add onion and red pepper; cook and stir until crisp-tender, 2-3 minutes. Add mushrooms; cook and stir until tender, 3-4 minutes. Stir in horseradish; cook 2 minutes more.

2. In a small bowl, whisk together remaining ingredients and remaining olive oil. Pour into skillet; cook and stir until eggs are thickened and no liquid egg remains.

1 serving: 274 cal., 24g fat (12g sat. fat), 234mg chol., 405mg sod., 4g carb. (2g sugars, 1g fiber), 11g pro.

MEAT LOVER OPTION
PAGE 320

SLOW-COOKER COCONUT GRANOLA

Here's a versatile treat with a taste of the tropics. Mix it up by subbing dried pineapple or tropical fruits for the cherries.
—Taste of Home *Test Kitchen*

Prep: 15 min. • **Cook:** 3½ hours + cooling
Makes: 6 cups

4	cups old-fashioned oats
1	cup sliced almonds
1	cup unsweetened coconut flakes
1	tsp. ground cinnamon
1	tsp. ground ginger
¼	tsp. salt
½	cup coconut oil, melted
½	cup maple syrup
1	cup dried cherries

1. Combine the oats, almonds, coconut, cinnamon, ginger and salt in a 3-qt. slow cooker. In small bowl, whisk together oil and maple syrup. Pour into slow cooker; stir to combine. Cook, covered, on low, stirring occasionally, 3½-4 hours. Stir in cherries.
2. Transfer mixture to a baking sheet; let stand until cool.
½ cup: 343 cal., 19g fat (12g sat. fat), 0 chol., 55mg sod., 41g carb. (18g sugars, 5g fiber), 6g pro.

TEST KITCHEN TIP

Pack granola in small containers for a portable snack throughout the work week.

CHILES RELLENOS SOUFFLE

After we spent the night at our friends' house in Arizona, we awoke to the tantalizing aroma of an egg souffle. This lovely southwest-inspired dish brings back wonderful memories.
—*Pat Coyne, Las Vegas, NV*

Prep: 15 min. • **Bake:** 45 min.
Makes: 8 servings

- 2 cans (4 oz. each) chopped green chiles
- ¼ cup sliced ripe olives
- ¼ cup finely chopped onion
- 2 cups sharp shredded cheddar cheese
- 4 large eggs
- 1½ cups biscuit/baking mix
- 2 cups 2% milk
- ¼ tsp. pepper
- 1 cup 4% small-curd cottage cheese
  Optional: Salsa and sour cream

1. Preheat oven to 350°. Spread green chiles in a greased 11x7-in baking dish; sprinkle with the olives, onion and cheese. In a large bowl, whisk eggs, biscuit mix, milk and pepper until blended. Stir in cottage cheese; pour over the top.

2. Bake, uncovered, until golden brown, puffed and a knife inserted in the center comes out clean, 45-50 minutes. Let stand 5-10 minutes before serving. If desired, serve with salsa and sour cream.

To make ahead: Refrigerate unbaked souffle, covered, several hours or overnight. To use, preheat oven to 350°. Remove souffle from refrigerator while oven heats. Bake as directed, increasing time as necessary until golden, puffed and a knife inserted in the center comes out clean. Let stand 5-10 minutes before serving.

1 piece: 305 cal., 17g fat (8g sat. fat), 128mg chol., 708mg sod., 23g carb. (5g sugars, 1g fiber), 16g pro.

RASPBERRY-BANANA BREAKFAST TACOS

My sweet take on breakfast tacos swaps in pancakes instead of tortillas! They're so easy and absolutely delicious. Choose fruits and berries depending on what's in season.
—*Joan Hallford, North Richland Hills, TX*

Prep: 25 min. • **Cook:** 5 min./batch
Makes: 4 servings

- ¾ cup all-purpose flour
- ¾ cup whole wheat flour
- 3 Tbsp. sugar
- 2 tsp. baking powder
- ¾ tsp. ground cinnamon
- ½ tsp. salt
- 1 large egg, room temperature
- 1 cup 2% milk
- 2 Tbsp. canola oil
- 1 tsp. vanilla extract
- ⅓ cup cream cheese, softened
- 3 Tbsp. vanilla yogurt
- 1 small banana, sliced
- 1 cup fresh raspberries

1. Whisk together flours, sugar, baking powder, cinnamon and salt. Combine egg, milk, canola oil and vanilla; stir into dry ingredients just until moistened.

2. Preheat a griddle over medium heat. Lightly grease griddle. Pour the batter by ½ cupfuls onto griddle; cook until bubbles on top begin to pop and bottoms are golden brown. Turn; cook until the second side is golden brown.

3. Meanwhile, beat together cream cheese and yogurt. Spread over pancakes; top with banana and raspberries. Fold up.

1 taco: 429 cal., 17g fat (6g sat. fat), 71mg chol., 651mg sod., 59g carb. (19g sugars, 6g fiber), 11g pro.

🕐 CRUNCHY FRENCH TOAST

This light version of classic French toast is perfect for quick meals or Sunday brunches. My kids love it, and so do I!
—*Barbara Arnold, Spokane, WA*

Takes: 20 min. • **Makes:** 4 servings

6	**large eggs**
⅓	**cup fat-free milk**
2	**tsp. vanilla extract**
⅛	**tsp. salt**
1	**cup frosted cornflakes, crushed**
½	**cup old-fashioned oats**
¼	**cup sliced almonds**
8	**slices whole wheat bread**
	Maple syrup

1. In a shallow bowl, whisk eggs, milk, vanilla and salt until blended. In another shallow bowl, toss cornflakes with oats and almonds.
2. Heat a griddle coated with cooking spray over medium heat. Dip both sides of bread in egg mixture, then in cereal mixture, patting to help coating adhere. Place on griddle; toast 3-4 minutes on each side or until golden brown. Serve with syrup.
2 slices: 335 cal., 11g fat (2g sat. fat), 196mg chol., 436mg sod., 43g carb. (8g sugars, 5g fiber), 17g pro. **Diabetic exchanges:** 3 starch, 1 medium-fat meat, ½ fat.

COLORFUL BROCCOLI CHEDDAR CASSEROLE

When we have houseguests, we make broccoli and cheese strata the night before so in the morning we can relax and visit while it bubbles in the oven.
—*Gale Lalmond, Deering, NH*

- -

Prep: 25 min. + chilling • **Bake:** 50 min.
Makes: 8 servings

- 1   Tbsp. olive oil
- 6   green onions, sliced
- 2   cups fresh broccoli florets, chopped
- 1   medium sweet red pepper, finely chopped
- 2   garlic cloves, minced
- ⅛   tsp. pepper
- 5   whole wheat English muffins, split, toasted and quartered
- 1½   cups shredded reduced-fat cheddar cheese, divided
- 8   large eggs
- 2½   cups fat-free milk
- 2   Tbsp. Dijon mustard
- ½   tsp. hot pepper sauce, optional

1. In a large skillet, heat oil over medium-high heat. Add green onions; cook and stir until tender. Add broccoli, red pepper and garlic; cook and stir 4-5 minutes or until tender. Transfer to a large bowl; season with pepper.
2. Place English muffins in a greased 13x9-in. baking dish, cut sides up. Top muffins with vegetable mixture and sprinkle with 1 cup shredded cheese.
3. In a large bowl, whisk eggs, milk, mustard and, if desired, hot sauce. Pour over top. Refrigerate, covered, overnight.
4. Remove from refrigerator 30 minutes before baking. Preheat oven to 350°. Bake, covered, 30 minutes. Sprinkle with remaining cheese. Bake, uncovered, 20-30 minutes longer or until egg mixture is set. Let stand 5 minutes before cutting.
1 piece: 273 cal., 12g fat (5g sat. fat), 228mg chol., 529mg sod., 25g carb. (9g sugars, 4g fiber), 19g pro. **Diabetic exchanges:** 2 medium-fat meat, 1½ starch, ½ fat.

LOADED QUINOA BREAKFAST BOWL

After I was diagnosed with multiple sclerosis in 2001, I embarked on a journey to improve my diet and live a healthier lifestyle. I began developing recipes that were not only delicious and satisfying, but also anti-inflammatory and highly nutritious.
—*Chantale Michaud, Guelph, ON*

- -

Prep: 15 min. + soaking • **Cook:** 15 min.
Makes: 1 serving

- ¾   cup water, divided
- ¼   cup tri-colored quinoa, rinsed
- 2   Tbsp. dried goji berries or dried cranberries
- 1   small banana
- ¼   cup unsweetened almond milk
- 1   Tbsp. maple syrup
- ⅛   tsp. ground cinnamon
- ⅛   tsp. vanilla extract
- ¼   cup fresh or frozen unsweetened blueberries
- 1   Tbsp. chopped walnuts
- 1   Tbsp. slivered almonds
- 1   Tbsp. fresh pumpkin seeds
  Additional unsweetened almond milk and maple syrup, optional

1. In a small saucepan, bring ½ cup water to a boil. Add the quinoa. Reduce heat; simmer, covered, until liquid is absorbed, 12-15 minutes. Meanwhile, soak berries in remaining water for 10 minutes; drain. Halve banana crosswise. Slice 1 banana half; mash the other.
2. Remove quinoa from heat; fluff with a fork. Mix in mashed banana, almond milk, maple syrup, cinnamon and vanilla. Transfer to an individual bowl; add blueberries, walnuts, almonds, pumpkin seeds, banana slices and goji berries. If desired, serve with additional almond milk and maple syrup.
1 serving: 475 cal., 13g fat (1g sat. fat), 0 chol., 85mg sod., 83g carb. (35g sugars, 10g fiber), 13g pro.

TEST KITCHEN TIP

Quinoa contains a natural substance called saponin, which has a bitter taste. Most (but not all) packaged quinoa has been rinsed to remove this coating. If your quinoa has not been pre-rinsed, simply rinse it under cold water in a fine-mesh strainer until the water runs clear.

🕐 SPICY BREAKFAST PIZZA

Eggs and hash browns have extra pizazz when they're served up on a pizza pan. My family requests this fun breakfast often, and it's a snap to make with ready-to-use pizza crust. I adjust the heat index of the toppings to suit the taste buds of my diners.
—*Christy Hinrichs, Parkville, MO*

Takes: 30 min. • **Makes:** 6 slices

- 2 cups frozen shredded hash brown potatoes
- ¼ tsp. ground cumin
- ¼ tsp. chili powder
- 2 Tbsp. canola oil, divided
- 4 large eggs
- 2 Tbsp. 2% milk
- ¼ tsp. salt
- 2 green onions, chopped
- 2 Tbsp. diced sweet red pepper
- 1 Tbsp. finely chopped jalapeno pepper
- 1 garlic clove, minced
- 1 prebaked 12-in. thin pizza crust
- ½ cup salsa
- ¾ cup shredded cheddar cheese

1. In a large nonstick skillet, cook the hash browns, cumin and chili powder in 1 Tbsp. oil over medium heat until golden. Remove and keep warm.

2. In a small bowl, beat the eggs, milk and salt; set aside. In the same skillet, saute the onions, peppers and garlic in the remaining oil until tender. Add egg mixture. Cook and stir over medium heat until almost set. Remove from the heat.

3. Place crust on an ungreased 14-in. pizza pan. Spread salsa over crust. Top with egg mixture. Sprinkle with hash browns and cheese. Bake at 375° for 8-10 minutes or until cheese is melted.

Note: Wear disposable gloves when cutting hot peppers; the oils can burn skin. Avoid touching your face.

1 slice: 320 cal., 16g fat (5g sat. fat), 138mg chol., 605mg sod., 31g carb. (2g sugars, 1g fiber), 13g pro. **Diabetic exchanges:** 2 starch, 1½ fat, 1 medium-fat meat.

MEDITERRANEAN BROCCOLI & CHEESE OMELET

My Italian mother-in-law taught me to make this omelet years ago—she would make it for breakfast, lunch or dinner and eat it on Italian bread. This is one of my favorite ways to use up leftover broccoli.

—Mary Licata, Pembroke Pines, FL

Takes: 30 min. • **Makes:** 4 servings

- 2½ cups fresh broccoli florets
- 6 large eggs
- ¼ cup 2% milk
- ½ tsp. salt
- ¼ tsp. pepper
- ⅓ cup grated Romano cheese
- ⅓ cup sliced pitted Greek olives
- 1 Tbsp. olive oil
  Shaved Romano cheese and minced fresh parsley

1. Preheat broiler. In a large saucepan, place steamer basket over 1 in. of water. Place broccoli in basket. Bring water to a boil. Reduce heat to a simmer; steam, covered, 4-6 minutes or until crisp-tender.
2. In a large bowl, whisk eggs, milk, salt and pepper. Stir in cooked broccoli, grated cheese and olives. In a 10-in. ovenproof skillet, heat oil over medium heat; pour in egg mixture. Cook, uncovered, 4-6 minutes or until eggs are nearly set.
3. Broil 3-4 in. from heat 2-4 minutes or until eggs are completely set. Let stand 5 minutes. Cut into wedges. Sprinkle with shaved cheese and parsley.
1 wedge: 229 cal., 17g fat (5g sat. fat), 290mg chol., 775mg sod., 5g carb. (1g sugars, 1g fiber), 15g pro.

MEAT LOVER OPTION PAGE 320

ENGLISH MUFFIN EGG SANDWICHES

You can't beat the delicious combination of mushrooms, onions, peppers and cream cheese! Leave out the red pepper flakes for a less spicy taste.

—Amy Lloyd, Madison, WI

Takes: 25 min. • **Makes:** 8 servings

- ½ lb. sliced fresh mushrooms
- 1 small sweet red pepper, chopped
- 1 small sweet onion, chopped
- ½ tsp. garlic salt
- ¼ tsp. pepper
- ¼ tsp. crushed red pepper flakes, optional
- 7 large eggs, lightly beaten
- 8 whole wheat English muffins, split and toasted
- 4 oz. reduced-fat cream cheese

1. Place a large nonstick skillet over medium-high heat. Add mushrooms, red pepper, onion and seasonings; cook and stir 5-7 minutes or until mushrooms are tender. Remove from pan.
2. Wipe skillet clean and coat with cooking spray; place skillet over medium heat. Add the eggs; cook and stir just until eggs are thickened and no liquid egg remains. Add vegetables; heat through, stirring gently.
3. Spread muffin bottoms with cream cheese; top with egg mixture. Replace tops.
1 sandwich: 244 cal., 9g fat (4g sat. fat), 173mg chol., 425mg sod., 30g carb. (7g sugars, 5g fiber), 14g pro. **Diabetic exchanges:** 2 starch, 1 medium-fat meat, ½ fat.

GREEK VEGGIE OMELET

This veggie-packed family favorite is a great way to sneak more veggies into your diet. Not only is it quick and satisfying, it's yummy.
—*Sharon Mannix, Windsor, NY*

Takes: 20 min. • **Makes:** 2 servings

- 4   large eggs
- 2   Tbsp. fat-free milk
- ⅛   tsp. salt
- 3   tsp. olive oil, divided
- 2   cups sliced baby portobello mushrooms
- ¼   cup finely chopped onion
- 1   cup fresh baby spinach
- 3   Tbsp. crumbled feta cheese
- 2   Tbsp. sliced ripe olives
      Freshly ground pepper

1. Whisk together eggs, milk and salt. In a large nonstick skillet, heat 2 tsp. oil over medium-high heat; saute mushrooms and onion until golden brown, 5-6 minutes. Stir in spinach until wilted; remove from pan.
2. In same pan, heat remaining oil over medium-low heat. Pour in egg mixture. As eggs set, push cooked portions toward the center, letting uncooked eggs flow underneath. When eggs are thickened and no liquid egg remains, spoon vegetables on 1 side; sprinkle with cheese and olives. Fold to close; cut in half to serve. Sprinkle with ground pepper.

½ omelet: 271 cal., 19g fat (5g sat. fat), 378mg chol., 475mg sod., 7g carb. (3g sugars, 2g fiber), 18g pro. **Diabetic exchanges:** 2 medium-fat meat, 2 fat, 1 vegetable.

OVERNIGHT MAPLE OATMEAL

I began my own muesli experiments at home after tasting muesli while on a trip to Switzerland. Keep things interesting (and avoid midmorning munchies) by adding different fruits and nuts every day.
—*Maddie Kirk, Springfield, PA*

Prep: 10 min. + chilling • **Makes:** 6 servings

- 2   cups old-fashioned oats
- 1   cup fat-free milk
- ¼   cup maple syrup
- 2   tsp. vanilla extract
- 1   cup vanilla yogurt
- ½   cup chopped walnuts, toasted
      Assorted fresh fruit

1. In a large bowl, combine oats, milk, syrup and vanilla. Refrigerate, covered, overnight.
2. Just before serving, stir in yogurt. Top with walnuts and fruit.
Note: To toast nuts, bake in a shallow pan in a 350° oven for 5-10 minutes or cook in a skillet over low heat until lightly browned, stirring occasionally.

½ cup: 249 cal., 9g fat (1g sat. fat), 3mg chol., 46mg sod., 36g carb. (16g sugars, 3g fiber), 9g pro. **Diabetic exchanges:** 2½ starch, 1 fat.
Health tip: Old-fashioned oats are 100% whole grain. They are slowly absorbed, giving you energy that will last.

CHEESE & FRESH HERB QUICHE

With herbs from the garden to use, I created a quiche with basil, parsley and dill along with feta, Swiss, Gruyere and mozzarella. Goat cheese is also delicious in the mix.
—*Sonya Labbe, West Hollywood, CA*

Prep: 15 min. • **Bake:** 25 min. + standing
Makes: 6 servings

- 1 sheet refrigerated pie crust
- ½ cup shredded part-skim mozzarella cheese
- ½ cup shredded Swiss cheese
- ½ cup shredded Gruyere or additional Swiss cheese
- ½ cup crumbled feta cheese
- 5 large eggs
- 1 cup half-and-half cream
- 1 Tbsp. minced fresh basil
- 1 Tbsp. minced fresh parsley
- 2 tsp. minced fresh dill

1. Preheat oven to 400°. Unroll crust into a 9-in. pie plate; flute edge. Sprinkle cheeses into crust. In a large bowl, whisk eggs and cream until blended. Stir in herbs; pour over top.
2. Bake on a lower oven rack 25-30 minutes or until a knife inserted in center comes out clean. Let stand 10 minutes before cutting.
1 piece: 394 cal., 26g fat (13g sat. fat), 209mg chol., 380mg sod., 21g carb. (3g sugars, 0 fiber), 17g pro.

EGG & ASPARAGUS BREAKFAST CROQUETTES

Trying to come up with something new for breakfast on the run, I thought this was an interesting way to combine the whole meal. If you want to get fancy, these are perfect with hollandaise sauce on top and sprinkled with paprika.
—Barbara J. Miller, Oakdale, MN

Prep: 30 min. + chilling • **Cook:** 5 min./batch
Makes: 6 servings

- 3   Tbsp. butter
- 3   Tbsp. all-purpose flour
- ¾   cup 2% milk
- 6   hard-boiled large eggs, chopped
- ½   cup chopped fresh asparagus
- ½   cup chopped green onions
- ⅓   cup shredded cheddar cheese
- 1   Tbsp. minced fresh tarragon
- ¼   tsp. salt
- ¼   tsp. pepper
- 1¾ cups panko bread crumbs
- 3   large eggs, beaten
      Oil for deep-fat frying

1. In a large saucepan, melt butter over medium heat. Stir in flour until smooth; cook and stir until lightly browned, 1-2 minutes. Gradually whisk in milk; cook and stir until thickened (mixture will be thick). Stir in next 7 ingredients. Refrigerate 2 hours.
2. Shape ¼ cupfuls of egg mixture into twelve 3-in.-long ovals. Place bread crumbs and eggs in separate shallow bowls. Roll logs in crumbs to coat, then dip in egg and roll again in crumbs, patting to help coating adhere. In a deep cast-iron or electric skillet, heat oil to 375°. Fry in batches until golden brown, about 3 minutes, turning occasionally. Drain on paper towels.
2 croquettes: 381 cal., 27g fat (8g sat. fat), 303mg chol., 348mg sod., 18g carb. (3g sugars, 1g fiber), 15g pro.

PRESSURE-COOKER APPLE PIE STEEL-CUT OATMEAL

I absolutely love this one-dish oatmeal. The steel-cut oats have so much flavor and texture. My family loves to sprinkle toasted pecans on top.
—Angela Lively, Conroe, TX

Prep: 10 min. + standing
Cook: 5 min. + releasing • **Makes:** 8 servings

- 6   cups water
- 1½ cups steel-cut oats
- 1½ cups unsweetened applesauce
- ¼   cup maple syrup
- 1½ tsp. ground cinnamon
- ½   tsp. ground nutmeg
- ⅛   tsp. salt
- 1   large apple, chopped
      Optional toppings: Sliced apples and toasted pecans

1. In a 6-qt. electric pressure cooker, combine the first 7 ingredients. Lock lid; close pressure-release valve. Adjust to pressure-cook on high for 5 minutes. Let pressure release naturally.
2. Stir in chopped apple. Let stand 10 minutes before serving (oatmeal will thicken upon standing). If desired, top servings with sliced apples, pecans and additional syrup.
1¼ cups: 171 cal., 2g fat (0 sat. fat), 0 chol., 39mg sod., 36g carb. (13g sugars, 4g fiber), 4g pro.

HOT SPINACH SPREAD
WITH PITA CHIPS, PAGE 253

SMALL BITES
& SNACKS

Treat your guests to a tempting array of dips, appetizers and snacks. These are so unique and flavorful, they're sure to win hearts everywhere they go. Some are downright good for you, too.

KALAMATA CHEESECAKE APPETIZER

The savory cheesecake filling tames the bold flavor of kalamata olives, so even those who shy away from kalamatas will be glad they sampled this dish. For a milder flavor, use the more common black or green olives.
—*Theresa Kreyche, Tustin, CA*

Prep: 30 min. • **Bake:** 25 min. + chilling
Makes: 24 servings

- 1¼ cups seasoned bread crumbs
- ½ cup finely chopped pecans
- ⅓ cup butter, melted

FILLING

- 11 oz. cream cheese, softened
- 1 cup sour cream
- 1 Tbsp. all-purpose flour
- ¼ tsp. salt
- ¼ tsp. pepper
- 1 large egg, room temperature
- 1 large egg yolk, room temperature
- ½ cup pitted kalamata olives, chopped
- 2 tsp. minced fresh rosemary
  Optional: Halved pitted kalamata olives and fresh rosemary sprigs

1. In a small bowl, combine bread crumbs and pecans; stir in butter. Press onto bottom of a greased 9-in. springform pan. Place pan on a baking sheet. Bake at 350° for 12 minutes. Cool on a wire rack.

2. In a large bowl, beat the cream cheese, sour cream, flour, salt and pepper until smooth. Add egg and egg yolk; beat on low speed just until combined. Fold in chopped olives and minced rosemary. Pour over crust. Return pan to baking sheet.

3. Bake for 25-30 minutes or until center is almost set. Cool on a wire rack for 10 minutes. Loosen edges of cheesecake from pan with a knife. Cool 1 hour longer. Refrigerate overnight.

4. Remove rim from the pan. If desired, top cheesecake with halved olives and rosemary sprigs.

1 slice: 142 cal., 12g fat (6g sat. fat), 45mg chol., 223mg sod., 6g carb. (1g sugars, 0 fiber), 3g pro.

READER RAVE

"Incredible flavor combination. The pecans in the crust balanced the saltiness of the olives. The creaminess of the cheesecake brought it all together. Served it at a dinner party to rave reviews and requests for the recipe."
—KMDKMDKMD, TASTEOFHOME.COM

CURRY CARROT DIP

The flavors of sweet carrots, mustard and curry blend deliciously in this appetizing dip. Raw veggies are the perfect partners.
—*Louise Weyer, Marietta, GA*

Takes: 30 min. • **Makes:** 1 cup

- 1 small onion, chopped
- 2 tsp. canola oil
- 4 medium carrots, sliced
- ⅓ cup water
- ¼ tsp. salt
- ¼ tsp. pepper
- ¼ tsp. curry powder
- 2 Tbsp. reduced-fat mayonnaise
- 2 tsp. prepared mustard
  Assorted raw vegetables

1. In a nonstick skillet, saute onion in oil. Add carrots, water, salt, pepper and curry. Bring to a boil. Reduce heat; cover and simmer for 6 minutes or until the vegetables are tender. Uncover; cook for 8 minutes or until liquid has evaporated. Cool.
2. Transfer to a food processor or blender; cover and process until smooth. Add the mayonnaise and mustard; mix well. Serve with vegetables.
2 Tbsp.: 40 cal., 3g fat (0 sat. fat), 1mg chol., 133mg sod., 4g carb. (2g sugars, 1g fiber), 0 pro.

PUMPKIN PINWHEELS

Cream cheese, mozzarella and roasted red peppers make these pretty pinwheels devilishly delightful. They were a hit at my last Halloween party.
—Anndrea Bailey, Huntington Beach, CA

Prep: 15 min. + chilling • **Bake:** 20 min.
Makes: 32 pinwheels

- 2 pkg. (8 oz. each) cream cheese, softened
- 1 cup shredded part-skim mozzarella cheese
- ½ cup chopped roasted sweet red peppers, drained
- ¼ tsp. Italian seasoning
- ¼ tsp. garlic salt
- ¼ tsp. onion powder
- 2 tubes (8 oz. each) refrigerated crescent rolls
  Optional: Pretzel sticks and fresh cilantro leaves

1. Preheat oven to 350°. Beat cream cheese until smooth. Beat in the mozzarella, red peppers and seasonings until blended. Unroll tubes of crescent dough and separate each into 2 rectangles; press perforations to seal.
2. Spread the cheese mixture over each rectangle. Roll up jelly-roll style, starting with a short side; pinch seam to seal. Wrap and chill at least 1 hour.
3. Cut each roll crosswise into 8 slices; place on ungreased baking sheets, cut side down. Bake until golden brown, 20-22 minutes. If desired, decorate with pretzel sticks and cilantro leaves to look like pumpkins.
1 pinwheel: 112 cal., 8g fat (3g sat. fat), 17mg chol., 204mg sod., 7g carb. (2g sugars, 0 fiber), 3g pro.

FRESH FROM THE GARDEN WRAPS

We moved into a house with a garden that needed tending. Using the herbs we found, we made these freshtastic wraps for our first dinner there.
—Chris Bugher, Asheville, NC

Prep: 20 min. + standing
Makes: 8 servings

- 1 medium ear sweet corn
- 1 medium cucumber, chopped
- 1 cup shredded cabbage
- 1 medium tomato, chopped
- 1 small red onion, chopped
- 1 jalapeno pepper, seeded and minced
- 1 Tbsp. minced fresh basil
- 1 Tbsp. minced fresh cilantro
- 1 Tbsp. minced fresh mint
- ⅓ cup Thai chili sauce
- 3 Tbsp. rice vinegar
- 2 tsp. reduced-sodium soy sauce
- 2 tsp. creamy peanut butter
- 8 Bibb or Boston lettuce leaves

1. Cut corn from cob and place in a large bowl. Add cucumber, cabbage, tomato, onion, jalapeno and herbs.
2. Whisk together chili sauce, vinegar, soy sauce and peanut butter. Pour over vegetable mixture; toss to coat. Let stand 20 minutes.
3. Using a slotted spoon, place ½ cup salad in each lettuce leaf. Fold lettuce over filling.
Note: Wear disposable gloves when cutting hot peppers; the oils can burn skin. Avoid touching your face.
1 filled lettuce wrap: 64 cal., 1g fat (0 sat. fat), 0 chol., 319mg sod., 13g carb. (10g sugars, 2g fiber), 2g pro. **Diabetic exchanges:** 1 vegetable, ½ starch.

PICKLED MUSHROOMS WITH GARLIC

I'm always asked to bring these tempting tidbits to holiday gatherings. Simple to make ahead and transport, they're something to celebrate on a festive relish tray.
—*Joyce Anderson, Chico, CA*

Prep: 10 min. + marinating • **Makes:** 4½ cups

- ⅔ cup white wine vinegar
- ½ cup vegetable oil
- 2 Tbsp. water
- 1 tsp. salt
  Dash pepper
  Dash hot pepper sauce
- 1 lb. small whole fresh mushrooms
- 1 medium onion, thinly sliced
- 2 to 4 garlic cloves, thinly sliced

In a large glass jar with a tight-fitting lid, combine the first 6 ingredients. Add the mushrooms, onion and garlic. Cover and shake gently to coat. Refrigerate for 8 hours or overnight. Drain before serving.

¼ cup: 25 cal., 2g fat (0 sat. fat), 0 chol., 132mg sod., 2g carb. (0 sugars, 0 fiber), 1g pro.

🕐 HOMEMADE GUACAMOLE

Ever wonder how to make guacamole? Just whip together this recipe for an easy dip with your favorite ingredients.
—*Joan Hallford, North Richland Hills, TX*

- -

Takes: 10 min. • **Makes:** 2 cups

- 3 medium ripe avocados, peeled and cubed
- 1 garlic clove, minced
- ¼ to ½ tsp. salt
- 2 medium tomatoes, seeded and chopped, optional
- 1 small onion, finely chopped
- ¼ cup mayonnaise, optional
- 1 to 2 Tbsp. lime juice
- 1 Tbsp. minced fresh cilantro

Mash avocados with garlic and salt. Stir in remaining ingredients.

¼ cup: 90 cal., 8g fat (1g sat. fat), 0 chol., 78mg sod., 6g carb. (1g sugars, 4g fiber), 1g pro. **Diabetic exchanges:** 1½ fat.

HOW-TO

Ripen Avocados Fast

- When life hands you hard, less-than-ripe avocados, here's how to ripen them ASAP. Place them in a paper bag with an apple or banana. Poke the bag a few times with a toothpick or scissors, and let the avocados ripen at room temperature for a day or 2. The more fruits (and ethylene gas they give off), the faster the results.
- Once cut, place avocado in a container with a few pieces of raw onion, and seal. The sulfur fumes from the onions help stop any discoloration.

VEGETABLE EGG ROLLS

It's nice to get a crunch from egg rolls that aren't deep-fried. Combined with sweet-hot dipping sauce, these vegetable egg rolls are a tasty alternative to less-healthy versions.
—*Pamela Thomas, Watchung, NJ*

- -

Prep: 25 min. • **Bake:** 25 min.
Makes: 14 servings

- 1 large green pepper, cut into thin strips
- 1 cup cut fresh green beans
- 1 Tbsp. olive oil
- 1¾ cups shredded cabbage
- 1 cup chopped fresh broccoli
- 1 cup shredded zucchini
- 1 Tbsp. plus ¾ tsp. herbes de Provence
- 1 tsp. pepper
- 14 egg roll wrappers

SAUCE

- ¼ cup apricot preserves
- ¼ cup orange marmalade
- 1½ tsp. grated orange zest
- 1½ tsp. reduced-sodium soy sauce
- ½ tsp. lime juice
- ¼ tsp. chili garlic sauce

1. In a large skillet over medium heat, cook the green pepper and green beans in oil until tender. Add the cabbage, broccoli, zucchini, herbes de Provence and pepper. Cook until vegetables are crisp-tender, 5-7 minutes longer.

2. Place 3 Tbsp. of vegetable mixture in center of 1 egg roll wrapper. (Keep remaining wrappers covered with a damp paper towel until ready to use.) Fold bottom corner over filling. Fold sides toward center over filling.

Moisten remaining corner with water; roll up tightly to seal. Repeat with remaining vegetable mixture and wrappers.

3. Place seam side down on a 15x10x1-in. baking pan coated with cooking spray. Bake at 425° until golden brown, 20-25 minutes, turning once.

4. Meanwhile, in a small saucepan, cook preserves and marmalade over medium heat until smooth, 8-10 minutes. Remove from heat; let stand for 5 minutes. Add remaining ingredients; mix well. Serve with egg rolls.

Note: Look for herbes de Provence in the spice aisle.

1 egg roll with 1 tsp. sauce: 142 cal., 2g fat (0 sat. fat), 3mg chol., 217mg sod., 29g carb. (7g sugars, 2g fiber), 4g pro.

MEAT
LOVER
OPTION
PAGE 320

HOT SPINACH SPREAD WITH PITA CHIPS

Warm and cheesy, this spread is absolutely scrumptious served on toasted pita wedges. Its colorful appearance makes a stunning addition to any buffet.
—*Teresa Emanuel, Smithville, MO*

Prep: 30 min. • **Bake:** 20 min.
Makes: 16 servings (4 cups spread)

- 2 cups shredded Monterey Jack cheese
- 1 pkg. (10 oz.) frozen chopped spinach, thawed and squeezed dry
- 1 pkg. (8 oz.) cream cheese, cubed
- 2 plum tomatoes, seeded and chopped
- ¾ cup chopped onion
- ⅓ cup half-and-half cream
- 1 Tbsp. finely chopped seeded jalapeno pepper
- 6 pita breads (6 in.)
- ½ cup butter, melted
- 2 tsp. lemon-pepper seasoning
- 2 tsp. ground cumin
- ¼ tsp. garlic salt

1. In a large bowl, gently combine the first 7 ingredients. Transfer to a greased 1½-qt. baking dish. Bake, uncovered, at 375° for 20-25 minutes or until bubbly.

2. Meanwhile, cut each pita bread into 8 wedges. Place in two 15x10x1-in. baking pans. Combine the butter, lemon pepper, cumin and garlic salt; brush over pita wedges.

3. Bake for 7-9 minutes or until crisp. Serve with spinach spread.

Note: Wear disposable gloves when cutting hot peppers; the oils can burn skin. Avoid touching your face.

¼ cup spread with 3 pita wedges: 231 cal., 16g fat (10g sat. fat), 46mg chol., 381mg sod., 15g carb. (1g sugars, 1g fiber), 8g pro.

CHEESE & GRAPE APPETIZERS

These small bites are well worth the time they take. Serve them as part of an antipasto platter or as a cheese course alongside your favorite wine.
—*Eleanor Grofvert, Kalamazoo, MI*

Prep: 35 min. • **Bake:** 10 min. + cooling
Makes: about 5 dozen

- 4 oz. sliced almonds (about 1 cup)
- 1 pkg. (8 oz.) cream cheese, softened
- 2 oz. crumbled blue cheese, room temperature
- 2 Tbsp. minced fresh parsley
- 2 Tbsp. heavy whipping cream, room temperature
  Appetizer skewers or toothpicks
- 1 to 1¼ lbs. seedless red or green grapes, rinsed and patted dry

1. Preheat oven to 275°. Pulse almonds in a food processor until finely chopped (do not overprocess). Spread in a 15x10x1-in. pan; bake until golden brown, 6-9 minutes, stirring occasionally. Transfer to a shallow bowl; cool slightly.

2. In another bowl, mix cream cheese, blue cheese, parsley and cream until blended. Insert a skewer into each grape. Roll grapes in cheese mixture, then in almonds; place on waxed paper-lined baking sheets. Refrigerate, covered, until serving.

5 appetizers: 146 cal., 11g fat (6g sat. fat), 28mg chol., 124mg sod., 8g carb. (7g sugars, 1g fiber), 4g pro.

PARTY CHEESE BREAD

You can't go wrong with this recipe. The cheesy, buttery loaf looks fantastic and is so simple to make—people just flock to it. The taste is positively sinful, and it's better than the usual garlic bread with pasta, too.
—*Karen Grant, Tulare, CA*

- -

Prep: 25 min. • **Bake:** 30 min.
Makes: 16 servings

1	round loaf sourdough bread (1 lb.)
1	lb. Monterey Jack cheese, sliced
½	cup butter, melted
2	Tbsp. lemon juice
2	Tbsp. Dijon mustard
1½	tsp. garlic powder
½	tsp. onion powder
½	tsp. celery salt
	Minced fresh chives, optional

1. Preheat oven to 350°. Cut bread into 1-in. slices to within ½ in. of bottom of loaf. Repeat cuts in opposite direction. Insert cheese in cuts.

2. Mix all remaining ingredients except chives; drizzle over bread. Wrap in foil; place on a baking sheet.

3. Bake 20 minutes. Unwrap; bake until cheese is melted, about 10 minutes. If desired, sprinkle with chives.

1 serving: 237 cal., 15g fat (9g sat. fat), 41mg chol., 468mg sod., 15g carb. (2g sugars, 1g fiber), 10g pro.

TEST KITCHEN TIP

Turn this loaf into a turtle or a hedgehog using additional small rolls, chopped vegetables, pickles and olives. So cute!

⏱ RAINBOW PEPPER APPETIZERS

Company will quickly polish off this colorful pepper medley. The crisp-tender veggies are topped with chopped olives and cheese.
—*Marion Karlin, Waterloo, IA*

Takes: 20 min. • **Makes:** 3 dozen

- ½ each medium green, sweet red, yellow and orange peppers
- 1 cup shredded Monterey Jack cheese
- 2 Tbsp. chopped ripe olives
- ¼ tsp. crushed red pepper flakes, optional

1. Cut each pepper half into 9 pieces. Place skin side down in an ungreased cast-iron or other ovenproof skillet; sprinkle with cheese, olives and, if desired, pepper flakes.
2. Broil 3-4 in. from the heat until peppers are crisp-tender and the cheese is melted, 5-7 minutes.

3 pieces: 34 cal., 2g fat (1g sat. fat), 7mg chol., 93mg sod., 2g carb. (1g sugars, 0 fiber), 3g pro. **Diabetic exchanges:** 1 vegetable.

SPICY SWEET POTATO CHIPS & CILANTRO DIP

This cool, creamy dip is a perfect partner for the spicy sweet potato chips. They're made for each other!
—*Elizabeth Godecke, Chicago, IL*

Prep: 20 min. • **Bake:** 25 min./batch
Makes: 12 servings (1½ cups dip)

- 2 to 3 large sweet potatoes (1¾ lbs.), peeled and cut into ⅛-in. slices
- 2 Tbsp. canola oil
- 1 tsp. chili powder
- ½ tsp. garlic powder
- ½ tsp. taco seasoning
- ¼ tsp. salt
- ¼ tsp. ground cumin
- ¼ tsp. pepper
- ⅛ tsp. cayenne pepper

DIP
- ¾ cup mayonnaise
- ½ cup sour cream
- 2 oz. cream cheese, softened
- 4½ tsp. minced fresh cilantro
- 1½ tsp. lemon juice
- ½ tsp. celery salt
- ⅛ tsp. pepper

1. Preheat oven to 400°. Place the sweet potatoes in a large bowl. In a small bowl, mix oil and seasonings; drizzle over potatoes and toss to coat.
2. Arrange half the sweet potatoes in a single layer in 2 ungreased 15x10x1-in. baking pans. Bake 25-30 minutes or until golden brown, turning once. Repeat with the remaining sweet potatoes.
3. In a small bowl, beat dip ingredients until blended. Serve with chips.

½ cup chips with about 1 Tbsp. dip: 285 cal., 16g fat (4g sat. fat), 8mg chol., 217mg sod., 33g carb. (14g sugars, 4g fiber), 3g pro.

APPETIZER TOMATO CHEESE BREAD

I found this recipe in a dairy cookbook, and it has become a family favorite. We milk 180 cows and have a large garden, so we welcome dishes that use both dairy and fresh vegetables. My husband and our two children are mostly meat-and-potato eaters, but I don't hear any complaints when I serve this irresistible bread!

—*Penney Kester, Springville, NY*

Prep: 20 min. • **Bake:** 25 min. + standing
Makes: 12 servings

- 2   Tbsp. butter
- 1   medium onion, minced
- 1   cup shredded cheddar cheese
- ½   cup sour cream
- ¼   cup mayonnaise
- ¾   tsp. salt
- ¼   tsp. pepper
- ¼   tsp. dried oregano
       Pinch rubbed sage
- 2   cups biscuit/baking mix
- ⅔   cup 2% milk
- 3   medium tomatoes, cut into ¼-in. slices
       Paprika

1. In a small skillet, heat butter over medium heat. Add onion and cook until tender. Remove from the heat. Stir in the cheese, sour cream, mayonnaise and seasonings; set aside.

2. In a bowl, combine the baking mix and milk to form a soft dough. Turn dough onto a well-floured surface; knead lightly 10-12 times. Pat into a greased 13x9-in. baking dish, pushing dough up sides of dish to form a shallow rim. Arrange tomato slices over top. Spread with topping; sprinkle with paprika.

3. Bake at 400° for 25 minutes. Let stand for 10 minutes before cutting.

1 piece: 209 cal., 14g fat (6g sat. fat), 26mg chol., 521mg sod., 17g carb. (3g sugars, 1g fiber), 5g pro.

⑤ⓛ CAMEMBERT & CRANBERRY PIZZA

Appetizer pizza takes several steps up in elegance with creamy Camembert cheese. Tangy, bright cranberries make this a welcome addition to any holiday party.
—*Sue Sans, Buckeye, AZ*

- -

Takes: 30 min. • **Makes:** 2 dozen pieces

- 1 tube (13.8 oz.) refrigerated pizza crust
- 1 can (14 oz.) whole-berry cranberry sauce
- 1 round (8 oz.) Camembert cheese, cut into ½-in. cubes
- ½ cup chopped pecans
  Chopped fresh parsley, optional

1. Preheat oven to 425°. Unroll and press dough onto bottom and ½ in. up sides of a greased 15x10-in. pan. Bake until golden brown, 6-8 minutes.
2. Place cranberry sauce in a bowl; stir to break up. Spoon over crust; top with cheese and pecans. Bake until cheese is melted, 6-8 minutes. If desired, sprinkle with parsley. Cool 5 minutes; cut into squares.
1 piece: 108 cal., 4g fat (2g sat. fat), 7mg chol., 183mg sod., 14g carb. (5g sugars, 1g fiber), 3g pro.

🍲 CLASSIC HUMMUS

We love hummus, and this version is really amazing. If you have a pressure cooker, this is an easy, tasty reason to pull it out! We pair hummus with fresh veggies for a meal or a healthy snack.
—*Monica and David Eichler, Lawrence, KS*

- -

Prep: 20 min. + soaking
Cook: 15 min. + chilling • **Makes:** 2½ cups

- 1 cup dried garbanzo beans or chickpeas
- 1 medium onion, quartered
- 1 bay leaf
- 4 cups water
- ¼ cup minced fresh parsley
- ¼ cup lemon juice
- ¼ cup tahini
- 4 to 6 garlic cloves, minced
- 1 tsp. ground cumin
- ¾ tsp. salt
- ⅛ tsp. cayenne pepper
- ¼ cup olive oil
  Assorted fresh vegetables

1. Rinse and sort beans; soak according to package directions.
2. Drain and rinse the beans, discarding liquid. Transfer to a 6-qt. electric pressure cooker; add the onion, bay leaf and water.
3. Lock the lid; close pressure-release valve. Adjust to pressure cook on high for 12 minutes. Let pressure release naturally. Drain mixture, reserving ½ cup cooking liquid. Discard the onion and bay leaf.
4. Place the beans, parsley, lemon juice, tahini, garlic, cumin, salt and cayenne in a food processor; cover and process until smooth. While processing, gradually add oil in a steady stream. Add enough reserved cooking liquid to achieve desired consistency.
5. Cover and refrigerate for at least 1 hour. Serve with vegetables.
¼ cup: 139 cal., 10g fat (1g sat. fat), 0 chol., 190mg sod., 14g carb. (1g sugars, 6g fiber), 5g pro. **Diabetic exchanges:** 1½ fat, 1 starch.

MINI GRILLED CHEESE

If you're looking for a fantastic make-ahead snack, try these. They're nice to have in the freezer for lunch with soup or a salad. My family loves to nibble on them anytime.
—*Anita Curtis, Camarillo, CA*

Takes: 30 min. • **Makes:** 8 dozen

- 1 cup butter, softened
- 2 jars (5 oz. each) sharp American cheese spread, softened
- 1 large egg
- 1 can (4 oz.) chopped green chiles, drained
- ¼ cup salsa
- 2 cups shredded cheddar cheese
- 2 loaves (1½ lbs. each) thinly sliced sandwich bread, crusts removed

1. Preheat oven to 350°. Cream butter, cheese spread and egg until smooth. Stir in chiles, salsa and cheddar cheese. Spread about 1 Tbsp. cheese mixture on each slice of 1 loaf of bread.

2. Top with remaining bread; spread with more cheese mixture. Cut each sandwich into 4 squares or triangles; place on a baking sheet lined with parchment. Bake until cheese is melted, 10-15 minutes.

Freeze option: Place in a single layer on a baking sheet. Freeze 1 hour. Transfer to an airtight container and store in the freezer. Bake frozen appetizers as directed until bubbly and browned, about 15-20 minutes.

2 pieces: 102 cal., 7g fat (4g sat. fat), 22mg chol., 213mg sod., 8g carb. (1g sugars, 0 fiber), 3g pro.

SPANISH MARINATED MUSHROOMS

I had some amazing marinated mushrooms in a little tapas bar in Seville when I was stationed in Spain with the U.S. Navy. A couple of months ago, I decided to see if I could make something close, and here's what I came up with. The longer you keep them refrigerated, the stronger the vinegar taste will be.
—*Patricia Mitchell, Ingleside, TX*

Prep: 15 min. + marinating
Makes: 6 cups

- 2 cups water
- 1 cup red wine vinegar
- 3 Tbsp. olive oil
- 1 Tbsp. sugar
- 1 Tbsp. dried basil
- 2 garlic cloves, minced
- 1½ tsp. salt
- 1 tsp. dried oregano
- ½ tsp. crushed red pepper flakes
- 2 lbs. small fresh mushrooms

1. In a large shallow dish, combine the first 9 ingredients. Add the mushrooms and turn to coat. Cover and refrigerate for at least 8 hours or overnight.

2. Drain mushrooms, discarding marinade.

¼ cup: 10 cal., 0 fat (0 sat. fat), 0 chol., 21mg sod., 1g carb. (0 sugars, 0 fiber), 1g pro.

SLOW-COOKER CAPONATA

This Italian eggplant dip preps quickly and actually gets better as it stands. Serve it warm or at room temperature. Try adding a little leftover caponata to scrambled eggs for a savory breakfast.

—*Nancy Beckman, Helena, MT*

- -

Prep: 20 min. • **Cook:** 5 hours
Makes: 6 cups

- 2 medium eggplants, cut into ½-in. pieces
- 1 medium onion, chopped
- 1 can (14½ oz.) diced tomatoes, undrained
- 12 garlic cloves, sliced
- ½ cup dry red wine
- 3 Tbsp. extra virgin olive oil
- 2 Tbsp. red wine vinegar
- 4 tsp. capers, undrained
- 5 bay leaves
- 1½ tsp. salt
- ¼ tsp. coarsely ground pepper
  French bread baguette slices, toasted
  Optional: Fresh basil leaves, toasted pine nuts and additional olive oil

Place first 11 ingredients in a 6-qt. slow cooker (do not stir). Cook, covered, on high for 3 hours. Stir gently; replace cover. Cook on high until vegetables are tender, about 2 hours longer. Cool slightly; discard bay leaves. Serve with toasted baguette slices, adding toppings as desired.

¼ cup: 34 cal., 2g fat (0 sat. fat), 0 chol., 189mg sod., 4g carb. (2g sugars, 2g fiber), 1g pro.

TEST KITCHEN TIP

For easy entertaining, serve warm directly from the slow cooker or at room temperature.

FLORENTINE ALMOND ARTICHOKE MOUNDS

I always enjoyed traditional spinach artichoke dip. For a party, I wanted to make a new appetizer that was a spin on that. This original creation is a bit reminiscent of the dip recipe and works well on a buffet.
—*Sherry Johnston, Green Cove Springs, FL*

Prep: 20 min. • **Bake:** 20 minutes
Makes: 8 servings

- 2 cans (14 oz. each) artichoke bottoms, drained
- 1 pkg. (16 oz.) frozen leaf spinach, thawed and squeezed dry
- ¾ cup heavy whipping cream
- ¾ cup shredded Swiss cheese
- ¾ cup chopped or sliced almonds, divided
- 2 large garlic cloves, minced
- 2 tsp. prepared horseradish
- ½ tsp. salt
- ¼ tsp. coarsely ground pepper

1. Preheat oven to 400°. Rinse artichoke bottoms; pat dry with paper towels. Combine spinach with cream, Swiss cheese and ½ cup almonds; mix in garlic, horseradish, salt and pepper. Place the artichoke bottoms on a parchment-lined baking sheet. Mound the spinach mixture on artichokes; sprinkle with remaining almonds.
2. Bake until almonds turn golden brown, 20-25 minutes. Serve hot or at room temperature.
1 appetizer: 243 cal., 18g fat (8g sat. fat), 35mg chol., 461mg sod., 12g carb. (3g sugars, 4g fiber), 10g pro.

HERBED LEEK TARTS

This savory tart recipe is a favorite among family and friends! It's delicious and different—and surprisingly easy to make.
—*Jean Ecos, Hartland, WI*

Prep: 25 min. • **Bake:** 20 min. + cooling
Makes: 2 tarts (8 servings each)

- 3 cups thinly sliced leeks (about 4 medium)
- ½ cup chopped sweet red pepper
- 4 garlic cloves, minced
- 2 Tbsp. olive oil
- 1½ cups shredded Swiss cheese
- 2 Tbsp. Dijon mustard
- 1 tsp. herbes de Provence
- 2 sheets refrigerated pie crust
- 1 tsp. 2% milk
- 2 Tbsp. chopped almonds or walnuts, optional

1. In a large skillet, saute the leeks, red pepper and garlic in oil until tender. Remove from the heat; cool for 5 minutes. Stir in the cheese, mustard and herbs; set aside.
2. On a lightly floured surface, roll each sheet of crust into a 12-in. circle. Transfer to parchment-lined baking sheets. Spoon leek mixture over crusts to within 2 in. of edges. Fold edges of crust over filling, leaving center uncovered. Brush folded crust with milk; sprinkle with nuts if desired.
3. Bake at 375° for 20-25 minutes or until crust is golden and filling is bubbly. Using parchment, slide tarts onto wire racks. Cool for 10 minutes before cutting. Serve warm. Refrigerate leftovers.
Note: Look for herbes de Provence in the spice aisle.
1 slice: 194 cal., 12g fat (5g sat. fat), 14mg chol., 177mg sod., 17g carb. (2g sugars, 1g fiber), 5g pro.

❄️🍲 HEALTHY GREEK BEAN DIP

This crowd-pleasing appetizer is healthy to boot! Folks will love to eat their veggies when they can dip them in this zesty, fresh alternative to hummus.
—*Kelly Silvers, Edmond, OK*

Prep: 15 min. • **Cook:** 2 hours • **Makes:** 3 cups

- 2 cans (15 oz. each) cannellini beans, rinsed and drained
- ¼ cup water
- ¼ cup finely chopped roasted sweet red peppers
- 2 Tbsp. finely chopped red onion
- 2 Tbsp. olive oil
- 2 Tbsp. lemon juice
- 1 Tbsp. snipped fresh dill
- 2 garlic cloves, minced
- ¼ tsp. salt
- ¼ tsp. pepper
- 1 small cucumber, peeled, seeded and finely chopped
- ½ cup fat-free plain Greek yogurt
  Additional snipped fresh dill
  Baked pita chips or assorted fresh vegetables

Process beans and water in a food processor until smooth. Transfer to a greased 1½-qt. slow cooker. Add the next 8 ingredients. Cook, covered, on low until heated through, 2-3 hours. Stir in cucumber and yogurt; cool slightly. Sprinkle with additional dill. Serve warm or cold with chips or assorted fresh vegetables.

Freeze option: Omitting cucumber, yogurt and additional dill, freeze cooled dip in freezer containers. To use dip, thaw in refrigerator overnight. To serve dip warm, heat through in a saucepan, stirring occasionally. Or serve cold. Stir cucumber and yogurt into finished dip; sprinkle with additional dill. Serve with chips or vegetables.

¼ cup: 86 cal., 3g fat (0 sat. fat), 0 chol., 260mg sod., 11g carb. (1g sugars, 3g fiber), 4g pro. **Diabetic exchanges:** 1 starch, ½ fat.

🕐 THREE-CHEESE FONDUE

I got this easy recipe from my daughter, who lives in France. It's become my go-to fondue, and I make it often for our family.
—*Betty Mangas, Toledo, OH*

Takes: 30 min. • **Makes:** 4 cups

- ½ lb. each Emmenthaler, Gruyere and Jarlsberg cheeses, shredded
- 2 Tbsp. cornstarch, divided
- 4 tsp. cherry brandy
- 2 cups dry white wine
- ⅛ tsp. ground nutmeg
- ⅛ tsp. paprika
  Dash cayenne pepper
  Cubed French bread baguette, boiled red potatoes and/or tiny whole pickles

1. In a large bowl, combine cheeses and 1 Tbsp. cornstarch. In a small bowl, combine remaining cornstarch and brandy; set aside. In a large saucepan, heat wine over medium heat until bubbles form around sides of pan.

2. Reduce heat to medium-low; add a handful of cheese mixture. Stir constantly, using a figure-8 motion, until cheese is almost completely melted. Continue adding cheese, one handful at a time, allowing cheese to almost completely melt between additions.

3. Stir brandy mixture; gradually stir into cheese mixture. Add spices; cook and stir until mixture is thickened and smooth.

4. Transfer to a fondue pot and keep warm. Serve with bread cubes, potatoes and/or pickles.

¼ cup: 191 cal., 12g fat (7g sat. fat), 37mg chol., 151mg sod., 3g carb. (1g sugars, 0 fiber), 12g pro.

DID YOU KNOW?

Nutmeg is the secret spice in many savory recipes. It's commonly used in white sauces, pastas and potato dishes. Be careful not to overdo it. A small amount goes a long way.

🔟 ROASTED BUTTERNUT SQUASH DIPPERS

When it comes to fries, I've made everything from apple and carrot to pumpkin and zucchini. The sour cream sauce is just heavenly with squash fries.
—*Paula Marchesi, Lenhartsville, PA*

Prep: 10 min. • **Bake:** 25 min.
Makes: 4 servings (⅔ cup dip)

- 1 small butternut squash (about 2 lbs.)
- 2 tsp. olive oil
- 1 tsp. Cajun seasoning
- ¼ tsp. salt
- ¼ tsp. pepper
DIP
- ½ cup sour cream
- 2 Tbsp. maple syrup

1. Preheat oven to 425°. Peel, halve and seed squash; cut into 3x½-in. strips. Spread in a greased foil-lined 15x10x1-in. pan; toss with oil. Roast until tender and lightly browned, 25-30 minutes, stirring once.

2. Sprinkle with seasonings. Mix the dip ingredients; serve with squash.

1 serving: 208 cal., 7g fat (4g sat. fat), 20mg chol., 303mg sod., 34g carb. (13g sugars, 8g fiber), 3g pro.

SLOW-COOKER SPICED MIXED NUTS

What slow cookers do for soups and stews, they'll do for mixed nuts, too. The scent of spices is delightful, and the nuts are delicious.
—Stephanie Loaiza, Layton, UT

Prep: 15 min. • **Cook:** 1 hour 50 min. + cooling
Makes: 6 cups

- 1 large egg white
- 2 tsp. vanilla extract
- 1 cup unblanched almonds
- 1 cup pecan halves
- 1 cup shelled walnuts
- 1 cup unsalted cashews
- 1 cup sugar
- 1 cup packed brown sugar
- 4 tsp. ground cinnamon
- 2 tsp. ground ginger
- 1 tsp. ground nutmeg
- ½ tsp. ground cloves
- ⅛ tsp. salt
- 2 Tbsp. water

1. In a large bowl, whisk egg white and vanilla until blended; stir in nuts. In a small bowl, mix sugars, spices and salt. Add to nut mixture and toss to coat.

2. Transfer to a greased 3-qt. slow cooker. Cook, covered, on high 1½ hours, stirring every 15 minutes. Gradually stir in water. Cook, covered, on low 20 minutes.

3. Spread onto waxed paper; cool nuts completely. Store in an airtight container up to 1 week.

⅓ cup: 261 cal., 15g fat (2g sat. fat), 0 chol., 26mg sod., 30g carb. (24g sugars, 2g fiber), 5g pro.

PRESSURE-COOKER LIGHT DEVILED EGGS

Our updated version of a classic appetizer uses only half the egg yolks of traditional deviled eggs and calls for soft bread crumbs to help firm up the filling. Light ingredients lower the fat grams even more.
—Taste of Home *Test Kitchen*

Prep: 20 min. • **Cook:** 5 min. + releasing
Makes: 16 pieces

- 8 large eggs
- ¼ cup fat-free mayonnaise
- ¼ cup reduced-fat sour cream
- 2 Tbsp. soft bread crumbs
- 1 Tbsp. prepared mustard
- ¼ tsp. salt
  Dash white pepper
- 4 pimiento-stuffed olives, sliced
  Paprika, optional

1. Place trivet insert and 1 cup water in a 6-qt. electric pressure cooker. Set eggs on trivet. Lock lid; close pressure-release valve. Adjust to pressure-cook on high for 5 minutes. Let pressure release naturally for 5 minutes; quick-release any remaining pressure. Immediately place eggs in a bowl of ice water to cool. Remove shells.

2. Cut eggs lengthwise in half. Remove yolks; refrigerate 8 yolk halves for another use. Set whites aside. In a small bowl, mash remaining yolks. Stir in mayonnaise, sour cream, bread crumbs, mustard, salt and pepper. Stuff or pipe into egg whites. Garnish with olives. If desired, sprinkle with paprika.

1 stuffed egg half: 32 cal., 2g fat (1g sat. fat), 46mg chol., 132mg sod., 1g carb. (1g sugars, 0 fiber), 3g pro.

TOMATO & CORN CHEESY PASTRY BITES

Local veggies and herbs have a magical knack for inspiring me to cook. After my CSA box arrived, I used the fresh ingredients to create this adorable appetizer.

—Kristen Heigl, Staten Island, NY

Prep: 25 min. • **Bake:** 20 min.
Makes: 8 pastries

- 1 Tbsp. olive oil
- ½ cup finely chopped onion
- 1 cup fresh corn
- 1 tsp. garlic powder
- ½ tsp. minced fresh parsley
- ¼ tsp. salt
- ⅛ tsp. pepper
- 1 pkg. (17.3 oz.) frozen puff pastry, thawed
- 1 large egg
- 1 Tbsp. water
- ¾ cup quartered cherry tomatoes
- ½ cup crumbled goat cheese
- ½ cup shredded provolone cheese
- 2 Tbsp. minced fresh basil

1. Preheat oven to 375°. In a large skillet, heat oil over medium heat. Add onion; cook and stir until tender, about 5 minutes. Stir in corn, garlic powder, parsley, salt and pepper; cook until corn is tender, about 2 minutes. Remove from heat.

2. Unfold puff pastry sheets. Using a floured 4-in. round cookie cutter, cut 4 circles in each sheet; place on parchment-lined baking sheets. Whisk together the egg and water; brush over pastries. Spoon 2 Tbsp. corn mixture onto each circle. Top with tomatoes and cheeses.

3. Bake until golden brown and cheese is melted, about 20 minutes. Sprinkle with basil.

1 pastry: 236 cal., 14g fat (5g sat. fat), 37mg chol., 279mg sod., 22g carb. (2g sugars, 3g fiber), 7g pro.

Health tip: Puff pastry is convenient but very rich. Lighten up this appetizer by serving the veggie mixture on toasted sliced French bread or English muffin halves. Decrease bake time.

⑤ THYME-SEA SALT CRACKERS

These homemade crackers are decidedly light and crispy. They are irresistible on their own as a snack or pair well with a sharp white cheddar.

—Jessica Wirth, Charlotte, NC

Prep: 25 min. • **Bake:** 10 min./batch
Makes: about 7 dozen

- 2½ cups all-purpose flour
- ½ cup white whole wheat flour
- 1 tsp. salt
- ¾ cup water
- ¼ cup plus 1 Tbsp. olive oil, divided
- 1 to 2 Tbsp. minced fresh thyme
- ¾ tsp. sea or kosher salt

1. Preheat oven to 375°. In a large bowl, whisk flours and salt. Gradually add water and ¼ cup oil, tossing with a fork until dough holds together when pressed.

2. Divide dough into 3 portions. On a lightly floured surface, roll each portion of dough to ⅛-in. thickness. Cut with a floured 1½-in. round cookie cutter. Place 1 in. apart on ungreased baking sheets. Prick each cracker with a fork; brush lightly with remaining oil. Mix the thyme and sea salt; sprinkle over the crackers.

3. Bake 9-11 minutes or until bottoms are lightly browned.

1 cracker: 23 cal., 1g fat (0 sat. fat), 0 chol., 45mg sod., 3g carb. (0 sugars, 0 fiber), 0 pro.

MUSHROOM & SMOKED GOUDA PUFF

It's so very easy, but it looks and tastes gourmet. Dinner party guests will be impressed with this perfect starter course. Serve it with a spicy mustard for dipping if desired.
—*Christina Singer, Bellefontaine, OH*

- -

Prep: 30 min. • **Bake:** 30 min. + standing
Makes: 8 servings

- 4½ tsp. butter
- ½ cup sliced fresh mushrooms
- ½ cup sliced baby portobello mushrooms
- ¼ cup chopped fresh shiitake mushrooms
- 1 shallot, minced
- 2 tsp. minced fresh thyme
- ¼ tsp. salt
- ⅛ tsp. pepper
- 1 sheet frozen puff pastry, thawed
- ½ cup shredded smoked Gouda cheese
- 1 large egg
- 2 Tbsp. water

1. Preheat oven to 350°. In a large skillet, heat butter over medium-high heat. Add mushrooms and shallot; cook and stir until tender, about 5 minutes. Stir in thyme, salt and pepper.

2. Unfold puff pastry. Spread mushroom mixture to within 1 in. of edges. Sprinkle with cheese. Roll up jelly-roll style; pinch the seam and ends to seal. Place on a parchment-lined baking sheet, seam side down. In a small bowl, whisk the egg and water; brush over pastry. Cut slits in top.

3. Bake until golden brown, about 30 minutes. Let stand for 10 minutes before cutting.

1 slice: 210 cal., 13g fat (5g sat. fat), 37mg chol., 260mg sod., 19g carb. (1g sugars, 2g fiber), 5g pro.

TEST KITCHEN TIP

You can experiment with the cheese here—try a sharp cheddar, a creamy provolone or a blend of different cheeses.

🕐 PUMPKIN HUMMUS

Traditional hummus gets an update for autumn with the addition of canned pumpkin. Hot pepper sauce lends just the right amount of heat.
—Taste of Home *Test Kitchen*

- -

Takes: 15 min. • **Makes:** 4 cups

  2 cans (15 oz. each) garbanzo beans or chickpeas, rinsed and drained
  1 can (15 oz.) solid-pack pumpkin
  ½ cup olive oil
  ⅓ cup tahini
  5 Tbsp. lemon juice
  2 tsp. hot pepper sauce
  2 garlic cloves, minced
  1 tsp. salt
     Baked pita chips
     Assorted fresh vegetables, optional

Place the first 8 ingredients in a food processor; cover and process until blended. Serve with chips and, if desired, vegetables.
¼ cup: 173 cal., 13g fat (2g sat. fat), 0 chol., 243mg sod., 12g carb. (2g sugars, 4g fiber), 5g pro.

MEAT LOVER OPTION PAGE 320

AVOCADO BRUSCHETTA

My mother shared this fabulous recipe with me, and I have shared it with my friends. They are always requesting this tasty appetizer—which is not a problem, because you can prepare it so quickly. The flavor explosion is something else. All this and healthy, too!

—*Stephanie Perenyi, Littleton, CO*

Takes: 20 min. • **Makes:** 2 dozen

- ½ cup olive oil
- ¼ cup lemon juice
- ¼ cup red wine vinegar
- 3 garlic cloves, minced
- 1½ tsp. salt
- 1 tsp. crushed red pepper flakes
- 1 tsp. dried oregano
- ½ tsp. pepper
- ½ cup chopped fresh cilantro
- ½ cup chopped fresh parsley
- ¼ cup chopped fresh basil
- 6 medium ripe avocados, peeled and cubed
- 24 slices French bread baguette (½ in. thick)

Preheat broiler. Whisk together the first 8 ingredients; stir in herbs. Fold in avocados. Place the bread on an ungreased baking sheet; broil 3-4 in. from heat until golden brown, 1-2 minutes per side. Top with the avocado mixture.

1 appetizer: 118 cal., 10g fat (1g sat. fat), 0 chol., 199mg sod., 8g carb. (0 sugars, 2g fiber), 2g pro.

CAPRESE SALAD KABOBS

Trade in the usual veggie party platter for these fun kabobs. I often make them for my family to snack on, and it's a wonderful recipe for the kids to help with.

—*Christine Mitchell, Glendora, CA*

Takes: 10 min. • **Makes:** 12 kabobs

- 24 grape tomatoes
- 12 cherry-size fresh mozzarella cheese balls
- 24 fresh basil leaves
- 2 Tbsp. olive oil
- 2 tsp. balsamic vinegar

On each of 12 appetizer skewers, alternately thread 2 tomatoes, 1 cheese ball and 2 basil leaves. To serve, whisk together oil and vinegar; drizzle over kabobs.

1 kabob: 44 cal., 4g fat (1g sat. fat), 5mg chol., 10mg sod., 2g carb. (1g sugars, 0 fiber), 1g pro. **Diabetic exchanges:** 1 fat.

CAYENNE PRETZELS

These seasoned pretzels were a huge hit at my daughter's graduation party. The longer they sit, the spicier they get!

—*Gayle Zebo, Warren, PA*

Prep: 10 min. • **Bake:** 1¼ hours • **Makes:** 3 qt.

- 1 cup canola oil
- 1 envelope ranch salad dressing mix
- 1 tsp. garlic salt
- 1 tsp. cayenne pepper
- 1 lb. (12 cups) pretzel sticks

1. In a small bowl, combine the oil, dressing mix, garlic salt and cayenne. Divide pretzels between 2 ungreased 15x10x1-in. baking pans. Pour the oil mixture over pretzels; stir to coat.

2. Bake at 200° for 1¼-1½ hours or until golden brown, stirring occasionally. Cool completely. Store in an airtight container.

¾ cup: 236 cal., 15g fat (2g sat. fat), 0 chol., 690mg sod., 24g carb. (1g sugars, 1g fiber), 3g pro.

GARLIC PUMPKIN SEEDS

What to do with all those leftover pumpkin seeds after carving your jack-o'-lantern? Try this yummy microwave-easy recipe. Works great for butternut or acorn squash, too.
—*Iola Egle, Bella Vista, AR*

Takes: 25 min. • **Makes:** 2 cups

- 1 Tbsp. canola oil
- ½ tsp. celery salt
- ½ tsp. garlic powder
- ½ tsp. seasoned salt
- 2 cups fresh pumpkin seeds

1. In a small bowl, combine the oil, celery salt, garlic powder and seasoned salt. Add pumpkin seeds; toss to coat. Spread a quarter of the seeds in a single layer on a microwave-safe plate. Microwave, uncovered, on high for 1 minute; stir.

2. Microwave 2-3 minutes longer or until the seeds are crunchy and lightly browned, stirring after each minute. Repeat with the remaining pumpkin seeds. Serve warm, or cool before storing in an airtight container.

¼ cup: 87 cal., 5g fat (1g sat. fat), 0 chol., 191mg sod., 9g carb. (0 sugars, 1g fiber), 3g pro. **Diabetic exchanges:** 1 fat, ½ starch.

⑤ SAVORY POTATO SKINS

For a simple hot snack on your holiday buffet, put together a plate of these crisp potato skins.

—*Andrea Holcomb, Torrington, CT*

Prep: 1¼ hours • **Broil:** 5 min.
Makes: 32 appetizers

- 4 large baking potatoes (about 12 oz. each)
- 3 Tbsp. butter, melted
- 1 tsp. salt
- 1 tsp. garlic powder
- 1 tsp. paprika
  Optional: Sour cream and chives

1. Preheat oven to 375°. Scrub potatoes; pierce several times with a fork. Place on a greased baking sheet; bake until tender, 1-1¼ hours. Cool slightly.
2. Cut each potato lengthwise in half. Scoop out pulp, leaving ¼-in.-thick shells (save pulp for another use).
3. Cut each half shell lengthwise into quarters; return to baking sheet. Brush insides with butter. Mix seasonings; sprinkle over butter.
4. Broil 4-5 in. from heat until golden brown, 5-8 minutes. If desired, mix sour cream and chives and serve with potato skins.
1 piece: 56 cal., 2g fat (1g sat. fat), 6mg chol., 168mg sod., 8g carb. (0 sugars, 1g fiber), 1g pro.

⑤ ⑥ BROCCOLI & CHIVE STUFFED MINI PEPPERS

Crunchy peppers perfectly balance the creamy filling in these party appetizers. Fresh chives help them stand out.

—*Jean McKenzie, Vancouver, WA*

Takes: 30 min. • **Makes:** 2 dozen

- 12 miniature sweet peppers
- 1 pkg. (8 oz.) cream cheese, softened
- ⅓ cup minced fresh chives
- ⅛ tsp. salt
- ⅛ tsp. pepper
- ⅔ cup finely chopped fresh broccoli
- ⅔ cup shredded cheddar cheese

1. Preheat oven to 400°. Cut peppers lengthwise in half; remove seeds. In a bowl, mix cream cheese, chives, salt and pepper; stir in broccoli. Spoon into pepper halves.
2. Place on a foil-lined baking sheet; bake until heated through, 9-11 minutes. Sprinkle with cheddar cheese. Bake until the cheese is melted, 3-4 minutes longer. Cool slightly before serving.
1 stuffed pepper half: 48 cal., 4g fat (2g sat. fat), 14mg chol., 68mg sod., 1g carb. (1g sugars, 0 fiber), 1g pro.

GRILLED TOMATO-PEACH PIZZA

This delicious pizza is unique, healthy and easy to make. The fresh flavors make it a perfect appetizer for a summer party.
—*Scarlett Elrod, Newnan, GA*

Prep: 20 min. + standing • **Grill:** 5 min.
Makes: 16 pieces

- 4 medium tomatoes, thinly sliced
- ¼ tsp. salt
- 2 medium peaches, halved
  Cooking spray
- 1 Tbsp. cornmeal
- 1 tube (13½ oz.) refrigerated
  pizza crust
- 4 oz. fresh mozzarella cheese, sliced
- 6 fresh basil leaves, thinly sliced
- ⅛ tsp. coarsely ground pepper

1. Sprinkle the tomatoes with salt; let stand 15 minutes. Drain tomatoes on paper towels and pat dry.
2. Coat grill rack lightly with cooking oil. Grill peaches, covered, over medium heat or broil 4 in. from heat until peaches have grill marks and are tender, 2-3 minutes on each side, turning once. Remove peaches; cool slightly. Cut into slices.
3. Coat a 15x10x1-in. baking pan with cooking spray; sprinkle with cornmeal. Unroll crust into pan, pressing into a 12x10-in. rectangle. Spritz with cooking spray. Invert crust onto grill. Grill, covered, over medium heat until bottom is lightly browned, 2-3 minutes. Remove from grill, inverting onto baking pan.
4. Layer grilled side of pizza with tomatoes, peaches and cheese. Return pizza to the grill. Cook, covered, until the crust is lightly browned and cheese is melted, 3-4 minutes, rotating halfway through cooking to ensure an evenly browned crust. Sprinkle with basil and pepper.

1 piece: 98 cal., 3g fat (1g sat. fat), 6mg chol., 208mg sod., 15g carb. (3g sugars, 1g fiber), 4g pro. **Diabetic exchanges:** 1 starch.

CHAMPIONSHIP BEAN DIP

My friends and neighbors expect me to bring this irresistible dip to every gathering. When I arrive, they ask, "You brought your bean dip, didn't you?" If there are any leftovers, we use them to make bean and cheese burritos the next day.
—*Wendi Wavrin Law, Omaha, NE*

Prep: 10 min. • **Cook:** 2 hours
Makes: 4½ cups

- 1 can (16 oz.) vegetarian refried beans
- 1 cup picante sauce
- 1 cup shredded Monterey Jack cheese
- 1 cup shredded cheddar cheese
- ¾ cup sour cream
- 3 oz. cream cheese, softened
- 1 Tbsp. chili powder
- ¼ tsp. ground cumin
  Tortilla chips and salsa

In a large bowl, gently combine the first 8 ingredients; transfer to a 1½-qt. slow cooker. Cover and cook on high for 2 hours or until heated through, stirring once or twice. Serve with chips and salsa.

2 Tbsp.: 57 cal., 4g fat (2g sat. fat), 12mg chol., 151mg sod., 3g carb. (1g sugars, 1g fiber), 2g pro.

MEAT LOVER OPTION PAGE 320

BAKED ONION CHEESE DIP

We like our onion dip with a kick, so we mix cheddar and cream cheese with pepper jack. Then we inhale the aroma of this baking dish.
—*Bonnie Hawkins, Elkhorn, WI*

Takes: 30 min. • **Makes:** 3 cups

- 2 **cups shredded cheddar cheese**
- 1 **cup shredded pepper jack cheese**
- 4 **oz. cream cheese, cubed**
- ¼ **tsp. dried thyme**
- 2 **cups chopped sweet onions, divided**
  Assorted crackers

1. In a food processor, combine the cheeses, thyme and 1 cup onions; cover and process until blended. Stir in remaining onions.
2. Transfer to a greased 3-cup baking dish. Bake, uncovered, at 375° for 20-25 minutes or until bubbly. Serve with crackers.
¼ cup: 208 cal., 19g fat (9g sat. fat), 44mg chol., 248mg sod., 2g carb. (1g sugars, 0 fiber), 7g pro.

FRIED ASPARAGUS

This battered asparagus is a favorite at events. It's fun to eat with a side of ranch dressing for dipping.
—*Lori Kimble, Montgomery, AL*

Takes: 30 min. • **Makes:** 2½ dozen

- 1 **cup all-purpose flour**
- ¾ **cup cornstarch**
- 1¼ **tsp. salt**
- 1¼ **tsp. baking powder**
- ¾ **tsp. baking soda**
- ¾ **tsp. garlic salt**
- ½ **tsp. pepper**
- 1 **cup beer or nonalcoholic beer**
- 3 **large egg whites**
- 2½ **lbs. fresh asparagus, trimmed**
  Oil for deep-fat frying
  Ranch salad dressing

1. In a large bowl, combine the first 7 ingredients. Combine beer and egg whites; stir into dry ingredients just until moistened. Dip asparagus into batter.
2. In a deep cast-iron or electric skillet, heat 1½ in. of oil to 375°. Fry asparagus in batches until golden brown, 2-3 minutes on each side. Drain on paper towels. Serve immediately with ranch dressing.
1 piece: 70 cal., 4g fat (0 sat. fat), 0 chol., 207mg sod., 7g carb. (1g sugars, 0 fiber), 1g pro.

TEST KITCHEN TIP

A thrifty alternative to purchased garlic salt is to mix your own: Simply combine 1 tsp. garlic powder with 3 tsp. table salt or other fine-grained salt. The ratio works the same for onion salt, too.

⏱ CILANTRO TOMATO BRUSCHETTA

This is an easy tomato appetizer that all of my family and friends love. The ingredients meld together for a delightful hors d'oeuvre that goes well with a variety of main dishes.
—*Lisa Kane, Milwaukee, WI*

Takes: 25 min. • **Makes:** about 2 dozen

- 1 loaf (1 lb.) French bread, cut into 1-in. slices
- ½ cup olive oil, divided
- 1 Tbsp. balsamic vinegar
- 3 small tomatoes, seeded and chopped
- ¼ cup finely chopped onion
- ¼ cup fresh cilantro leaves, coarsely chopped
- ¼ tsp. salt
- ¼ tsp. pepper
- ¼ cup shredded part-skim mozzarella cheese

1. Preheat oven to 325°. Place bread slices on ungreased baking sheets; brush with ¼ cup oil. Bake until golden brown, 10-12 minutes.
2. In a small bowl, whisk together vinegar and remaining oil. Stir in tomatoes, onion, cilantro, salt and pepper.
3. To serve, spoon scant 1 Tbsp. tomato mixture onto each slice of bread. Top with shredded cheese.
1 piece: 98 cal., 5g fat (1g sat. fat), 1mg chol., 147mg sod., 11g carb. (1g sugars, 1g fiber), 2g pro. **Diabetic exchanges:** 1 starch, 1 fat.

CUCUMBER PARTY SANDWICHES

This is one of my favorite appetizers. We have lots of pig roasts here in Kentucky, and these small sandwiches are perfect to serve while the pig is cooking.

—*Rebecca Rose, Mount Washington, KY*

Prep: 20 min. + standing • **Makes:** 2½ dozen

- 1   pkg. (8 oz.) cream cheese, softened
- 2   Tbsp. mayonnaise
- 2   tsp. Italian salad dressing mix
- 30 slices cocktail rye or pumpernickel bread
- 60 thin cucumber slices
      Optional: Fresh dill sprigs and slivered red pearl onions

1. Beat cream cheese, mayonnaise and dressing mix until blended; let stand for 30 minutes.

2. Spread cream cheese mixture on bread. Top each with 2 cucumber slices and, if desired, dill and red onion slivers. Refrigerate, covered, until serving.

1 open-faced sandwich: 53 cal., 4g fat (2g sat. fat), 8mg chol., 92mg sod., 4g carb. (1g sugars, 1g fiber), 1g pro.

✳ BUTTERNUT-GOUDA POT STICKERS

My family can't get enough butternut squash. I had some left over, so I used pot sticker wraps and other veggies to create these fun little appetizers.

—Carla Mendres, Winnipeg, MB

Prep: 45 min. • **Cook:** 15 min.
Makes: about 4 dozen

- 1 small butternut squash (about 2½ lbs.)
- 1 Tbsp. butter
- 1 small sweet red pepper, finely chopped
- 1 small onion, finely chopped
- 2 cups shredded Gouda cheese
- ½ tsp. salt
- ½ tsp. minced fresh thyme or ⅛ tsp. dried thyme
- ½ tsp. pepper
- 1 pkg. (10 oz.) pot sticker or gyoza wrappers
- 3 Tbsp. canola oil, divided
- ¾ cup water, divided

1. Halve squash lengthwise; discard seeds. Place squash in a microwave-safe dish, cut side down; add ½ in. of water. Microwave, covered, on high until soft, 15-20 minutes; cool slightly. Scoop out flesh and mash.

2. In a skillet, heat butter over medium heat; saute pepper and onion until tender, 4-6 minutes. Add to squash; stir in the cheese, salt, thyme and pepper.

3. Place 1 Tbsp. filling on each wrapper (keep remaining wrappers covered with a damp towel). Moisten edge of wrapper with water; fold over to enclose filling, while pleating the front side to form a pouch. Stand on a work surface to flatten bottom, curving ends slightly.

4. In a large nonstick skillet, heat 1 Tbsp. oil over medium heat. Place a third of the pot stickers in pan; cook until the bottoms are lightly browned, 1-2 minutes. Add ¼ cup water (water may spatter); cook, covered, until filling is heated through, 3-4 minutes. Uncover; cook until bottoms are crisp and water is evaporated, 1-2 minutes. Repeat twice.

Freeze option: Cover and freeze uncooked pot stickers on lightly floured baking sheets until firm. Transfer to airtight freezer containers; return to freezer. To use, cook pot stickers as directed, increasing time as necessary to heat through.

1 pot sticker: 55 cal., 3g fat (1g sat. fat), 7mg chol., 84mg sod., 7g carb. (1g sugars, 1g fiber), 2g pro.

APPETIZER TORTILLA PINWHEELS

A friend gave me this recipe, and whenever I serve these pretty and delicious appetizers, people ask me for the recipe, too! Besides being attractive and tasty, the pinwheels can be made ahead of time and then sliced just before serving, leaving you time for other last-minute party preparations.

—*Pat Waymire, Yellow Springs, OH*

Prep: 20 min. + chilling
Makes: about 4 dozen

- 1   pkg. (8 oz.) cream cheese, softened
- 1   cup shredded cheddar cheese
- 1   cup sour cream
- 1   can (4¼ oz.) chopped ripe olives
- 1   can (4 oz.) chopped green chiles, well drained
- ½   cup chopped green onions
      Garlic powder to taste
      Seasoned salt to taste
- 5   flour tortillas (10 in.)
      Salsa, optional

1. Beat cream cheese, cheese and sour cream until blended. Stir in olives, green chiles, green onions and seasonings.
2. Spread over the tortillas; roll up tightly. Wrap each in plastic, twisting ends to seal; refrigerate several hours.
3. Unwrap. Cut into ½- to ¾-in. slices, using a serrated knife. If desired, serve with salsa.
1 pinwheel: 63 cal., 4g fat (2g sat. fat), 8mg chol., 115mg sod., 5g carb. (1g sugars, 0 fiber), 2g pro.

TEST KITCHEN TIP

This recipe is super versatile. For a Greek twist, for example, swap in feta cheese, use kalamata olives and trade diced tomatoes for the chiles.

STRAWBERRY TOMATO SALSA

Here's a sweet and tangy salsa that's miles away from the spicy version people expect. Serve it as an appetizer with tortilla chips for scooping, or make it part of the main event by serving it over chicken or pork.

—*Amy Hinkle, Topeka, KS*

Takes: 25 min. • **Makes:** 6 cups

- 2   pints cherry tomatoes, quartered
- 1   pint fresh strawberries, chopped
- 8   green onions, chopped
- ½   cup minced fresh cilantro
- 6   Tbsp. olive oil
- 2   Tbsp. balsamic vinegar
- ½   tsp. salt

In a large bowl, combine the tomatoes, strawberries, green onions and cilantro. In a small bowl, whisk oil, vinegar and salt; gently stir into tomato mixture. Refrigerate until serving.
¼ cup: 41 cal., 4g fat (0 sat. fat), 0 chol., 53mg sod., 3g carb. (2g sugars, 1g fiber), 0 pro.

ZUCCHINI CUPCAKES
PAGE 295

ROOM FOR DESSERT

Ready to try your hand at vegan peanut butter cookies or summery fruit pops? How about a scrumptious pie or majestic cake? Here are dozens of fresh, wholesome, easy ways to end any meal.

LEMON ZUCCHINI DROPS

When we lived on the East Coast, a nearby fruit and vegetable stand had a bakery featuring these soft, cakelike cookies. We missed every bite when we moved away, so I developed this recipe.

—*Barbara Franklin, Tucson, AZ*

Prep: 20 min. • **Bake:** 10 min./batch + cooling
Makes: about 3½ dozen

- ½ cup butter, softened
- 1 cup sugar
- 1 large egg, room temperature
- 1 cup finely shredded zucchini
- 1 tsp. grated lemon zest
- 2 cups all-purpose flour
- 1 tsp. baking soda
- 1 tsp. baking powder
- 1 tsp. ground cinnamon
- ½ tsp. salt
- ½ cup raisins
- ½ cup chopped walnuts

LEMON GLAZE

- 2 cups confectioners' sugar
- 2 to 3 Tbsp. lemon juice

1. In a large bowl, cream the butter and granulated sugar until light and fluffy. Beat in egg, zucchini and lemon zest. Combine the flour, baking soda, baking powder, cinnamon and salt; gradually add to the creamed mixture and mix well. Stir in raisins and walnuts.

2. Drop by tablespoonfuls 3 in. apart onto lightly greased baking sheets. Bake at 375° for 8-10 minutes or until lightly browned. Remove to wire racks to cool.

3. For glaze, combine confectioners' sugar and enough lemon juice to reach a thin spreading consistency. Spread or drizzle over cooled cookies.

1 cookie: 99 cal., 3g fat (2g sat. fat), 10mg chol., 89mg sod., 17g carb. (12g sugars, 0 fiber), 1g pro.

51 WATERMELON SORBET

Summertime and watermelon go hand in hand. My melon sorbet is fresh, fruity and without the gluten and eggs you get in many other frozen desserts.

—*Rachel Lewis, Danville, VA*

Prep: 15 min. + chilling
Process: 30 min. + freezing • **Makes:** 1 qt.

- 1 cup sugar
- ½ cup water
- 3 cups chopped seedless watermelon
- 1 cup orange juice
- 2 Tbsp. lime juice
- ½ cup miniature semisweet chocolate chips, optional

1. In a small saucepan, bring sugar and water to a boil. Reduce heat; simmer, uncovered, 5 minutes, stirring occasionally to dissolve sugar. Cool slightly.

2. Place watermelon in a food processor; process until pureed. Add orange juice, lime juice and cooled syrup; process until blended. Transfer to a large bowl; refrigerate, covered, until cold, about 3 hours.

3. Pour into cylinder of ice cream freezer. Freeze according to the manufacturer's directions; if desired, add chocolate chips during the last 10 minutes of processing. Transfer sorbet to freezer containers, allowing headspace for expansion. Freeze until firm, 2-4 hours.

½ cup: 129 cal., 0 fat (0 sat. fat), 0 chol., 1mg sod., 33g carb. (32g sugars, 0 fiber), 1g pro.

SPICED DEVIL'S FOOD CAKE

One of my mom's friends gave her this recipe when I was a child, and it has been a family favorite ever since. When your chocolate sweet tooth acts up, this really hits the spot!
—*Linda Yeamans, Ashland, OR*

Prep: 25 min. • **Bake:** 30 min. + cooling
Makes: 12 servings

- 1 cup butter, softened
- 1½ cups sugar
- 3 large eggs, room temperature
- 1 tsp. vanilla extract
- 2 cups all-purpose flour
- ¼ cup baking cocoa
- 1 tsp. baking powder
- 1 tsp. baking soda
- 1 tsp. ground cinnamon
- ½ to 1 tsp. ground nutmeg
- ¼ to ½ tsp. ground cloves
- 1 cup buttermilk

MOCHA ICING
- 3¾ cups confectioners' sugar
- ¼ cup baking cocoa

- 6 Tbsp. strong brewed coffee
- 6 Tbsp. butter, melted
- 1 tsp. vanilla extract
  Toasted whole or chopped almonds, optional

1. Preheat oven to 350°. Cream butter and sugar until light and fluffy. Add 1 egg at a time, beating well after each addition. Add the vanilla.
2. Sift together all dry ingredients; add to creamed mixture alternately with buttermilk. Pour into 2 greased and floured 9-in. round baking pans.
3. Bake until a toothpick inserted in center comes out clean, 30-35 minutes. Cool on wire racks for 10 minutes before removing from pans.
4. In a small bowl, combine all the icing ingredients except nuts. Spread frosting between layers and over the top and sides of cake. If desired, top with almonds.
1 slice: 543 cal., 23g fat (14g sat. fat), 110mg chol., 389mg sod., 82g carb. (61g sugars, 1g fiber), 5g pro.

CHOCOLATE-COVERED STRAWBERRY COBBLER

This cobbler came about because I love chocolate-covered strawberries. Top it with whipped cream, either plain or with a little chocolate syrup stirred in.
—*Andrea Bolden, Unionville, TN*

Prep: 15 min. • **Bake:** 35 min. + standing
Makes: 12 servings

- 1 cup butter, cubed
- 1½ cups self-rising flour
- 2¼ cups sugar, divided
- ¾ cup 2% milk
- 1 tsp. vanilla extract
- ⅓ cup baking cocoa
- 4 cups fresh strawberries, quartered
- 2 cups boiling water
  Whipped cream and additional strawberries

1. Preheat oven to 350°. Place butter in a 13x9-in. baking pan; heat pan in oven until butter is melted, 3-5 minutes. Meanwhile, in a large bowl, combine flour, 1¼ cups sugar, milk and vanilla until well blended. In a small bowl, mix cocoa and remaining sugar.
2. Remove baking pan from oven; add batter. Sprinkle with the strawberries and the cocoa mixture; pour boiling water evenly over top (do not stir). Bake 35-40 minutes or until a toothpick inserted into the cake portion comes out clean. Let stand 10 minutes. Serve warm with whipped cream and additional strawberries.
1 serving: 368 cal., 16g fat (10g sat. fat), 42mg chol., 316mg sod., 55g carb. (41g sugars, 2g fiber), 3g pro.

HUMBLE BUMBLE CRUMBLE BARS

While developing a treat for my bingo group, I asked my husband for ideas. He suggested a fruity bar. This berry bar is lightly sweet and so easy.

—*Nancy Phillips, Portland, ME*

Prep: 30 min. • **Bake:** 45 min. + cooling
Makes: 15 servings

- ½ cup butter, softened
- ¾ cup sugar
- 1 large egg, room temperature
- 2½ cups all-purpose flour
- ½ tsp. baking powder
- ¼ tsp. salt
- ¼ cup packed brown sugar
- 1 tsp. ground cinnamon

FILLING
- 2 cups chunky applesauce
- ½ tsp. ground cinnamon
- ⅛ tsp. ground nutmeg
- 2 cups fresh blackberries
- 2 cups fresh raspberries

1. Preheat oven to 350°. In a large bowl, cream butter and sugar until light and fluffy. Beat in egg. In another bowl, whisk flour, baking powder and salt; gradually beat into creamed mixture. Reserve ½ cup crumb mixture for topping. Press remaining mixture onto bottom of a greased 13x9-in. baking pan. Bake until lightly browned, 12-15 minutes. Cool on a wire rack.

2. Stir brown sugar and cinnamon into reserved topping; set aside. In a large bowl, combine applesauce, cinnamon and nutmeg until blended. Spread over crust; top with berries and reserved topping. Bake until golden brown, 30-35 minutes. Cool in pan on a wire rack. Cut into bars.

1 piece: 228 cal., 7g fat (4g sat. fat), 29mg chol., 109mg sod., 39g carb. (20g sugars, 3g fiber), 3g pro.

BLACK BEAN BROWNIES

You'd never guess that these rich, velvety chocolate treats contain a can of black beans.
—*Kathy Hewitt, Cranston, RI*

Prep: 15 min. • **Bake:** 20 min. + cooling
Makes: 1 dozen

- 1 can (15 oz.) black beans, rinsed and drained
- ½ cup semisweet chocolate chips, divided
- 3 Tbsp. canola oil
- 3 large eggs, room temperature
- ⅔ cup packed brown sugar
- ½ cup baking cocoa
- 1 tsp. vanilla extract
- ½ tsp. baking powder
- ⅛ tsp. salt

1. Place the beans, ¼ cup chocolate chips and oil in a food processor; cover and process until blended. Add eggs, brown sugar, cocoa, vanilla, baking powder and salt; cover and process until smooth.

2. Transfer to a parchment-lined 8-in. square baking pan. Sprinkle with remaining chocolate chips. Bake at 350° for 20-25 minutes or until a toothpick inserted in center comes out clean. Cool on a wire rack. Cut into bars.

1 brownie: 167 cal., 7g fat (2g sat. fat), 53mg chol., 131mg sod., 24g carb. (16g sugars, 2g fiber), 4g pro. **Diabetic exchanges:** 1½ starch, 1 fat.

READER RAVE

"I was intrigued by this recipe, so I just had to give it a try... and I was pleasantly surprised! The texture is more cakelike than that of a brownie, but it's definitely a fudgy treat that you can feel good about eating. I will certainly be making these again!"

—SGRONHOLZ, TASTEOFHOME.COM

TART & TANGY LEMON TART

Our family adores lemon desserts. I often make this cheery tart for brunch and for extra-special events in my heart-shaped tart pan.
—*Joyce Moynihan, Lakeville, MN*

Prep: 15 min. + chilling
Bake: 45 min. + cooling • **Makes:** 14 servings

- ¾ cup butter, softened
- ½ cup confectioners' sugar
- 1½ cups all-purpose flour

FILLING

- ¾ cup sugar
- 1 Tbsp. grated lemon zest
- ¾ cup lemon juice
- 3 large eggs, room temperature
- 3 large egg yolks, room temperature
- 4 oz. cream cheese, softened
- 1 Tbsp. cornstarch
  Sweetened whipped cream, optional

1. Preheat oven to 325°. In a large bowl, cream butter and confectioners' sugar until smooth. Gradually beat in flour. Press dough onto bottom and up sides of an ungreased 11-in. fluted tart pan with removable bottom. Refrigerate 15 minutes.

2. Line the unpricked crust with a double thickness of foil. Fill with pie weights, dried beans or uncooked rice. Bake until edges are lightly browned, 18-22 minutes. Remove foil and weights; bake until the bottom is golden brown, 5-7 minutes longer. Cool on a wire rack.

3. In a large bowl, beat sugar, lemon zest, lemon juice, eggs, egg yolks, cream cheese and cornstarch until blended; pour into crust. Bake until filling is set, 18-22 minutes. Cool on a wire rack. If desired, serve with whipped cream. Refrigerate leftovers.

Note: Let pie weights cool before storing. Beans and rice may be reused for pie weights, but not for cooking.

1 slice: 254 cal., 15g fat (9g sat. fat), 114mg chol., 125mg sod., 27g carb. (16g sugars, 0 fiber), 4g pro.

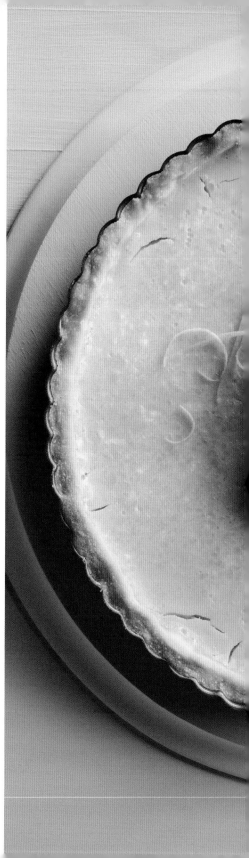

5i CHOCOLATE CINNAMON TOAST

Looking for a fun dessert or snack? Toast cinnamon bread in a skillet and top with chocolate and fresh fruit. Add a small dollop of whipped cream to each slice to make it extra indulgent.
—*Jeanne Ambrose, Milwaukee, WI*

Takes: 10 min. • **Makes:** 1 serving

- 1 slice cinnamon bread
- 1 tsp. butter, softened
- 2 Tbsp. 60% cacao bittersweet chocolate baking chips
  Optional: Sliced banana and strawberries

Spread both sides of bread with butter. In a small skillet, toast bread over medium-high heat 2-3 minutes on each side, topping with chocolate chips after turning. Remove from heat; spread melted chocolate evenly over toast. If desired, top with fruit.

1 slice: 235 cal., 13g fat (8g sat. fat), 10mg chol., 131mg sod., 29g carb. (19g sugars, 3g fiber), 4g pro.

⑤ CARROT DUMP CAKE

Because our family adores carrot cake, I experimented to find an easier way to make it so we could enjoy it more often. This super moist version guarantees smiles all around the table.

—*Bonnie Hawkins, Elkhorn, WI*

Prep: 10 min. • **Bake:** 25 min. + cooling
Makes: 12 servings

- 1 can (8 oz.) crushed pineapple
- 1 cup shredded carrots (2 medium carrots)
- 1 cup finely chopped walnuts
- 1 pkg. spice cake mix (regular size)
- ¾ cup unsalted butter, melted
  Whipped cream, optional

1. Preheat oven to 350°. Mix pineapple, carrots and walnuts; spread into a greased 11x7-in. baking dish. Sprinkle with cake mix; drizzle with butter.
2. Bake until golden brown, 25-30 minutes. Cool on a wire rack. If desired, serve with whipped cream.

1 piece: 339 cal., 21g fat (9g sat. fat), 31mg chol., 263mg sod., 37g carb. (20g sugars, 1g fiber), 4g pro.

CHOCOLATE ESPRESSO-NUT TORTE

I love chocolate and nuts, and they come together deliciously in this torte. Serve it with sweetened whipped cream or your favorite ice cream.

—*Thomas Faglon, Somerset, NJ*

- -

Prep: 40 min. • **Bake:** 35 min. + chilling
Makes: 14 servings

- 5 large eggs, separated
- 1 tsp. baking cocoa
- 1 cup hazelnuts, toasted and skins removed
- 3 Tbsp. dark brown sugar
- ½ cup butter, softened
- ⅔ cup sugar
- 6 oz. bittersweet chocolate, melted and cooled
- 1 tsp. instant espresso powder
- 1 tsp. almond extract
- ¼ tsp. salt

GANACHE
- 6 oz. bittersweet chocolate, chopped
- ½ cup heavy whipping cream
- ½ cup finely chopped almonds, toasted

1. Place egg whites in a large bowl; let stand at room temperature for 30 minutes. Line the bottom of a greased 9-in springform pan with waxed paper; grease the paper and dust with cocoa. Set aside.

2. Place hazelnuts and brown sugar in a food processor; cover and process until ground. In a second large bowl, cream butter and sugar until light and fluffy, about 5 minutes. Add 1 egg yolk at a time, beating well after each addition. Beat in the melted chocolate, espresso powder, extract and salt. Gradually add hazelnut mixture.

3. In the first large bowl, with clean beaters beat egg whites until stiff peaks form. Fold into batter. Spread into prepared pan. Place pan on a baking sheet.

4. Bake at 375° for 35-40 minutes or until a toothpick inserted in the center comes out with a few moist crumbs. Cool on a wire rack to room temperature. Remove sides of pan and invert onto a serving plate.

5. Place chocolate in a small bowl. In a small saucepan, bring cream just to a boil. Pour over chocolate; whisk until smooth. Cool, stirring occasionally, to room temperature or until the ganache reaches a spreading consistency, about 30 minutes.

6. Spread ganache over top and sides of cake; press almonds onto sides. Cover and refrigerate for 30 minutes or until set.

1 slice: 387 cal., 32g fat (13g sat. fat), 104mg chol., 118mg sod., 28g carb. (22g sugars, 4g fiber), 7g pro.

DATE-NUT PINWHEELS

Pinwheel cookies with dates and walnuts are a family treasure. There are a few steps when prepping, so I sometimes freeze the dough and bake later.
—*Frieda Whiteley, Lisbon, CT*

Prep: 30 min. + chilling • **Bake:** 10 min./batch
Makes: about 9 dozen

- 1 cup butter, softened
- 1 cup sugar
- 1 cup packed brown sugar
- 2 large eggs, room temperature
- 4 cups all-purpose flour
- ½ tsp. baking soda

FILLING
- 2 pkg. (8 oz. each) pitted dates
- 1 cup water
- ½ cup sugar
- ½ cup chopped walnuts

1. In a large bowl, cream butter and sugars until light and fluffy. Beat in eggs. In another bowl, whisk flour and baking soda; gradually beat into creamed mixture. Divide dough into 3 portions. Shape each into a disk. Cover and refrigerate 1 hour or until firm enough to roll.

2. For filling, place dates, water and sugar in a large saucepan. Bring to a boil. Reduce heat; simmer, uncovered, until dates are tender and liquid is almost evaporated. Stir in walnuts; cool completely.

3. Roll each dough portion between 2 sheets of waxed paper into a 12x10-in. rectangle. Refrigerate for 30 minutes. Remove waxed paper. Spread a third of the filling over each rectangle. Roll up tightly jelly-roll style, starting with a long side. Wrap securely. Refrigerate until firm.

4. Preheat oven to 350°. Unwrap and cut dough crosswise into ⅓-in. slices. Place 2 in. apart on greased baking sheets. Bake 10-12 minutes or until set. Remove from pans to wire racks to cool.

1 cookie: 67 cal., 2g fat (1g sat. fat), 8mg chol., 21mg sod., 12g carb. (7g sugars, 1g fiber), 1g pro.

ZUCCHINI BROWNIES

A fast-to-fix peanut butter and chocolate frosting tops these moist brownies that are a sweet way to use up your green garden squash. We really like the cakelike texture of the bars.
—*Allyson Wilkins, Amherst, NH*

Prep: 20 min. • **Bake:** 35 min. + cooling
Makes: 1½ dozen

- 1 cup butter, softened
- 1½ cups sugar
- 2 large eggs, room temperature
- ½ cup plain yogurt
- 1 tsp. vanilla extract
- 2½ cups all-purpose flour
- ¼ cup baking cocoa
- 1 tsp. baking soda
- ½ tsp. salt
- 2 cups shredded zucchini

FROSTING
- ⅔ cup semisweet chocolate chips
- ½ cup creamy peanut butter

1. Preheat oven to 350°. In a large bowl, cream butter and sugar until light and fluffy. Add 1 egg at a time, beating well after each addition. Beat in yogurt and vanilla. In another bowl, combine flour, cocoa, baking soda and salt; gradually add to creamed mixture. Stir in zucchini.

2. Pour into a greased 13x9-in. baking pan. Bake until a toothpick inserted in the center comes out clean, 35-40 minutes.

3. For frosting, in a small saucepan, combine chocolate chips and peanut butter. Cook and stir over low heat until smooth. Spread over warm brownies. Cool on a wire rack. Cut into bars.

1 piece: 307 cal., 17g fat (8g sat. fat), 52mg chol., 283mg sod., 37g carb. (21g sugars, 2g fiber), 5g pro.

TRIPLE PEAR PIE

One year, I won a giveaway and received three kinds of pears. After giving a few to family, I decided to use the rest to prepare a pie for Easter. Serve this majestic pie with vanilla ice cream for the perfect pairing!

—*Jenn Tidwell, Fair Oaks, CA*

- -

Prep: 30 min. + chilling
Bake: 50 min. + cooling • **Makes:** 10 servings

- 2   Tbsp. fat-free milk
- 1   tsp. lemon juice
- ¾   cup all-purpose flour
- ½   cup whole wheat flour
- 2   Tbsp. sugar
- ⅛   tsp. salt
- ⅓   cup cold butter, cubed
- 1   to 3 Tbsp. ice water

FILLING
- ½   cup sugar
- ⅓   cup all-purpose flour
- ½   tsp. ground cinnamon
- ⅛   tsp. salt
- 2   medium ripe Anjou pears
- 2   medium ripe Bartlett pears
- 2   medium Bosc pears
- 3   Tbsp. lemon juice

STREUSEL
- ¼   cup all-purpose flour
- ¼   cup packed brown sugar
- 2   Tbsp. butter, softened

1. Mix the milk and lemon juice; let stand 5 minutes. Place flours, sugar and salt in a food processor; pulse until blended. Add butter; pulse until butter is the size of peas. While pulsing, add milk mixture and just enough ice water to form moist crumbs. Shape dough into a disk; wrap in plastic. Refrigerate 1 hour or overnight.

2. Preheat oven to 375°. On a lightly floured surface, roll dough into a ⅛-in.-thick circle; transfer to a 9-in. deep-dish pie plate. Trim crust to ½ in. beyond rim of plate; flute edge.

3. Mix sugar, flour, cinnamon and salt. Peel and thinly slice pears; toss with sugar mixture and lemon juice. Place in crust.

4. Using a fork, mix streusel ingredients until crumbly; sprinkle over filling. Bake on a lower oven rack until golden brown and filling is bubbly, 50-60 minutes. Cool on a wire rack.

1 piece: 288 cal., 9g fat (5g sat. fat), 22mg chol., 130mg sod., 52g carb. (29g sugars, 4g fiber), 3g pro.

CANTALOUPE A LA MODE

This special dessert is a refreshing finale to a warm-weather meal.
—*Nancy Walker, Granite City, IL*

Takes: 15 min.
Makes: 4 servings (1 cup sauce)

½	cup water
½	cup sugar
2	Tbsp. lemon juice
1	Tbsp. cornstarch
1	tsp. grated lemon zest
1	cup fresh or frozen blueberries
2	small cantaloupes, halved and seeded
2	cups vanilla ice cream
	Fresh mint, optional

In a small saucepan, combine the first 5 ingredients; bring to a boil over medium heat. Boil and stir until thickened, about 2 minutes. Add blueberries; cook until heated through. Fill cantaloupe with ice cream; top with sauce. Garnish with mint if desired.
1 serving: 337 cal., 8g fat (5g sat. fat), 29mg chol., 74mg sod., 67g carb. (56g sugars, 3g fiber), 5g pro.

51 TRIPLE FRUIT FREEZE

These pops won't turn your tongue blue or neon green like many store-bought pops because they're made with fresh grapes, blueberries and kiwi. What could be better?
—*Colleen Ludovice, Wauwatosa, WI*

- -

Prep: 20 min. + freezing • **Makes:** 10 pops

- 1 cup sliced peeled kiwifruit (about 3 medium)
- 1 cup water, divided
- 2 Tbsp. sugar, divided
- 10 wooden pop sticks and 10 freezer pop molds or 10 paper cups (3 oz. each)
- 1 cup fresh blueberries or frozen unsweetened blueberries
- ½ cup seedless red grapes
- ½ cup red grape juice

1. Place kiwi, ½ cup water and 1 Tbsp. sugar in a food processor; pulse until combined. Pour into molds or paper cups. Top molds or paper cups with foil and insert sticks through foil. Freeze until firm, about 2 hours.

2. Place blueberries and the remaining water and sugar in food processor; pulse until combined. Spoon over kiwi layer. Freeze, covered, until firm, about 2 hours.

3. Wipe food processor clean. Repeat with grapes and grape juice. Spoon over blueberry layer. Freeze, covered, until firm.

1 pop: 50 cal., 0 fat (0 sat. fat), 0 chol., 3mg sod., 12g carb. (10g sugars, 1g fiber), 0 pro. **Diabetic exchanges:** 1 starch.

ZUCCHINI CUPCAKES

I asked my grandmother for this recipe after enjoying these irresistible spice cupcakes at her house. I love their creamy caramel frosting. They're such a scrumptious dessert, you actually forget you're eating your vegetables, too!

—*Virginia Lapierre, Greensboro Bend, VT*

Prep: 20 min. • **Bake:** 20 min. + cooling
Makes: about 1½ dozen

- 3 **large eggs, room temperature**
- 1⅓ **cups sugar**
- ½ **cup canola oil**
- ½ **cup orange juice**
- 1 **tsp. almond extract**
- 2½ **cups all-purpose flour**
- 2 **tsp. ground cinnamon**
- 2 **tsp. baking powder**
- 1 **tsp. baking soda**
- 1 **tsp. salt**
- ½ **tsp. ground cloves**
- 1½ **cups shredded zucchini**

FROSTING
- 1 **cup packed brown sugar**
- ½ **cup butter, cubed**
- ¼ **cup 2% milk**
- 1 **tsp. vanilla extract**
- 1½ **to 2 cups confectioners' sugar**

1. Preheat oven to 350°. Beat the first 5 ingredients. Combine dry ingredients; gradually add to egg mixture and blend well. Stir in zucchini.

2. Fill paper-lined muffin cups two-thirds full. Bake until a toothpick inserted in the center comes out clean, 20-25 minutes. Cool 10 minutes before removing to a wire rack.

3. For frosting, combine the brown sugar, butter and milk in a large saucepan. Bring to a boil over medium heat; cook and stir until thickened, 1-2 minutes. Remove from heat; stir in vanilla. Cool to lukewarm.

4. Gradually beat in the confectioners' sugar until frosting reaches spreading consistency. Frost cupcakes.

1 cupcake: 327 cal., 12g fat (4g sat. fat), 45mg chol., 305mg sod., 52g carb. (38g sugars, 1g fiber), 3g pro.

GINGER APPLE-PEAR CRISP

Enjoy autumn aromas—apples, cinnamon and spices—in this delicious recipe. It's even better with a scoop of vanilla or pumpkin ice cream! Whipped cream is always an option.
—*Holly Battiste, Barrington, NJ*

Prep: 20 min. • **Bake:** 40 min.
Makes: 8 servings

- 4 medium tart apples, peeled and sliced
- 4 medium pears, peeled and sliced
- ¼ cup sugar
- 1 Tbsp. lemon juice
- 1 Tbsp. grated fresh gingerroot
- ½ tsp. salt
- ½ tsp. vanilla extract

TOPPING

- 1 cup old-fashioned oats
- ½ cup all-purpose flour
- ½ cup packed brown sugar
- 1 tsp. ground cinnamon
- ¼ tsp. ground nutmeg
- ⅛ tsp. salt
- ⅓ cup cold butter, cubed

1. Preheat oven to 375°. In a large bowl, toss the first 7 ingredients. Transfer to a greased 2½-qt. baking dish.
2. In another bowl, mix the first 6 topping ingredients; cut in butter until crumbly. Sprinkle over fruit.
3. Bake until golden brown and fruit is tender, 40-45 minutes. Serve warm.
1 serving: 295 cal., 9g fat (5g sat. fat), 20mg chol., 250mg sod., 55g carb. (35g sugars, 5g fiber), 3g pro.

OLIVE OIL CAKE

A good olive oil cake isn't overly sweet, so it can just as easily be a breakfast treat or an afternoon snack as it can be a dessert.
—*Lisa Kaminski, Wauwatosa, WI*

Prep: 15 min. • **Bake:** 45 min. + cooling
Makes: 16 servings

- 3 large eggs
- 1½ cups sugar
- ¾ cup extra virgin olive oil
- ¾ cup ground almonds
- ½ cup 2% milk
- 4 tsp. grated orange zest
- 1 tsp. vanilla extract
- 1¾ cups all-purpose flour
- 2 tsp. baking powder
- ½ tsp. salt
- ¾ cup confectioners' sugar
- 2 to 3 Tbsp. orange juice
  Sliced almonds, toasted, optional

1. Preheat oven to 350°. Grease and flour a 10-in. fluted tube pan. In a large bowl, beat eggs on high speed 3 minutes. Gradually add sugar, beating until thick and lemon-colored. Gradually beat in oil. Beat in ground almonds, milk, orange zest and vanilla. In another bowl, whisk the flour, baking powder and salt; fold into egg mixture. Transfer batter to the prepared pan, spreading evenly. Bake until a toothpick inserted in cake comes out clean, 45-50 minutes. Cool in pan 15 minutes before removing to a wire rack to cool completely.
2. For the icing, in a small bowl, whisk the confectioners' sugar and enough orange juice to achieve a drizzling consistency. Drizzle over cake. If desired, sprinkle with almonds.
1 piece: 279 cal., 14g fat (2g sat. fat), 35mg chol., 152mg sod., 37g carb. (25g sugars, 1g fiber), 4g pro.

TEST KITCHEN TIP

Try this cake with ground pistachios and lemon zest instead of almonds and orange zest.

CRUMB-TOPPED APPLE & PUMPKIN PIE

This special recipe combines all the warm flavors of the season and makes a truly unique presentation. It gets rave reviews each year and has become a holiday tradition at our house.

—*Trisha Fox, Plainfield, IL*

Prep: 35 min. • **Bake:** 50 min. + cooling
Makes: 10 servings

- 1 sheet refrigerated pie crust
- 2 cups thinly sliced peeled tart apples
- ¼ cup sugar
- 2 tsp. all-purpose flour
- 1 tsp. lemon juice
- ¼ tsp. ground cinnamon

PUMPKIN FILLING
- 1½ cups canned pumpkin
- 1 cup fat-free evaporated milk
- 2 large eggs, room temperature
- ½ cup sugar
- ¾ tsp. ground cinnamon
- ¼ tsp. salt
- ⅛ tsp. ground nutmeg

TOPPING
- ½ cup all-purpose flour
- 3 Tbsp. sugar
- 4½ tsp. cold butter
- 3 Tbsp. chopped walnuts

1. On a lightly floured surface, unroll crust. Transfer crust to a 9-in. deep-dish pie plate. Trim crust to ½ in. beyond edge of plate; flute edges. In a large bowl, combine the apples, sugar, flour, lemon juice and cinnamon. Spoon into crust.

2. In another large bowl, whisk the pumpkin filling ingredients. Pour over apple mixture. Bake at 375° for 30 minutes.

3. For topping, combine flour and sugar. Cut in butter until crumbly; stir in walnuts. Sprinkle over pie.

4. Bake 20-25 minutes longer or until a knife inserted into pumpkin layer comes out clean (cover edge with foil during the last 15 minutes to prevent overbrowning if necessary).

5. Cool on a wire rack. Refrigerate leftovers.

1 piece: 350 cal., 12g fat (6g sat. fat), 142mg chol., 220mg sod., 55g carb. (33g sugars, 3g fiber), 7g pro.

READER RAVE

"Made this at the request of my 14- and 19-year-old sons for Thanksgiving. They asked for an apple/pumpkin pie in one pie. I thought I should see if there was a good recipe rather than scoff at the idea. This recipe looked like a winner and boy did it deliver the goods!"

— CALIQUEENBEE, TASTEOFHOME.COM

🔵 NUTELLA-STUFFED STRAWBERRIES

Gourmet strawberries are pricey to order but easy to make. We serve strawberries with hazelnut spread as a crowd-pleasing appetizer or dessert.
—*Darlene Brenden, Salem, OR*

Prep: 15 min. + chilling • **Makes:** 1 dozen

- 12 **large fresh strawberries**
- ¼ **cup Nutella**
- 1 **cup milk chocolate chips, melted**
- ¼ **cup chopped hazelnuts**
  Confectioners' sugar

1. Remove stems from strawberries. Using a paring knife, cut out centers; pipe Nutella into strawberries.

2. Insert a toothpick into the side of each strawberry. Holding toothpick, quickly dip stem end of each strawberry into melted chocolate; allow excess to drip off. Sprinkle with hazelnuts; place strawberries on a waxed paper-lined baking sheet, point side up. Remove toothpicks; refrigerate the strawberries until set. Just before serving, dust with confectioners' sugar.

1 stuffed strawberry: 100 cal., 6g fat (2g sat. fat), 2mg chol., 10mg sod., 11g carb. (9g sugars, 1g fiber), 2g pro.

WATERMELON PIZZA

Start with grilled melon slices and layer on the tangy, salty and sweet toppings for a summer-fresh appetizer.
—*Ellen Riley, Murfreesboro, TN*

Prep: 25 min. • **Grill:** 10 min. + chilling
Makes: 8 servings

- 8 wedges seedless watermelon, about 1 in. thick
- 1 cup heirloom cherry tomatoes, sliced
- 1 cup fresh baby arugula
- ½ cup fresh blueberries
- ⅓ cup crumbled feta cheese
- ⅓ cup pitted Greek olives, halved
- 1 Tbsp. olive oil
- ⅛ tsp. kosher salt
- ⅛ tsp. coarsely ground pepper
  Balsamic glaze, optional

1. Grill watermelon, covered, on a greased grill rack over medium-high direct heat until seared, 5-6 minutes on each side. Remove from heat; transfer to a platter. Chill.

2. To serve, top chilled watermelon with tomatoes, arugula, blueberries, feta and olives. Drizzle with olive oil; season with salt and pepper. If desired, drizzle with balsamic glaze.

1 slice: 91 cal., 4g fat (1g sat. fat), 3mg chol., 169mg sod., 13g carb. (11g sugars, 1g fiber), 2g pro. **Diabetic exchanges:** 1 fruit, 1 fat.

BLUEBERRY ZUCCHINI SQUARES

I saw a bar recipe on a box of muffin mix using apple and lemon zest. I tried it from scratch using shredded zucchini and fresh blueberries instead. It's a tasty combo.
—*Shelly Bevington, Hermiston, OR*

- -

Prep: 30 min. • **Bake:** 30 min. + cooling
Makes: 2 dozen

2	**cups shredded zucchini (do not pack)**
½	**cup buttermilk**
1	**Tbsp. grated lemon zest**
3	**Tbsp. lemon juice**
1	**cup butter, softened**
2½	**cups sugar**
2	**large eggs, room temperature**
3¼	**cups plus 2 Tbsp. all-purpose flour, divided**
1	**tsp. baking soda**
½	**tsp. salt**
2	**cups fresh or frozen blueberries**

GLAZE

2	**cups confectioners' sugar**
¼	**cup buttermilk**
1	**Tbsp. grated lemon zest**
2	**tsp. lemon juice**
⅛	**tsp. salt**

1. Preheat oven to 350°. Grease a 15x10x1-in. baking pan.

2. In a small bowl, combine the zucchini, buttermilk, lemon zest and lemon juice; toss to combine. In a large bowl, cream butter and sugar until light and fluffy. Beat in 1 egg at a time. In another bowl, whisk 3¼ cups flour, baking soda and salt; gradually add to the creamed mixture alternately with the zucchini mixture, mixing well after each addition. Toss blueberries with the remaining flour; fold into batter.

3. Transfer batter to prepared pan, spreading evenly (pan will be full). Bake 30-35 minutes or until light golden brown and a toothpick inserted in center comes out clean. Cool completely in pan on a wire rack.

4. In a small bowl, mix glaze ingredients until smooth; spread over top. Let stand until set.
Note: If using frozen blueberries, use without thawing to avoid discoloring the batter.
1 piece: 270 cal., 8g fat (5g sat. fat), 36mg chol., 197mg sod., 47g carb. (33g sugars, 1g fiber), 3g pro.

HOW-TO

Make Your Own Buttermilk

For each cup of buttermilk needed, combine 1 Tbsp. lemon juice or white vinegar plus enough milk to measure 1 cup. Stir, then let stand 5 minutes before using.

❄ CARROT COOKIE BITES

These soft and delicious cookies are an all-time family favorite. Their aroma while baking is absolutely irresistible! I'm always asked for the recipe.

—Jeanie Petrik, Greensburg, KY

Prep: 15 min. • **Bake:** 10 min./batch
Makes: 7 dozen

- ⅔ cup shortening
- 1 cup packed brown sugar
- 2 large eggs, room temperature
- ½ cup buttermilk
- 1 tsp. vanilla extract
- 2 cups all-purpose flour
- 1 tsp. ground cinnamon
- ½ tsp. salt
- ¼ tsp. baking powder
- ¼ tsp. baking soda
- ¼ tsp. ground nutmeg
- ¼ tsp. ground cloves
- 2 cups quick-cooking oats
- 1 cup shredded carrots
- ½ cup chopped pecans

1. In a large bowl, cream the shortening and brown sugar until light and fluffy. Beat in the eggs, buttermilk and vanilla. Combine the flour, cinnamon, salt, baking powder, baking soda, nutmeg and cloves; gradually add to creamed mixture. Stir in the oats, carrots and pecans.

2. Drop dough by rounded teaspoonfuls 2 in. apart onto ungreased baking sheets. Bake at 375° for 6-8 minutes or until lightly browned. Remove to wire racks to cool.

Freeze option: Drop dough by rounded teaspoonfuls onto parchment-lined baking sheets. Freeze until firm. Transfer cookie dough balls to resealable freezer containers; seal tightly and freeze for up to 3 months. To bake, place frozen dough 2 in. apart on ungreased baking sheets. Bake at 375° until lightly browned, 10-15 minutes. Remove to wire racks to cool.

1 cookie: 50 cal., 2g fat (0 sat. fat), 5mg chol., 24mg sod., 6g carb. (3g sugars, 0 fiber), 1g pro. **Diabetic exchanges:** ½ starch, ½ fat.

⏱ GINGER-GLAZED GRILLED HONEYDEW

If you've never grilled fruit like this before, you're in for a real treat! I love the idea of cooking everything from appetizers to desserts on the grill. This dish is both sweet and light.

—Jacqueline Correa, Landing, NJ

Takes: 25 min. • **Makes:** 6 servings

- ¼ cup peach preserves
- 1 Tbsp. lemon juice
- 1 Tbsp. finely chopped crystallized ginger
- 2 tsp. grated lemon zest
- ⅛ tsp. ground cloves
- 1 medium honeydew melon, cut into 2-in. cubes

1. In a small bowl, combine the first 5 ingredients. Thread honeydew onto 6 metal or soaked wooden skewers; brush with half of the glaze.

2. On a lightly oiled rack, grill honeydew, covered, over medium-high heat or broil 4 in. from the heat just until melon begins to soften and brown, 4-6 minutes, turning and basting frequently with remaining glaze.

1 skewer: 101 cal., 0 fat (0 sat. fat), 0 chol., 18mg sod., 26g carb. (23g sugars, 1g fiber), 1g pro. **Diabetic exchanges:** 1 fruit, ½ starch.

Health tip: These honeydew skewers are a sweet (and delicious) way to get a healthy dose of vitamin C and potassium.

ROASTED STRAWBERRY SHEET CAKE

My Grandma Gigi loved summer berry cakes. Almost any time I'd call her during the warmer months, she'd invite me over to taste her latest masterpiece. This cake is an ode to her.
—*Kristin Bowers, Rancho Palos Verdes, CA*

- -

Prep: 1 hour • **Bake:** 30 min. + cooling
Makes: 24 servings

- 4 lbs. halved fresh strawberries
- ½ cup sugar

CAKE
- 1 cup butter, softened
- 1½ cups sugar
- 2 large eggs, room temperature
- 2 tsp. almond extract
- 3 cups all-purpose flour
- 3 tsp. baking powder
- 2 tsp. salt
- 1 cup whole milk
- ¼ cup turbinado (washed raw) sugar

TEST KITCHEN TIP

It's important to just halve the strawberries, not quarter them. If they're too small, they will sink into the cake. When roasting the strawberries, be sure to use a rimmed baking sheet to catch all the juices that will be released.

1. Preheat oven to 350°. Place strawberries on a parchment-lined rimmed baking sheet. Sprinkle with sugar and toss to coat. Bake until just tender, 35-40 minutes. Cool slightly.

2. Meanwhile, grease a 15x10x1-in. baking pan. In a large bowl, cream butter and sugar until light and fluffy. Add 1 egg at a time, beating well after each addition. Beat in extract. In another bowl, whisk flour, baking powder and salt; add to creamed mixture alternately with milk, beating well after each addition (batter may appear curdled).

3. Transfer to prepared pan. Top with 3 cups roasted strawberries; sprinkle with turbinado sugar. Reserve remaining strawberries for serving. Bake until a toothpick inserted in center comes out clean, 30-35 minutes. Cool completely in pan on a wire rack. Serve with reserved roasted strawberries.

1 piece: 235 cal., 9g fat (5g sat. fat), 37mg chol., 329mg sod., 37g carb. (23g sugars, 2g fiber), 3g pro.

CINNAMON APPLE PAN BETTY

I found this recipe soon after I was married decades ago. You will need just a few ingredients that you probably have on hand. It's super quick to put together and a favorite of ours during fall and winter, when apples are at their best.
—*Shirley Leister, West Chester, PA*

Takes: 15 min. • **Makes:** 6 servings

- 3 medium apples, peeled and cubed
- ½ cup butter
- 3 cups cubed bread
- ½ cup sugar
- ¾ tsp. ground cinnamon

In a large skillet, saute apples in butter until tender, 4-5 minutes. Add bread cubes. Stir together sugar and cinnamon; sprinkle over apple mixture and toss to coat. Saute until bread is warmed.

½ cup: 279 cal., 16g fat (10g sat. fat), 41mg chol., 208mg sod., 34g carb. (25g sugars, 2g fiber), 2g pro.

⑤ COCONUT MILK STRAWBERRY-BANANA POPS

These four-ingredient freezer pops are a delicious way to use up a pint of fresh strawberries. You'll love the hint of tropical flavor, thanks to the coconut milk.
—Taste of Home *Test Kitchen*

Prep: 10 min. + freezing • **Makes:** 12 servings

- 1 can (13.66 oz.) coconut milk
- 1 pint fresh strawberries, chopped, divided
- 1 medium banana, sliced
- 2 Tbsp. maple syrup
- 12 freezer pop molds or 12 paper cups (3 oz. each) and wooden pop sticks

Place coconut milk, 1½ cups strawberries, banana and syrup in a blender; cover and process until smooth. Divide remaining strawberries among 12 molds or paper cups. Pour pureed mixture into molds or cups, filling ¾ full. Top molds with holders. If using cups, top with foil and insert sticks through foil. Freeze until firm, at least 4 hours.

1 pop: 51 cal., 3g fat (3g sat. fat), 0 chol., 5mg sod., 7g carb. (5g sugars, 1g fiber), 1g pro.

PERFECT PLUM & PEACH PIE

I created this recipe to fit with in-season summer fruit. The plums give the pie a splash of color as well as flavor, and the crumb topping is both easy and excellent!
—*Rachel Johnson, Shippensburg, PA*

Prep: 25 min. • **Bake:** 40 min. + cooling
Makes: 8 servings

- 1 sheet refrigerated pie crust
FILLING
- 6 medium peaches, peeled and sliced
- 6 medium black plums, sliced
- ½ cup all-purpose flour
- ½ cup confectioners' sugar
- ½ tsp. ground cinnamon
- ½ tsp. ground nutmeg
TOPPING
- ¼ cup all-purpose flour
- ¼ cup packed brown sugar
- 2 Tbsp. butter, softened
- ¼ tsp. ground cinnamon

1. Preheat oven to 375°. Unroll the crust onto a lightly floured surface; roll into a 12-in. circle. Transfer to a 9-in. deep-dish pie plate; trim and flute edge. Refrigerate while preparing filling.
2. Toss peaches and plums with flour, sugar and spices; transfer to crust. Using a fork, mix topping ingredients until crumbly; sprinkle over fruit.
3. Bake on a lower oven rack until golden brown and bubbly, 40-50 minutes. Cool on a wire rack.
1 piece: 311 cal., 10g fat (5g sat. fat), 13mg chol., 125mg sod., 53g carb. (29g sugars, 3g fiber), 4g pro.
Health tip: Using a crumb topping instead of a top pastry crust is an easy way to lighten up your favorite fruit pie. Here it saves over 50 calories and 5g fat per serving.

CHAI-SPICED BREAD PUDDING

Nothing says the holidays to me more than the heartwarming scent of chai spices. This bread pudding incorporates chai flavors to make a dessert that everyone raves about.
—*Jess Apfe, Berkeley, CA*

Prep: 25 min. + standing • **Bake:** 35 min.
Makes: 9 servings

- 4 large eggs, room temperature, lightly beaten
- 2 cups 2% milk
- ½ cup packed brown sugar
- 1 tsp. ground cinnamon
- 1 tsp. vanilla extract
- ¾ tsp. ground ginger
- ½ tsp. ground cardamom
- ¼ tsp. salt
- ⅛ tsp. ground cloves
- 2 Tbsp. rum, optional
- 6 slices day-old French bread (1 in. thick), cubed
- ⅓ cup slivered almonds
  Vanilla ice cream or sweetened whipped cream

1. Preheat oven to 350°. In a large bowl, whisk together first 9 ingredients and, if desired, rum. Gently stir in bread; let stand 15 minutes or until bread is softened.
2. Transfer to a greased 8-in. square baking dish. Sprinkle with almonds.
3. Bake, uncovered, until puffed, golden and a knife inserted in the center comes out clean, 35-40 minutes. Serve warm with ice cream.
1 piece: 180 cal., 6g fat (2g sat. fat), 87mg chol., 218mg sod., 24g carb. (15g sugars, 1g fiber), 7g pro. **Diabetic exchanges:** 1½ starch, 1 fat.

VEGAN PEANUT BUTTER COOKIES

Even without butter or eggs, these vegan peanut butter cookies are still soft and chewy. No one will be able to tell they're vegan! If you want a little extra texture, feel free to use chunky peanut butter or add ¼ cup crushed peanuts to the dough.
—Katie Bandurski, Shorewood, WI

Prep: 15 min. • **Bake:** 10 min. + cooling
Makes: 3 dozen

- 1 cup creamy peanut butter
- ½ cup sugar
- ½ cup packed brown sugar
- 1 Tbsp. vanilla extract
- ⅓ cup unsweetened almond milk
- 1 cup all-purpose flour
- 1 tsp. baking soda
- ½ tsp. baking powder
- ½ tsp. salt

1. In a large bowl, cream peanut butter, sugars and vanilla extract until light and fluffy, about 4 minutes. Beat in almond milk. In another bowl, whisk flour, baking soda, baking powder and salt; gradually beat into creamed mixture.
2. Shape level tablespoonfuls into balls. Place 2 in. apart on parchment-lined baking sheets; flatten with a fork. Bake at 350° until set, for 8-10 minutes. Cool 5 minutes; remove to wire cooling racks to cool completely.
1 cookie: 78 cal., 4g fat (1g sat. fat), 0 chol., 107mg sod., 10g carb. (7g sugars, 1g fiber), 3g pro.

> **TEST KITCHEN TIP**
>
> **Letting the cookies rest once they're out of the oven is very important. Since they contain no butter or eggs, they need a little time to firm up. If you remove them from the pan too early, they'll crumble.**

🄑 FRUIT JUICE POPS

I've used this recipe for years as a refreshing treat. My children enjoyed these pops more than any store-bought ones I ever brought home. They're tasty with either pineapple or orange juice. Try freezing and serving in cups made from hollowed-out oranges.
—Barbara Stewart, Garland, TX

Prep: 25 min. + freezing • **Makes:** 1 dozen

- 2 cups water
- 1½ cups sugar
- 4 cups unsweetened apple juice
- 1 cup unsweetened pineapple or orange juice
- ½ cup lemon juice
- 12 freezer pop molds or 12 paper cups (3 oz. each) and wooden pop sticks

1. In a large saucepan, combine water and sugar; bring to a boil. Reduce heat; simmer, uncovered, for 3-4 minutes or until sugar is dissolved, stirring occasionally. Remove from the heat; stir in juices.
2. Fill molds or cups with ¼ cup juice mixture. Top molds with holders. If using cups, top with foil and insert sticks through foil. Freeze until firm.
1 serving: 149 cal., 0 fat (0 sat. fat), 0 chol., 3mg sod., 38g carb. (36g sugars, 0 fiber), 0 pro.

CLASSIC CARROT CAKE

I entered this moist cake in a Colorado Outfitters Association dessert contest, and it took first place.
—*Cheri Eby, Gunnison, CO*

Prep: 30 min. • **Bake:** 35 min. + cooling
Makes: 15 servings

- 1   can (8 oz.) unsweetened crushed pineapple
- 4   large eggs, room temperature
- 2   cups shredded carrots (about 4 medium)
- 1   cup sugar
- 1   cup packed brown sugar
- 1   cup canola oil
- 2   cups all-purpose flour
- 2   tsp. baking soda
- 2   tsp. ground cinnamon
- ¼   tsp. salt
- ¾   cup chopped walnuts

FROSTING
- 2   pkg. (8 oz. each) cream cheese, softened
- ¼   cup butter, softened
- 2   tsp. vanilla extract
- 1½ cups confectioners' sugar

1. Preheat oven to 350°. Grease a 13x9-in. baking dish.

2. Drain pineapple, reserving 2 Tbsp. juice (discard remaining juice or save for another use). In a large bowl, beat eggs, carrots, sugars, oil, drained pineapple and reserved juice until well blended. In another bowl, whisk together flour, baking soda, cinnamon and salt; gradually beat into carrot mixture until blended. Stir in walnuts. Transfer to prepared dish. Bake until a toothpick inserted in center comes out clean, 35-40 minutes. Cool completely on a wire rack.

3. For frosting, in a large bowl, beat cream cheese and butter until smooth. Beat in vanilla. Gradually beat in confectioners' sugar. Spread over cake.

1 piece: 555 cal., 34g fat (10g sat. fat), 88mg chol., 361mg sod., 59g carb. (44g sugars, 2g fiber), 6g pro.

VEGAN CHOCOLATE CHIP COOKIES

As a competitive figure skater, I came up with this high-energy recipe. Whenever I bring these cookies to the rink, coaches are always sneaking two or three. I also like them with macadamia nuts.
—*Cassandra Brzycki, Wauwatosa, WI*

Prep: 15 min. + chilling • **Bake:** 10 min./batch
Makes: 3½ dozen

- 1¼ cups packed dark brown sugar
- ½   cup canola oil
- 6   Tbsp. vanilla soy milk
- ¼   cup sugar
- ¼   cup unsweetened applesauce
- 2   tsp. vanilla extract
- 2¼ cups all-purpose flour
- 1   tsp. baking soda
- ¾   tsp. salt
- 1   cup dairy-free semisweet chocolate chips
- ½   cup finely chopped walnuts

1. In a large bowl, beat the first 6 ingredients until well blended. Combine the flour, baking soda and salt; gradually add to sugar mixture and mix well. Stir in chocolate chips and nuts. Cover and refrigerate for 1 hour.

2. Drop by rounded tablespoonfuls 2 in. apart onto parchment-lined baking sheets. Bake at 375° for 10-12 minutes or until edges are lightly browned. Cool for 1 minute before removing from pans to wire racks.

1 cookie: 111 cal., 5g fat (1g sat. fat), 0 chol., 76mg sod., 16g carb. (10g sugars, 1g fiber), 1g pro.

CRANBERRY ZUCCHINI WEDGES

I try to slip zucchini into as many dishes as possible. These cake wedges have wonderful flavor and a tender texture. They are pretty, too, with bits of pineapple, cranberries and zucchini. And they're perfect for brunch.

—*Redawna Kalynchuk, Rochester, AB*

Prep: 15 min. • **Bake:** 30 min. + cooling
Makes: 2 cakes (8 wedges each)

- 1 can (20 oz.) pineapple chunks
- 3 cups all-purpose flour
- 1¾ cups sugar
- 1 tsp. baking powder
- 1 tsp. baking soda
- 1 tsp. salt
- 3 large eggs, room temperature
- 1 cup canola oil
- 2 tsp. vanilla extract
- 1 cup tightly packed shredded zucchini
- 1 cup fresh or frozen cranberries, halved
- ½ cup chopped walnuts
  Confectioners' sugar
  Sugared cranberries, optional

1. Drain pineapple, reserving ⅓ cup juice (save remaining juice for another use). Place the pineapple and reserved juice in a blender; cover and process until smooth. Set aside.
2. In a large bowl, combine the flour, sugar, baking powder, baking soda and salt. In a small bowl, whisk the eggs, oil, vanilla and pineapple mixture; stir into the dry ingredients until blended. Fold in zucchini, cranberries and nuts.
3. Pour into 2 greased and floured 9-in. round baking pans. Bake at 350° for 30-35 minutes or until a toothpick inserted in the center comes out clean.
4. Cool 10 minutes before removing from pans to wire racks to cool completely. Just before serving, dust with confectioners' sugar. Top cakes with sugared cranberries if desired.
1 slice: 354 cal., 17g fat (2g sat. fat), 40mg chol., 264mg sod., 47g carb. (27g sugars, 1g fiber), 5g pro.

PEANUT BUTTER PRETZEL BARS

My secret to these rich, no-bake bites?
Pretzels in the crust. They add a salty crunch
to the classic peanut butter and chocolate
pairing. The irresistible treats were the first
to sell out at our PTA bake sale!
—*Jennifer Beckman, Falls Church, VA*

Prep: 15 min. + chilling • **Makes:** 4 dozen

- 1   pkg. (16 oz.) miniature pretzels
- 1½ cups butter, melted
- 1½ cups peanut butter
- 3   cups confectioners' sugar
- 2   cups (12 oz.) semisweet
      chocolate chips
- 1   Tbsp. shortening

1. Line a 13x9-in. baking pan with foil, letting
ends extend up sides. Set aside 1½ cups
pretzels for topping. Pulse remaining pretzels
in a food processor until fine crumbs form.
In a large bowl, mix butter, peanut butter,
confectioners' sugar and pretzel crumbs.
2. Press into prepared pan. In a microwave,
melt chocolate chips and shortening; stir until
smooth. Spread over the peanut butter layer.
Break reserved pretzels and sprinkle over top;
press down gently. Refrigerate, covered, until
set, about 1 hour. Lifting with foil, remove
from pan. Cut into 48 bars.
1 piece: 201 cal., 13g fat (6g sat. fat), 15mg
chol., 233mg sod., 22g carb. (12g sugars, 1g
fiber), 3g pro.

🍲 SLOW-COOKED BREAD PUDDING

This warm and hearty dessert is perfect on
any cold, blustery winter evening. And the
slow cooker fills your kitchen with an amazing
aroma. My stomach is growling just thinking
about it!
—*Maiah Miller, Montclair, VA*

Prep: 15 min. • **Cook:** 3 hours
Makes: 8 servings

- 4   whole wheat bagels, split
      and cut into ¾-in. pieces
- 1   large tart apple, peeled and chopped
- ½   cup dried cranberries
- ¼   cup golden raisins
- 2   cups fat-free milk
- 4   large eggs
- ½   cup sugar
- 2   Tbsp. butter, melted
- 1   tsp. ground cinnamon
- 1   tsp. vanilla extract
      Confectioners' sugar, optional

1. In a 3-qt. slow cooker coated with cooking
spray, combine the bagels, apple, cranberries
and raisins. In a large bowl, whisk the milk,
eggs, sugar, butter, cinnamon and vanilla.
Pour over bagel mixture and stir to combine;
gently press bagels down into milk mixture.
2. Cover and cook on low for 3-4 hours or
until a knife inserted in the center comes
out clean. If desired, dust servings with
confectioners' sugar.
1 serving: 245 cal., 5g fat (3g sat. fat), 102mg
chol., 232mg sod., 45g carb. (27g sugars, 4g
fiber), 8g pro.

JUICY CHERRY PIE

Tart, or sour, cherry season is in the heart of summer. Choose fresh tart cherries that are bright in color, shiny and plump. They should feel relatively firm when pressed lightly.
—*Karen Berner, New Canaan, CT*

Prep: 35 min. + chilling
Bake: 55 min. + cooling • **Makes:** 8 servings

- 2½ **cups all-purpose flour**
- ½ **tsp. salt**
- ⅔ **cup cold unsalted butter, cubed**
- ⅓ **cup shortening**
- 6 **to 10 Tbsp. ice water**

FILLING
- 5 **cups fresh tart cherries, pitted**
- 2 **tsp. lemon juice**
- ¼ **tsp. almond extract**
- 1 **cup sugar**
- ⅓ **cup all-purpose flour**
- 1 **tsp. ground cinnamon**

SUGAR TOPPING
- 1 **Tbsp. 2% milk**
- 1 **tsp. sugar**

1. In a large bowl, mix flour and salt; cut in butter and shortening until crumbly. Gradually add ice water, tossing with a fork until dough holds together when pressed. Divide dough in half. Shape each into a disk; wrap in plastic. Refrigerate 1 hour or overnight.

2. Preheat oven to 375°. For filling, place cherries in a large bowl; drizzle with lemon juice and almond extract. In a small bowl, mix sugar, flour and cinnamon. Sprinkle over cherries and toss gently to coat.

3. On a lightly floured surface, roll 1 dough portion into a ⅛-in.-thick circle; transfer to a 9-in. pie plate. Trim crust even with rim. Add filling.

4. Roll remaining dough into a ⅛-in.-thick circle; cut out stars or other shapes using cookie cutters. Place top crust over filling. Trim, seal and flute edge. If desired, decorate top with cutouts.

5. Bake 40 minutes. For topping, brush top of pie with milk; sprinkle with sugar. Bake 15-20 minutes longer or until crust is golden brown and filling is bubbly. Cool on wire rack.

1 piece: 521 cal., 24g fat (12g sat. fat), 41mg chol., 155mg sod., 72g carb. (34g sugars, 3g fiber), 6g pro.

`HOW-TO`

Give Pies Decorative Flair

A reverse-cutout finishing technique adds flair to pies you'd otherwise give a simple double crust or lattice top.
- Roll out top dough as usual. Then, using a medium or small cookie cutter, cut out select parts of the crust. Be sure not to place cutouts too close together.
- Then lay the crust on top, crimp and finish as you see fit.

BAKED APPLE SURPRISE

This sweet-savory recipe is a favorite. Use Brie instead of blue cheese if you like things creamier. My tip? Bake the apples in a muffin tin so they won't roll around.
—*Jessica Levinson, Nyack, NY*

Prep: 10 min. • **Bake:** 35 min.
Makes: 2 servings

- 2 medium apples
- 2 Tbsp. crumbled blue cheese, divided
- 2 Tbsp. quick-cooking oats
- 2 Tbsp. bran flakes
- 1 Tbsp. golden raisins
- 1 Tbsp. raisins
- 1 Tbsp. brown sugar

1. Cut apples in half lengthwise; remove cores. Place in an ungreased 8-in. square baking dish. Place 1 tsp. of blue cheese into each half.
2. Combine oats, bran flakes, golden raisins, raisins and brown sugar; spoon into apples. Top with remaining cheese. Bake, uncovered, at 350° until tender, 35-40 minutes.
2 filled apple halves: 181 cal., 3g fat (2g sat. fat), 6mg chol., 141mg sod., 39g carb. (27g sugars, 5g fiber), 3g pro.

RECIPE INDEX

A

Acorn Squash Slices............185
African Peanut Sweet Potato
    Stew......................49
Appetizer Tomato Cheese
    Bread....................256
Appetizer Tortilla Pinwheels......279
Apple-Cinnamon Pudgy Pie.......120
Apple, White Cheddar & Arugula
    Tarts.....................47
Apple-White Cheddar Grilled
    Cheese...................122
Artichoke Caprese Platter........194
Asian Tofu.....................32
Asparagus Tofu Stir-Fry..........49
Autumn Bisque.................152
Avocado & Garbanzo Bean Quinoa
    Salad....................139
Avocado Bruschetta............268

B

Baked Apple Surprise...........315
Baked Cheddar Eggs &
    Potatoes.................215
Baked Onion Cheese Dip.........274
Balsamic Zucchini Saute........195
Basic Pizza Crust...............80
Berry Smoothie Bowl...........231
Better than Egg Salad...........120
Black Bean & Corn Quinoa.......129
Black Bean & Rice Enchiladas.....42
Black Bean & Sweet Potato Rice
    Bowls...................142
Black Bean & White Cheddar
    Frittata..................210
Black Bean Brownies...........286
Black Bean Bulgur Salad........136

Black Bean Chip & Dip Burgers....110
Black Bean-Tomato Chili.........174
Blueberry Cantaloupe Salad......222
Blueberry Zucchini Squares......301
Bow Tie & Spinach Salad........202
Broccoli & Chive Stuffed Mini
    Peppers..................271
Broccoli Cheeseburgers with Spicy
    Sweet Potatoes...........103
Butternut & Portobello
    Lasagna..................73
Butternut-Gouda Pot Stickers.....277
Butternut Squash with Whole
    Grains...................144

C

Camembert & Cranberry
    Pizza....................257
Cantaloupe a la Mode...........293
Caprese Salad Kabobs..........268
Caribbean Fruit Soup...........160
Carrot Cookie Bites............303
Carrot Dump Cake.............288
Cast Iron Scrambled Eggs.......229
Cauliflower & Tofu Curry.........18
Cauliflower Casserole..........192
Chai-Spiced Bread Pudding......307
Championship Bean Dip.........272
Chard & White Bean Pasta........81
Cheddar Bean Burritos...........18
Cheddary Mushroom Burgers.....124
Cheese & Fresh Herb Quiche......241
Cheese & Grape Appetizers.......253
Cheesy Black Bean Nachos........39
Cheesy Chile Casserole..........29
Cheesy Spinach-Stuffed
    Shells....................76

Cherry Tomato Mozzarella
    Saute....................199
Chickpea & Red Onion Burgers.....93
Chickpea Mint Tabbouleh........139
Chickpea Tortilla Soup..........178
Chiles Rellenos Sandwiches.......88
Chiles Rellenos Souffle.........234
Chili-Lime Mushroom Tacos.......18
Chocolate Cinnamon Toast......287
Chocolate-Covered Strawberry
    Cobbler..................284
Chocolate Espresso-Nut Torte....289
Chunky Vegetarian Chili.........181
Cilantro Tomato Bruschetta......275
Cinnamon Apple Pan Betty.......305
Classic Carrot Cake............310
Classic Hummus...............257
Coconut Curry Cauliflower
    Soup....................168
Coconut Curry Vegetable
    Soup....................160
Coconut Milk Strawberry-Banana
    Pops....................306
Colorful Broccoli Cheddar
    Casserole................236
Confetti Quinoa...............131
Contest-Winning Eggplant
    Parmesan.................20
Cranberry Zucchini Wedges......311
Creamy Butternut Squash & Sage
    Soup....................154
Creamy Cauliflower Pakora
    Soup....................159
Creamy Egg Salad.............108
Creamy Eggplant & Mushroom Monte
    Cristo...................109

Creamy Lentils with Kale Artichoke
  Saute...........................11
Creamy Polenta with Balsamic
  Glaze..........................142
Crumb-Topped Apple & Pumpkin
  Pie 298
Crunchy French Toast............236
Cucumber Party Sandwiches 276
Cucumber Sandwiches............94
Curried Quinoa & Chickpeas 141
Curried Vegetable Soup 179
Curry Carrot Dip.................247
Curry Scramble 221

D

Date-Nut Pinwheels 291
Delicata Squash Boats 30
Deluxe Black Bean Burgers.......115

E

Easy Chana Masala...............40
Easy Egg Pad Thai................84
Easy Southwestern Veggie
  Wraps 118
Edamame & Soba Noodle
  Bowl...........................15
Egg & Asparagus Breakfast
  Croquettes 242
Eggplant Fries 204
Eggplant Rollatini 37
English Muffin Egg
  Sandwiches 239

F

Farmers Market Enchiladas 16
Farmers Market Orzo Salad 204
Favorite Deep-Dish Pizza.........58
Fennel Carrot Soup..............174
Festive Corn & Broccoli 206
Festive Rice....................147

Fettuccine with Black Bean
  Sauce..........................55
Fiesta Corn & Beans 133
Florentine Almond Artichoke
  Mounds 261
Fluffy Banana Pancakes..........220
Fontina & Sweet Potato Pizza.....84
French Onion Soup for 2 172
Fresh Corn & Tomato
  Fettuccine......................75
Fresh from the Garden
  Wraps 248
Fresh Mozzarella Basil
  Sandwiches 94
Fresh Vegetable Stew............154
Fresh Veggie Pockets 107
Fried Asparagus.................274
Fried Onions & Apples 201
Fruit & Nut Baked Oatmeal 219
Fruit & Nut Bulgur Pilaf 128
Fruit Juice Pops 308
Fruity Peanut Butter Pitas........121
Full Garden Frittata..............218

G

Garbanzo Bean Burgers..........123
Garden-Fresh Pizza Sauce 80
Garlic Pumpkin Seeds 270
Ginger Apple-Pear Crisp 296
Ginger-Glazed Grilled
  Honeydew.....................303
Gnocchi with Pesto Sauce 13
Gnocchi with White Beans........27
Golden Beet & Peach Soup with
  Tarragon 169
Great Grain Burgers 98
Greek Brown & Wild Rice
  Bowls..........................146
Greek Salad Ravioli...............63
Greek Sandwich Bites............97
Greek Veggie Omelet............240

Grilled Bean Burgers 90
Grilled Brussels Sprouts 195
Grilled Caprese Quesadillas 22
Grilled Cheese & Pepper
  Sandwiches 100
Grilled Cheese & Tomato Soup
  Bake...........................35
Grilled Chiles Rellenos 43
Grilled Eggplant Pita Pizzas 66
Grilled Eggplant Sandwiches 94
Grilled Garden Veggie Pizza 83
Grilled Tomato-Peach Pizza 272
Grilled Vegetable Sandwich.......110
Grilled Veggies with Caper
  Butter 200

H

Hazelnut Asparagus Soup........163
Healthy Greek Bean Dip 263
Hearty Asian Lettuce Salad......199
Hearty Chickpea Potpie 45
Hearty Multigrain Pancakes 227
Hearty Potato Soup..............158
Hearty Veggie Sandwiches 89
Heavenly Earth Burgers..........106
Herbed Leek Tarts...............261
Homemade Guacamole,..........251
Homemade Ricotta Gnocchi with
  Spinach & Gorgonzola 38
Hot Spinach Spread with Pita
  Chips 253
Humble Bumble Crumble
  Bars..........................285
Hummus & Veggie Wrap-Up 103

I

Indian Spiced Chickpea Wraps 89
Italian Cheese Loaf 90
Italian Herb-Lentil Patties with
  Mozzarella 44
Italian Spaghetti Squash 207

J

Jasmine Rice with Coconut & Cherries 133
Juicy Cherry Pie 314

K

Kalamata Cheesecake Appetizer 246

L

Lactose-Free Veggie-Stuffed Shells 64
Lemon Garlic Mushrooms 197
Lemon Zucchini Drops 282
Lentil Loaf 17
Linguine Primavera 67
Linguine with Broccoli Rabe & Peppers 78
Loaded Mexican Pizza 74
Loaded Quinoa Breakfast Bowl 237

M

Mango Barley Salad 145
Market Basket Soup 157
Meatless Chili Mac 58
Meatless Taco Salad 186
Mediterranean Broccoli & Cheese Omelet 239
Mediterranean Bulgur Bowl 147
Mediterranean Chickpeas 34
Mexican Grilled Cheese Sandwiches 106
Mexican Street Corn Bake 196
Mini Grilled Cheese 258
Mint-Cucumber Tomato Sandwiches 99
Minty Peas & Onions 190
Muffin-Tin Lasagnas 71
Mushroom & Smoked Gouda Puff 266

Mushroom-Bean Bourguignon 166
Mushroom Pear Melts 124
Mushrooms Marsala with Barley 140

N

Nutella-Stuffed Strawberries 299

O

Olive Oil Cake 296
Open-Faced Pizza Sandwiches 122
Orange-Glazed Beets 203
Over-the-Rainbow Minestrone 160
Overnight Maple Oatmeal 240

P

Party Cheese Bread 254
Pasta Pizza 78
Peanut Butter, Apple & Raisin Sandwich 104
Peanut Butter Pretzel Bars 313
Peanut Ginger Pasta 83
Pear Waldorf Pitas 92
Pepper Ricotta Pasta 69
Perfect Plum & Peach Pie 307
Pickled Mushrooms with Garlic 250
Poached Egg Buddha Bowls 130
Polenta Chili Casserole 31
Portobello Melts 102
Pressure-Cooked Broccoli Egg Cups 228
Pressure-Cooker Apple Pie Steel-Cut Oatmeal 242
Pressure-Cooker Chickpea & Potato Curry 29
Pressure-Cooker Greek-Style Soup 171

Pressure-Cooker Homemade Chunky Applesauce 210
Pressure-Cooker Lentil Pumpkin Soup 173
Pressure-Cooker Lentil Stew 21
Pressure-Cooker Light Deviled Eggs 264
Pumpkin Hummus 267
Pumpkin Pinwheels 248

Q

Quick Taco Wraps 113
Quick Veggie Potpies 22
Quickpea Curry 51
Quinoa & Black Bean-Stuffed Peppers 10
Quinoa Tabbouleh 149
Quinoa with Peas & Onion 137

R

Rainbow Pepper Appetizers 255
Rainbow Quiche 224
Raspberry-Banana Breakfast Tacos 234
Raspberry-Coconut French Toast 216
Raspberry Peach Puff Pancake 228
Refried Bean Tostadas 50
Ricotta-Stuffed Portobello Mushrooms 46
Rise & Shine Parfait 214
Roasted Butternut Squash Dippers 263
Roasted Strawberry Sheet Cake 304
Roasted Sweet Potato & Chickpea Pitas 115
Roasted Vegetable Strata 231
Rutabaga Carrot Casserole 197

S

Salsa Bean Burgers 118
Salsa Spaghetti Squash. 24
Satisfying Tomato Soup 163
Savory Potato Skins 271
Savory Zucchini Bread
    Pudding. .202
Scented Rice in Baked
    Pumpkin .128
Scored Potatoes. 206
Shakshuka Breakfast Pizza. 232
Sheet-Pan Curried Dinner 23
Shiitake & Manchego
    Scramble 232
Shredded Gingered Brussels
    Sprouts 184
Simple Lemon Parsley
    Potatoes .187
Simple Maple Baked Beans. 201
Skillet Mac & Cheese 62
Slow-Cooked Bread Pudding. 313
Slow-Cooked Stuffed Peppers 24
Slow-Cooker Caponata. 260
Slow-Cooker Coconut
    Granola 233
Slow-Cooker Frittata
    Provencal 223
Slow-Cooker Potluck Beans 184
Slow-Cooker Spiced Mixed
    Nuts. 264
Slow-Cooker Vegan Baked
    Beans 191
Smoked Gouda Veggie Melt. 97
So-Easy Gazpacho. 167
Southern Peanut Butter Mayo
    Sandwich 112
Southwest Hash with Adobo-Lime
    Crema 217
Spanish Marinated
    Mushrooms 258

Spiced Apricot Baked
    Oatmeal. .212
Spiced Devil's Food Cake 284
Spicy Breakfast Pizza. 238
Spicy Grilled Broccoli 189
Spicy Lentil & Chickpea Stew 171
Spicy Sweet Potato Chips
    & Cilantro Dip. 255
Spinach & Artichoke Pizza. 64
Spinach & Tortellini Soup. 153
Spinach Feta Turnovers 85
Spinach Rice. 134
Spinach-Stuffed Pizza 61
Spring Onion Pimiento Cheese
    Grits. 149
Strawberry Tomato Salsa 279
Summer Squash Flatbreads. 77
Sweet Potato & Mushroom
    Potpies 12

T

Tart & Tangy Lemon Tart 286
Tasty Lentil Tacos 25
The Best Marinara Sauce. 56
The Ultimate Grilled Cheese 95
Three-Cheese Fondue. 263
Thyme-Sea Salt Crackers 265
Tofu Chow Mein 60
Tofu-Veggie Pad Thai. 72
Tomato & Avocado
    Sandwiches 117
Tomato & Corn Cheesy Pastry
    Bites. 265
Tomato Baguette Pizza. 55
Tomato-Garlic Lentil Bowls 33
Triple Fruit Freeze. 294
Triple Pear Pie 292
Tropical French Toast 215
Tropical Fruit Salad. 219
Tuscan Portobello Stew 155

V

Veg Jambalaya. 15
Vegan Butternut Squash Soup 165
Vegan Cabbage Soup 165
Vegan Carrot Soup 181
Vegan Chocolate Chip Cookies 310
Vegan Cream of Mushroom
    Soup 177
Vegan Green Bean Casserole 191
Vegan Mac & Cheese. 69
Vegan Peanut Butter Cookies 308
Vegan Quinoa Salad 189
Vegan Tortilla Soup 157
Vegetable Barley Saute 145
Vegetable Couscous Salad. 135
Vegetable Egg Rolls. 252
Vegetable Lentil Soup. 176
Vegetarian Reubens 113
Veggie Bean Burgers 105
Veggie-Cashew Stir-Fry. 37
Veggie Nicoise Salad. 192
Veggie Power Crispy Tacos 21
Veggie Tacos. 49

W

Warm Grapefruit with
    Ginger-Sugar. 213
Watermelon Sorbet. 282
Watermelon Pizza 300
Wheat Berry Salad 196
Whole Wheat Veggie Pizza. 70

Z

Zesty Veggie Pitas 125
Zippy Egg Salad. 101
Zucchini & Gouda Skillet
    Frittata 227
Zucchini Brownies 291
Zucchini Burgers 117
Zucchini Cupcakes. 295

Need an option for hungry meat lovers? No problem!

We've paired easy-prep, affordable meats with more than 30 recipes.

RECIPE NAME	SHREDDED ROTISSERIE CHICKEN	DELI TURKEY OR HAM	CUBED COOKED HAM	SLICED SMOKED SAUSAGE	CRUMBLED COOKED ITALIAN SAUSAGE	TACO MEAT	COOKED BEEF STEAK
Black Bean Bulgur Salad, 136	•					•	
Bow Tie & Spinach Salad, 202			•	•			
Caprese Salad Kabobs, 268			•	•			
Championship Bean Dip, 272						•	
Cheddar Bean Burritos, 18						•	
Chunky Vegetarian Chili, 181						•	
Creamy Polenta with Balsamic Glaze, 142					•		
Easy Southwestern Veggie Wraps, 118	•					•	
Edamame & Soba Noodle Bowl, 15							•
English Muffin Egg Sandwiches, 239		•			•		
Favorite Deep-Dish Pizza, 58				•	•		
Fiesta Corn & Beans, 133						•	•
Fresh Veggie Pockets, 107	•	•					
Gnocchi with White Beans, 27				•	•		
Greek Brown & Wild Rice Bowls, 146	•						•
Grilled Caprese Quesadillas, 22		•					
Hearty Asian Lettuce Salad, 199	•		•				•
Hearty Potato Soup, 158			•				
Mango Barley Salad, 145	•		•				
Market Basket Soup, 157					•		
Meatless Taco Salad, 186						•	
Peanut Ginger Pasta, 83							•
Pear Waldorf Pitas, 92	•	•					
Pepper Ricotta Pasta, 69			•				
Quickpea Curry, 51	•						
Rainbow Quiche, 224			•				
Shakshuka Breakfast Pizza, 232							•
Southwest Hash with Adobo-Lime Crema, 217				•			
Spring Onion Pimiento Cheese Grits, 149			•				
Tuscan Portobello Stew, 155					•		
Vegan Cabbage Soup, 165				•			
Vegetable Egg Rolls, 252	•						•
Veggie Nicoise Salad, 192		•	•				